Educational Administration Under Municipal Corporations

Educational Administration Under Municipal Corporations

P.V. Prasad
P.W. Purushotham

KANISHKA PUBLISHERS, DISTRIBUTORS
NEW DELHI-110 002

KANISHKA PUBLISHERS, DISTRIBUTORS
4697/5-21 A, Ansari Road, Daryaganj
New Delhi-110 002
Phones : 2327 0497, 2328 8285
Fax : 011-2328 8285
E-mail: kanishka_publishing@yahoo.co.in

Educational Administration under Municipal Corporations

First Published 2010

ISBN 978-81-8457-243-8

PRINTED IN INDIA

Published by Madan Sachdeva for Kanishka Publishers, Distributors, 4697/5-21A, Ansari Road, Daryaganj, New Delhi-110 002, Typeset by Sunshine Graphics, Delhi, and Printed at Rajdhani Printers, Delhi.

Dedicated

to Our

Beloved Parents

and Family

Preface

The advent and advancement of democracy and the extension of the horizons of education prompted the need for an efficient, effective and appropriate system of educational administration in India. Education has been emerged as one of the prominent and largest human enterprises undertaken by modern governments. Educational administration constitutes the objectives and procedures which promote literacy, learning and education. Educational institutions now-a-days have been transpired as the agencies of eradicating and impending the twin social evils of illiteracy and ignorance in all developing as well as modern societies. The spirit of a country is inherent in its culture and civilization and the main function of education is to transmit the same to its future generations. Thus, education has been acclaimed as a beating heart of a progressive nation and life-blood of national heritage.

The civilization of any country is adjudged by the rate of literacy in that country and its progress depends largely on education which it provides to its citizens. In fact, the Third World countries are normally at their lower ebb in the level of increasing their literacy rate to modernize their social and cultural aspects. Establishment of local self-governments and entrusting them with the responsibility of promoting and providing developmental activities as well as civic amenities in general and besides these, literacy and education in particular have become *prima facie* activities of these countries. India as a developing Nation is also following the path line equally and putting efforts to promote literacy rate both among rural as well as urban folk. Enactment of legislations for the creation of rural as well as urban local self-governments in India is a right and judicious step in this direction.

Institutional changes in India since independence have been prompted by two fundamental urges. One is the urge for democratization and the other is the urge for development. These two urges resulted in the emergence of local self-governments in India which touched the lives and needs of all categories of people at an immense length especially effecting the twin fields of Literacy and Education.

The legislation for creation of urban local bodies like Municipalities and Municipal Corporations and structuring their organization and devising their administration, financing and flow of funds, exercising of supervision and control over the personnel and properties and on their functions and responsibilities have become part of their administrative activities in various states in India.

Municipal Corporations are constituted in Andhra Pradesh in accordance with the comprehensive Andhra Pradesh Municipal Corporations Act of 1965. The Andhra Pradesh State Legislature in consonance with the Seventy Fourth Constitutional Amendment Act, enacted Andhra Pradesh Municipal Corporation Act in 1994. Consequently the earlier Acts governing the Municipal Corporations in the State were amended and at the Municipal Corporations were brought under the governance of the newly enacted Act, i.e., A.P. Municipal Corporations Act of 1994. The Municipal Corporations at Warangal, Guntur, Rajahmundry and Kurnool were created newly in the year 1994 making the total number of Municipal Corporations to Fifteen. Except the Greater Hyderabad Municipal Corporation the organizational structure pattern is same and uniform for all Municipal Corporations.

The Andhra Pradesh Municipal Corporation Act, 1994 provided numerous functions and responsibilities to the Municipal Corporations for the growth and development of their respective local areas. The working of these Municipal Corporations in the State is dual in character. Primarily they are concerned with the administrative aspects followed by the developmental programmes. The programmes of expansion of education and literacy is one among their many objectives and various other developmental programmes. In fact to afford, to impact and to expand school education through democratic means is the core concept of Municipal Administration found in all the categories of Municipalities and Municipal Corporations in Andhra Pradesh including the Kurnool Municipal Corporation as is provided by the Act.

The success of any urban local body in general and the Kurnool Municipal Corporation in particular in fulfilling its avowed objectives of providing school education in general and secondary education in particular to all its school aged children and also promotion of the concept of literacy always depends invariably upon its organizational set up and the mode and method through which it operates its educational administration in particular. The organizational structure must be such that it provides effective means and appliances for furthering efficient educational administration and the educational administrative system inturn must provide for well standard performance of the educational institutions kept under its control. The organizational structure and the educational administrative systems of the Municipal Corporation must enable to keep all its schools away from various administrative and operational problems and also keep these institutions away from forsaking its basic objectives.

But the present controversy and altercation focused from various sections is that the Kurnool Municipal Corporation which is entrusted with the responsibility of facilitating its people with good standard, qualitative and suitable programmes of education through effective management of secondary schools is not successful in fulfilling the above objectives under the present organizational and administrative setup. There is also lot of criticism prevailing with regard to its mode and media through which it is operating the educational administration. The various lapses in its organizational structure especially in respect of its organizational branch which is dealing with school education, matters relating to schools administration, nature and scope of supervision and control over the schools and the various other personnel and operational problems being encountered by secondary schools and so on are all at brickbats. The enormous omissions pin-pointed at various quarters and at various levels with regard to the pupil enrollment rate, percentage of attendance, teaching staff and their performance, the manpower planning, teacher-pupil ratio, various problems of accommodations, and other physical facilities, students performance in public examinations, its various other personnel and financial problems and more particularly the degree of morale and motivation prevailing in its schools all reveal that all is not well with the educational administration under Kurnool Municipal Corporation.

Scope of the Study

Hence, an attempt is made in this book to study the administrative and organizational structure of Kurnool Municipal Corporation in general and its educational administration in particular in the light of the management of secondary education, the day-to-day working of its secondary schools, and their operational predicaments and various other related flaws with a view to brighten the performance, enhance the academic standards and promote administrative efficiency and functional efficacy with a sincere aim of making these schools more academic-oriented and pupil-spirited.

In the complexion of this book we received all kinds of help, advice and guidance from various authorities of the Kurnool Municipal Corporation in general and all the Headmasters and Headmistresses of all secondary schools and their staff and students under Kurnool Municipal Corporation who fed us with valuable information and suggestions. The pupils of all the secondary schools in general and pupil respondents in particular also deserve gratitude for their cooperation in responding to the questionnaire.

The Kanishka Publishing House deserves a special mention for publishing this book very neatly on priority basis within a very short period despite several difficulties that the Publishers are facing today.

Contents

Abbreviations

AD	Assistant Director
AE	Adult Education
AIFEA	All India Federation of Employees Associations
AP	Andhra Pradesh
APER	Andhra Pradesh Education Rules
APETF	Andhra Pradesh Elementary Teachers Federation
APPRTU	Andhra Pradesh Panchayati Raj Teachers Union
APRJUP	Andhra Pradesh Rashtra Jatiya Upadhyaya Parishad
APSHU	Andhra Pradesh State Headmasters Union
APTF	Andhra Pradesh Teachers Federation
APUTF	Andhra Pradesh United Teachers Federation
Asst.	Assistant
BC	Backward Classes
B.Ed.	Bachelor of Education
BJP	Bharatiya Janata Party
B.Li.Sc.	Bachelor of Library Science
CCT	Coordination Committee of Teachers
CGR	Compound Growth Rate
CCRTU	Coordination Committee of Recognised Teachers Unions

CL	Casual Leave
CPI	Communist Party of India
CPI (ML)	Communist Party of India (Marxist & Leninist)
DA	Dearness Allowance
DD	Deputy Director
DEO	District Educational Officer
Dept.	Department
DHE	Director of Higher Education
DIET	District Institute of Education and Training
Dip. P.Ed.	Diploma in Physical Education
DIS	Deputy Inspectors of Schools
DPI	Director of Public Instruction
DSC	District Selection Committee
DSE	Director of School Education
Dy. EO	Deputy Educational Officer
EL	Earned Leave
EM	English Medium
FAC	Full Additional Charge
FAPTO	Federation of Andhra Pradesh Teachers Organizations
FR	Fundamental Rules
FW	Finance Wing
GO	Government Order
Govt.	Government
Gr.	Grade
HG	Higher Grade
HM	Head Master/Head Mistress
HRD	Human Resource Development
IAS	Indian Administrative Service
IR	Interim Relief

JA	Junior Assistant
KMC	Kurnool Municipal Corporation
LGR	Linear Growth Rate
LSG	Local Self-Government
MA	Master of Arts
MC	Municipal Commissioner
ME	Municipal Engineer
M.Ed.	Master of Education
MEO	Mandal Educational Officer/Mandal Educational Office
MHO	Municipal Health Officer
	Municipal Educational Officer
NCERT	National Council for Education, Research and Training
NFE	Non-Formal Education
NSSO	National Sample Survey Organisation
OBB	Operation Black Board
PC	Planning Commission
PET	Physical Education Teacher
PR	Panchayati Raj
PVTC	Pre-Vocational Training Course
RD	Regional Director
RDMA	Regional Director of Municipal Administration
RJD	Regional Joint Director
SA	Senior Assistant/School Assistant
SC	Scheduled Castes
SCERT	State Council for Education, Research and Training
Sec.	Section
SG	Secondary Grade/Selection Grade

SGBT	Secondary Grade Basic Training
SO	Special Officer
ST	Scheduled Tribes
SSC	Secondary School Certificate
STUAP	State Teachers Union of Andhra Pradesh
SUPW	Socially Useful Productive Works
TDP	Telugu Desam Party
TIR	Terminal Inspection Reports
TM	Telugu Medium
UD	Urban Development
UP	Upper Primary
UT	Union Territory
VR	Voluntary Retirement
ZP	Zilla Parishad

1

Educational System in India

The march of time leaves its prints on the history of a nation. Education is an important national enterprise and it has come to stay as a force to be reckoned with in the mainstream of national life in the progress and prosperity of the country. It has been rightly said that a nation must take care of her education or face the peril. This fact has vehemently been recognized in the past century and particularly so in recent decades.[1]

India had to face the problems of political, economic and social development in the shortest possible time in the wake of independence. For facing all these problems the creation of a trained manpower was the first requisite. It was possible only through an efficient educational system. The government of free India, therefore, had to moderate its educational system.[2]

The story of Indian education is as interesting as it is enlightening. When we peep into the distant past and try to understand the present, we find that the roots of the present system of education in India did bear sweet fruit and love of learning did exercise powerful influence on the succeeding ages. But the shadows of the passing time darkened the glorious paths of India's great heritage, thus throwing every great tradition into oblivion.

Meaning of Education

Education is a means of transformation of human nature and culture. The term education has been derived from the Latin word 'Educare' which "means" 'to educate', 'to bring up', 'to raise' or 'to elevate'. It is also a means of bringing out what is the best within a man. It is also responsible for bringing out the latent potentialities of a person. It is also a part of training.[3]

Education as defined by Plato (428-348 B.C.) as:

> "that training which is given by suitable habits to the first instincts of virtue in children......which leads you always to hate what you ought to hate, and love what you ought to love from the beginning of the life to the end ...... in my view, will be rightly called education.

Aristotle (348-322 B.C.) another eminent philosopher of Greece has defined education in the following words:

> "........education of the young requires the special attention of the law giver. Indeed the neglect of this in states is injurious to their constitution, for education ought to be adapted to the particular form of constitution."

In his famous book 'Emile' Rousseau has defined education in the following words:

> "All that we are not possessed of at birth and which we acquire when grown up, is bestowed on us by education. This education we receive from men or from circumstances. The constitutional exertion of our organ and faculties is the education of nature: the uses we are taught to make of that exertion, constitute the education given to us by men; and in the acquisitions made by our own experience, on the objects that surround us, consists our education from circumstances."

Mahatma Gandhi fully realized the importance of education. He knew that it was a powerful instrument for changing the man and society. He in his work has dealt on various aspects of education. His best definition is as follows:[4]

> "By education, I mean an allround training out of the best in child and man body, mind and spirit."

These definitions very clearly mean that education is the process of the development of the innate qualities of man and bringing about allround development of the personality. In other words, it means that through education it is possible to bring about not only the allround development of the personality but also his internal faculties and social qualities.

Formal and Informal Education

Generally it is these two types of education that are very much in vogue. Formal education is more or less artificial and voluntary. It is complementary to the informal education. Since formal education is artificial its agencies which form its period is prescribed, curricular is laid down, the place is fixed and so is the case with the method of teaching and teachers. It is not necessary for everybody to clear this type of education. One who completes this prescribed education, gets a certificate at the end.

The education that is important in the schools, colleges, universities and other formal agencies, such education is called formal education.

Informal Education

It is the natural or non-prescribed type of education. Every person who acquires this type of education is learner while every person who imparts such education is teacher. Neither the learner knows that he is being taught nor it is the teacher who knows that he is imparting education. It is this type of education which has been termed as a social process and which contains from the cradle to the court-yard. There are no prescribed agencies of the informal education but since man is social animal it is imparted by social agencies like family, society, play field etc.[5]

Direct and Indirect Education

Direct Education

This type of education is the result of direct contract between the teacher and the taught. In this process the teacher imparts his knowledge to the student according to his aims and objects. This is more or less a type of direct education.

Indirect Education

This is a type of informal education in which teacher, unknowingly imparts knowledge to his educand. The agencies of indirect or informal education are not prescribed one.

Types of Education

Broadly speaking, education is divided into three branches viz., formal, informal and non-formal education. Formal education is deliberately and consciously planned and its curriculum is predesigned and goals also pre-determined. It comprises direct schooling and tuition intended for pupils of particular age group. For example, schools and colleges impart formal education. Informal education is predominant in the developing and underdeveloped countries and also in advanced countries. This is also called as incidental education which is received by living with others. But it is not provided consciously and deliberately. Finally, Non-formal education is offered at any convenient place, time and level of understanding or psychological growth of children or adults. Education in India can be divided into the following sub-heads.

(a) Pre-primary Education
(b) Primary Education
(c) Secondary Education
(d) Social Education
(e) Special Education
(f) Rural Higher Education
(g) Urban Education
(h) Physical Education
(i) Technical Education
(j) College Education
(k) University Education and
(l) Research and Training

Analysis of Table 1.1 reveals that the educational system in India is inter linked with each other types of education through the nature, purpose, mode and method but objectives vary from each other. The important arrangement in this system is that educational facilities are seen both at rural and urban levels. Physical education found its place in all levels and Research and Training is linked to both General and Technical education. The adult education is also found its place with the participation of State Governments, Universities and other Voluntary Organisations. In India Rural Education comprising of pre-primary, primary and secondary education is imparted by schools under Panchayati Raj system. The urban education comprising of primary and secondary education is offered by the primary as well as secondary schools managed by the municipalities on which the present study is made.

Agencies of Education

Society has developed number of specialized institutions to carryout the functions of education and these institutions are known as the

Table–1.1
Educational System in India
↓
Central and State Governments
↓
(Education under Concurrent List)

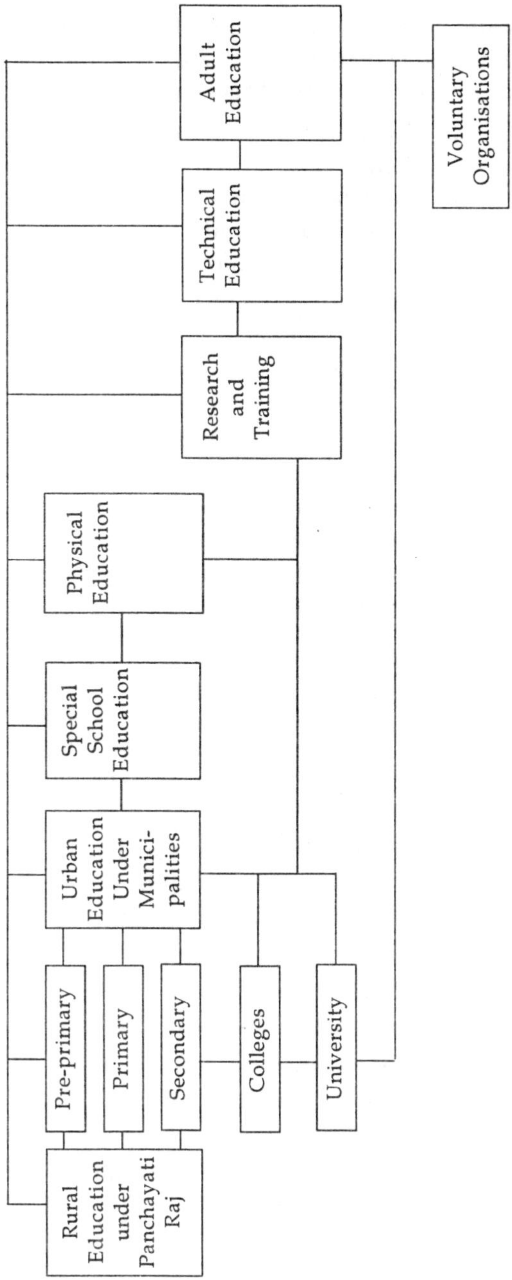

agencies of education. The agencies of education are generally divided into *(a)* Formal and *(b)* Informal. The formal agencies of education are those which are set up by men and less deliberately by society. The formal agencies of education are:

(a) School
(b) Library
(c) Recreation Centres
(d) Reading rooms and
(e) Religious Institutions

The informal agencies of education has a wider connotation. It should be understood in terms of learning. There are certain institutions other than formal agencies which educate people without definite rules or special curriculum. Here people are educated with their own activities. The informal agencies of education are:

(a) Home or Family
(b) Religious Organizations
(c) Drama and Cinemas
(d) News Papers
(e) Radios and Televisions, and
(f) Libraries

Schools as formal agencies of education managed by Local Bodies in general and Municipal Corporations in particular especially in respect of secondary education is discussed in succeeding chapters.

Education in India comprises two distinct stages, namely, the stage of school education and the stage of higher education. The period of school education may be further divided into three stages:

(i) Pre-primary education (the stage of informal education)
(ii) Primary education
(iii) Secondary education } (the two stages of formal education)

These three stages of school education correspond the three developmental stages in a child's life, namely, infancy, childhood and adolescence.

Importance of Secondary Education

Secondary education is very important from individual, social, economic and educational points of view.

1. *Secondary Education and Adolescence*

Secondary education deals with the adolescence period of child's development. It is the most crucial period which requires utmost care for the healthy development of child. Secondary education plays a significant role in the development of well-balanced personality of man.

2. *Secondary Education and Socio-Economic Reconstruction*

Secondary education plays an important role in training the youth of the country to take an effective part in the social reconstruction and economic development. Virtually it is the secondary education on which depends the social, economic, technical and cultural efficiency of the nation. During the British Rule, the secondary education aimed at creating 'Babus'. But now the situation has changed. Now vocationalisation of secondary education is emphasized. The reason is very obvious. Since secondary-stage marks the final stage of education for majority of the students, it has to prepare them for various vocations.

3. *Importance of Secondary Education in Qualitative Improvement of Education*

Secondary education determines the quality of education both at the primary and higher stages of education. Most of the teachers working in primary schools have attained academic qualification upto secondary stage i.e., matriculation. They can make or mar the standard of primary education. Similarly secondary schools supply students for universities and other centres of higher learning. So, secondary education colleges, is a very important link between the primary and higher stages of education.

Because of its vital importance it is essential that secondary education should be of the highest quality.

The Historical Background of Secondary Education in India (During the British Rule)

(A) From Macaulay's Minute to 1902

As a matter of fact, there was no systematic system of education before the advent of the English in India. With the efforts of Christian Missionaries some institutions were established. These institutions imparted education for the propagation of Christianity.

1. Macaulay's Minute

The present system of Secondary education can be traced to Lord's Macaulay's Minute and Government Resolution of 1835 which led to the establishment of English schools. Macaulay[6] wanted to create "a class of persons Indian in blood and colour but English in tastes, in opinions, in morals and in intellect."[7]

Keeping this view of Macaulay in mind, same schools were established to impart the knowledge of European literature and Science to the natives of India.

Lord Hardinge's Proclamation (1844)

In 1844 Lord Hardinge issued a proclamation that those who were educated in English schools would be given preference for services in public offices. This resulted to development of secondary education because it was considered to be a passport for entering government service.

Wood's Despatch, 1854[8]

The first government effort in secondary education was made after the acceptance of Wood's Despatch. The Despatch recommended the following:

(i) *Department of Public Instruction:* Departments of Public Instruction should be established in every province.
(ii) *Establishment of Universities:* Universities should be established in Calcutta, Bombay and Madras.
(iii) *Grant-in-Aid System:* Grant-in-Aid system should be introduced for giving financial help to Indian educational institutions.

Implementing the recommendations of Wood's Despatch, the departments of public instructions were set up in all the provinces, universities were established in Bombay, Madras and Calcutta and system of grant-in-aid was also started. Many secondary schools were opened and universities dominated and controlled secondary education. In spite of the implementation of the recommendations of Wood's Despatch, these remained many defects in secondary education such as:[9]

(i) It was isolated from the real life of the students.
(ii) The mother tongue was not recognized as the medium of instruction.

(iii) Necessity of training the teachers for secondary education was ignored.

(iv) No provision was made for technical and vocational education. As a result, the secondary education became academic.

(v) The only aim of secondary education was to pass matriculation examination and find out some government job or seek admission in university.

Hunter Commission, 1882

The Hunter Commission reviewed the progress of education in India and suggested:[10]

(i) *Private Enterprise:* Expansion of secondary education should be left to private enterprise because it is very costly for the Government to maintain secondary schools. The Government may open secondary schools only at such places where private schools can't be opened.

(ii) *Grant-in-aid System:* Grant-in-aid system should be intensified to help the private enterprise to work enthusiastically in this field.

(iii) *Diversification of Courses:* There should be diversification of courses at the secondary stage of education.

The recommendation of diversification of courses was very important as the Commission wanted that secondary education should adopt two courses—one leading to entrance examination of the university and the other leading to commercial, vocational of non-literary pursuits. But this recommendations was neither appreciated by the government nor by the people. It was virtually deposed and secondary education continued to remain in the same rut.

University Commission—1902

Due to the recommendations of University Commission (1902), secondary education was brought under more domination of the universities. Indian University Act 1904 made it compulsory for secondary schools to get recognition from the universities.[11]

Sadler Commission or Calcutta University Commission (1917-19)

The main purpose of this Commission was to suggest improvement in the functioning of Calcutta University. But it also made some valuable recommendations for secondary education. Some of its major recommendations are as under:[12]

(i) *Improvement of Secondary Education:* Improvement of secondary education is essential for the improvement of university education.

(ii) *Diversification of Courses:* There should be provision of diversification of courses at secondary stage of education.

(iii) *Intermediate Colleges:* There should be an intermediate course between Secondary and University courses. Intermediate colleges should be set up and they should provide instructions in Art, Science, Medicine, Engineering, Teaching etc.

(iv) *Boards of Secondary and Intermediate Education:* Secondary and Intermediate stages should not be under the control of Universities. For this, Boards of Secondary and Intermediate Education should be set up in each province.

(v) *Vernaculars as Media of Instruction:* Vernaculars should be adopted as media of education at the high school stage, except for Teaching of Mathematics and English.

The Commission also pointed out the defects of examination-ridden system of education, miserable condition of teaching service, inefficiency of teachers, predominance of English etc. Some of its recommendations were implemented. Intermediate colleges were set up and Boards of Secondary and Intermediate Education were established. Secondary education expanded more and the number of secondary schools began to increase in both urban and rural areas. But nothing was done towards qualitative improvement of secondary education. The problems of teachers remained unsolved and secondary education continued to be academic.

Hartog Committee (1929)

Hartog Committee (1929) expressed that Matriculation Examination dominated the whole of secondary education. The Committee, however, admitted that secondary education was well advanced in comparison with mass-education. It also pointed out that large number of failures at the matriculation examination was sheer wastage. To eliminate this wastage, the Committee suggested:[13]

(i) Diversion of more boys to industrial and commercial careers at the end of the middle stage.

(ii) Vernacular Middle schools be remodeled and adapted to rural requirements.

Sargent Report (1945)

The main recommendations of Sargent Report, so far as Secondary Education is concerned, are as follows:[14]

1. *Six-year High School Courses:* The high school course should cover six years and the normal age of admission should be about eleven;
2. *Selective Basis for High School Entry:* Entry to high school should be on selective basis. Only those students should be admitted to high schools who show special aptitude and promise for higher studies.
3. In accordance with the general principle set out in (2) above, places in high school should be provided for at least one child in every five of the appropriate age-group.
4. *Varied Curriculum:* Curriculum in all cases should be as varied as possible.
5. *Two Types of High Schools:* High Schools should be of two main types:
   (*a*) Academic and
   (*b*) Technical: Their aim should be to provide a good, all round education combined with some preparation for future careers which students will enter on leaving school.
6. *Mother-tongue as Medium:* Mother tongue should be made the medium of instruction.

All the above mentioned efforts made with regard to Secondary Education resulted in an enormous expansion of it.

Defects in Secondary Education during British Rule

No doubt there was considerable expansion of secondary education, but its general condition was far from satisfactory. Mr. H.V. Hampton has pointed out the following defects in secondary education during British Rule.

1. *Bookish and Theoretical:* Secondary education was bookish and theoretical and it had no attraction for those students who had practical turn of mind.
2. *Not Keeping Pace with the Change:* Secondary education

during British Rule could not keep pace with new social, economic, political and industrial changes of India.

3. *Excessive use of English:* Too much emphasis was laid on use of English in secondary education during British Rule. This resulted in psychological burden both on students and teachers. It crushed their interest in education.
4. *Neglect of Scientific and Practical Subjects:* No place was given to scientific and practical subjects. They were virtually neglected.
5. *Encouragement of Cramming:* Because of excessive use of English as medium of instruction. Cramming got encouragement, Cramming further made teaching-learning process dull and lifeless.
6. *Inadequate Provision for Out-door Games:* Provision for out-door games and recreational activities was inadequate in secondary schools.
7. *Rigid and Monotonous:* There was no flexibility. Because of rigidity and monotony the process of education was boring.

Secondary Education After Independence

Aims and functions of secondary education in 1947, at the time of attainment of Independence were disappointing. The same bookish education, the same stress on the preparation for matric examination, the same memorization and the same unpsychological teaching methods were in practice. Secondary education with many such serious defects was unable to contribute in the reconstruction of new India. It was felt by the leaders and the educationists that secondary education should be reframed in such a way that it should keep pace with forthcoming development and should extend healthy and constructive contribution in solving its various problems. So various education Commissions were appointed after independence for studying critically the problems of education and recommending suitable measures for bringing necessary reforms. To study the condition of secondary education after independence, it is essential to know the recommendations made by various Commissions and Committees.[15]

1. *Dr. Tara Chand Committee-1948*

In 1948, the Government of India appointed a Committee under the Chairmanship of Dr. Tara Chand to recommend the reorganization of Secondary Education in India. The Committee's major recommendations were as under:

(i) Secondary schools should be of multi-purpose type.

(ii) There should be a four years' Higher Secondary course, after the completion of which a student should be considered eligible for admission to degree classes.

(iii) Pay scales and service conditions of the teachers should be improved.

(iv) All India Council of Education to be set up for coordination between the Centre and the States.

2. *Radhakrishnan or University Education Commission–1948*

In order to meet the requirement of scientific, technical and agricultural braches and also to provide research facilities at the university stage, a University Commission was appointed in 1948 under the Chairmanship of Dr. Radhakrishnan. Although it was primarily concerned with the university education, yet it suggested improvement in secondary education as well. Criticizing the existing secondary education, the Commission stated:

"Our secondary education remains the weakest link in our educational machinery and needs urgent reforms".

The important recommendations of the Commissions with regards to secondary education were as under:

(i) There should be a twelve years secondary course instead of ten years course.

(ii) An exhaustive list of subjects for general and special education at the secondary stage should be given.

(iii) Liberal grant and better facilities should be provided.

(iv) Lot of the teachers should be improved.

3. *Secondary Education Commission (1952)*

On the recommendations of the Tara Chand Committee and the Central Advisory Board of Education, the Government of India appointed a Commission on September 23, 1925 under the Chairmanship of Dr. A. Lakshmanaswami Mudaliar, the Vice-Chancellor of Madras University. The Commission was directed to examine the existing system of secondary education in the country and to suggest suitable measures for its reorganization and improvement. The Commission after careful survey of the matter submitted its report in June, 1953 and offered detailed recommendations on various aspects of educational reconstruction and reorganization. Its major recommendations were as under:

1. Secondary education should start after four years of Primary education or Junior Basic stage. It should include three years of Middle or Senior Basic and four years of higher secondary.
2. There should be multi-purpose schools at higher-secondary level and students should be encouraged to join professional and technical courses after higher secondary, according to their interests and aptitudes.
3. Public schools should continue and the State Government should open some residential schools in the rural areas.
4. The regional or mother tongue should be made medium of instruction.
5. Trained Guidance Officers and Career Masters should be appointed in all secondary schools to help the students in choosing the most suitable vocation for themselves.
6. School medical service be provided for thorough medical examination of every student and for occasional check up afterwards.
7. Teachers of physical education and first-aid training should be appointed for giving regular training in sports, games and community and social activities to students.
8. Due credit should be given to internal school tests and cumulative records maintained in school for every student at the time of final assessment.
9. A Board of Secondary Education in each state with Director of Public Instruction (D.P.I.) as Chairman should be constituted. State Advisory Boards of Education should guide and advise the education department.
10. State or Central Governments should provide funds to schools for playgrounds, buildings, science-equipment and appliances, library books, art and craft equipment and agricultural farms.

Sufficient financial aid should be given to those government and private high schools which are converted to Higher Secondary Pattern.

Kothari Education Commission 1964-66

Indian Education Commission was appointed in 1964 to advise the Government of India on the national pattern of education and the general principles and policies for the development of education at all stages and in all aspects. Prof. D.S. Kothari, Chairman, University Grants Commission, was its Chairman. The Commission submitted its report on 29 June, 1966. The report of the Commission is a landmark in the history of Indian Education as it deals with general aspects of educational reconstruction, reorientation of educational system to national objectives, structural reorganization, enrolment policies, problems of curriculum, evaluation and administration, improvement of teachers etc. As the scope of the Commission was wider, it applied constructive thinking to almost all the aspects of education. The Commission was in favour of drastic reconstruction of educational system by improving primary education, introducing work experience as an integral part of general education, vocationalising secondary education, improving the quality of teachers at all levels, liquidating illiteracy and paying special attention to education and research in agriculture.

National Policy on Education 1968

On the basis of the recommendations of Kothari Education Commission and the Report of the Committee of Members of Parliament on Education, a National Policy of Education (Secondary Education) 1968, has been formulated. This included the following:

1. Educational opportunity at the secondary level is a major instrument for bringing social change and transformation. So this opportunity should be extended to all classes of people.
2. Facilities for Technical and Vocational education should be increased at this stage.
3. Facilities for secondary and vocational education should conform broadly to the real employment opportunities and requirements of developing economy.
4. Technical and vocational education should be suitably diversified to cover a large number of fields such as agriculture, industry, trade and commerce, medicine and public health, home management, arts and crafts, secretarial training etc.

The Central Government is making every attempt to implement the national policy of education. But without the active cooperation of the State Governments, nothing substantial can be achieved in this respect. Now that the country's all-round development is integrally linked with secondary education, it is essential that secondary education should be framed in accordance with the needs of national reconstruction.

The National Education Policy 1986

The National Educational Policy considered education in general and secondary and higher education in particular as a great challenge. Attention has been focused on vocationalisation of education at +2 stage. A large number of vocational streams were recommended. Three-language formula, mother tongue as medium of instruction were also recommended. Navodaya Vidyalayas were recommended by the Commission. Its objective was to provide free secondary and higher education to talented students who belonged to the rural areas. Under the New Policy of Education, well established secondary schools would strive for excellence, national integration and personality development of pupils.[16]

The progress of education in the post-independence era was mainly because of the English medium of education and it became the foundation for the modern system of education in India which was largely responsible for the transmission of western culture and civilization. Besides the Central and State Governments, the local bodies like Panchayat Raj Institutions in rural areas, the Municipalities and Municipal Corporations in urban areas were also brought into their fold for promotion of primary and secondary education in the country.

Constitutional Base of Education

The Indian Constitution has provided due place to the subject of education. An analysis of Table 1.2 reveals that education is one of the Fundamental Rights of the Constitution. Articles 29 and 30 of Indian Constitution ensure the various constitutional provisions regarding education in India are in accordance with our political, economic, social and culture needs. These provisions aimed at fulfilling the aspirations of the people through the medium of education. The subject of education was first placed under State List. Consistent with the 42nd Constitutional Amendment made in the year 1976, it brought education under Concurrent List with a new sharing of responsibility between Union Government and the States in all its ramification-substantive, administrative and financial.[17] The Constitution of India provides the following main areas of education to the country as given in Table 1.2.

Table-1.2
Main Provisions in the Constitution Relating to Education

S. No.	*Provision*	*Article of the Constitution*
1.	Free and compulsory education for children upto the age of 14 years	45
2.	Right of Minorities to establish and administer educational institutions	29, 30
3.	Facilities for instruction in mother tongue at primary stage of education	350 (A)
4.	Promotion of Hindi	351
5.	Provision regarding religious education and religious worship in educational institutions	25, 28
6.	Education of the socially and educationally backward classes of citizens	46
7.	Education of Women—15 (1)(3) 16 (1)	List I, II and
8.	Educational functions of State and Central Governments	III including 42 amendment

Source: Saxena, R.N. The Constitutional Law of India, (Allahabad: Central Law Agency, 1989).

Article 29 and 30 of Indian Constitution ensure every citizen the protection of their language, script or culture. Article 29 provides that:

> "No citizen shall be denied admission into any educational institution maintained by the States or receiving aid out of State funds on ground only of religion, race, caste, language or any of them."[18]

Article 30

> "Guarantees to all minorities whether based on religion or language the right to establish and administer educational institutions of their choice and declares that in granting aid to educational institutions, the State shall not

> discriminate against any educational institutions on the ground that it is managed by a religious or linguistic minority."[19]

The Part IV of Indian Constitution which deals with the Directive Principles of State Policy under Articles 36 to 52 clearly mentioned that:

> "The State shall strive to provide for free and compulsory education for all children until they complete the age of fourteen years."[20]

It has been realized and also evident from the above that the elementary education should be the strong base on which the fabric of Secondary Education could be constructed.

Article 46 of the Indian Constitution says that:

> "The State shall promote with special care the educational and economic interests of the weaker sections of the people and in particular of the Scheduled Castes and Scheduled Tribes education."

Before 1976, education was the exclusive responsibility of the States. The Constitutional Amendment of 1976, which included education in the Concurrent List, was a far-reaching step. The substantive, financial and administrative implication required a new sharing of responsibility between the Union Government and the States. While the role and responsibility of the States in education remained largely unchanged, the Union Government accepted a larger responsibility of reinforcing the National and integrative character of education, maintaining quality and standards including those of the teaching profession at all levels, and the study and monitoring of the educational requirements of the country.

The Central Government continues to play a leading role in the evolution and monitoring of educational policies and programmes, the most notable of which are the National Policy of Education (NPE), 1986 and the Programme of Action (POA), 1986 as updated in 1992. The modified policy envisages a National System of Education to bring uniformity in education, making adult education programmes a mass movement, providing universal access, retention and quality of elementary education, special emphasis on education of girls, establishment of pace-setting schools like Navodaya

Vidyalayas in each district, vocationalisation of secondary education, synthesis of knowledge and inter-disciplinary research in higher education, starting more Open Universities in the States, strengthening of the All India Council of Technical Education, encouraging sports, physical education, Yoga and adoption of an effective evaluation method, etc. Besides, a decentralized management structure had also been suggested to ensure popular participation in education. The POA lays down a detailed strategy for the implementation of the various policy parameters by the implementing agencies.

The National System of Education as envisaged in the NPE is based on a national curricular framework, which envisages a common core alongwith other flexible and region-specific components. While the policy stresses widening of opportunities for the people, it calls for consolidation of the existing system of higher and technical education. It also emphasizes the need for a much higher level of investment in education of atleast six per cent of the national income.[21]

Expenditure on Education

In line with the commitment of augmenting resources for education, the allocation for education has, over the years, increased significantly. The Plan outlay on education has increased from Rs. 151.20 crore on the First Five Year Plan to Rs. 43,825 crore in the Tenth Five Year Plan (2002-07).[22] Vide Table 1.3.

General Structure of School Education

A uniform structure of school education viz., the 10+2 system has been adopted by all the States and UTs of India. However, within the States and the UTs, there are variations in the number of classes constituting the Primary, Upper Primary, High and Higher Secondary schools, age for admission to Class I, medium of instruction, stages of public examinations, teaching of Hindi and English, number of working days in a year, academic session, vacation periods, fee structure compulsory education etc.

Stages of School Education in India

The Primary Stage consists Classes I-V, i.e., of five year duration, in 20 States/UTs namely Andhra Pradesh, Arunachal Pradesh, Bihar, Haryana, Himachal Pradesh, Jammu & Kashmir, Madhya Pradesh,

Table–1.3
Plan Expenditure on Different Sectors of Education

(In Percentage)

Sector	*First Plan Expdt. 1951-56*	*Second Plan Expdt. 1956-61*	*Third Plan Expdt. 1961-66*	*Plan Holiday Expdt. 1966-69*	*Fourth Plan Expdt. 1969-74*	*Fifth Plan Expdt. 1974-79*	*Sixth Plan Expdt. 1980-85*	*Seventh Plan Expdt. 1985-90*	*1990-92 Expdt.*	*Eighth Plan Expdt. 1992-97*	*Ninth Plan Outlay (1997-02) (Central Sector)*	*Ninth Plan Expdt. (1997-07) (Central Sector)*	*Tenth Plan Outlay (2002-07) (Central Sector)*
1	2	3	4	5	6	7	8	9	10	11	12	13	14
Elementary Education	58 (870)	35 (950)	34 (2010)	24 (750)	50 (3743)	52 (5913)	32 (8414)	37 (28494)	37 (17290)	48 (103940)	66 (163696)	65.7 (145233)	65.6 (287500)
Secondary Education	5 (83)	19 (510)	18 (1030)	16 (530)	@	@	20 (5344)	24 (18315)	22 (10530)	24 (52311)	10 (26035)	10.5 (23227)	9.9 (43250)
Adult Education					2 (126)	2 (248)	6 (1533)	6 (4696)	9 (4160)	5 (11421)	3 (6304)	2.4 (5204)	2.9 (12500)
Higher Education	8 (117)	18 (480)	15 (870)	24 (770)	25 (1883)	28 (3188)	28 (3188)	16 (12011)	12 (5880)	10 (20944)	10 (25000)	10.3 (22709)	9.5 (41765)
Others	15 (227)	10 (300)	12 (730)	11 (370)	13 (936)	9 (1071)	11 (2729)	3 (1980)	2 (1180)	3 (7398)	2 (4314)	1.6 (3492)	1.4 (6235)
Technical Education	14 (215)	18 (490)	21 (1250)	25 (810)	10 (786)	9 (1015)	10 (2563)	14 (10833)	17 (8230)	10 (21987)	9 (23735)	9.5 (21095)	10.7 (47000)
Total	100 (1512)	100 (2730)	100 (5890)	100 (3230)	100 (7474)	100 (11435)	100 (26187)	100 (76329)	100 (47270)	100 (218001)	100 (249084)	100 (220960)	100 (438250)

Source: Five Year Plan Documents, Planning Commission and Analysis of Budget Expenditure, Ministry of HRD.

Note: 1. Figures in parenthesis in millions of rupees.

2. Figures in col. 2 to col. 11 includes the share of States/UTs.

@ Included under Elementary Education.

Manipur, Orissa, Punjab, Rajasthan, Sikkim, Tamil Nadu, Tripura, Uttar Pradesh, West Bengal, Andaman & Nicobar Islands, Chandigarh, Delhi and Karaikal and Yanam regions of other regions of Pondicherry. The primary stage consists of Classes I-IV in Assam, Goa, Gujarat, Karnataka, Kerala, Maharashtra, Meghalaya, Mizoram, Nagaland, Dadra & Nagar Haveli, Daman & Diu, Lakshadweep and Mahe region of Pondicherry.

The Middle Stage of education comprises Classes VI-VIII in as many as 18 States/UTs viz., Arunachal Pradesh, Bihar, Haryana, Himachal Pradesh, Jammu & Kashmir, Madhya Pradesh, Manipur, Punjab, Rajasthan, Sikkim, Tamil Nadu, Tripura, Uttar Pradesh, West Bengal, Andhra Pradesh, Andaman & Nicobar Islands, Chandigarh, Delhi and Karaikal region of Pondicherry, Classes V-VIII in Assam, Goa, Gujarat, Karnataka, Kerala, Maharashtra, Meghalaya, Mizoram, Dadra & Nagar Haveli, Daman & Diu Lakshadweep and Mahe region of Pondicherry and Classes VI-VII in Andhra Pradesh, Orissa and Yanam region of Pondicherry and Nagaland Classes V-VIII constitute the Upper Primary stage.[23]

The Secondary Stage consists of Classes IX-X in 19 States/UTs viz., Arunachal Pradesh, Bihar, Haryana, Himachal Pradesh, Andhra Pradesh, Jammu & Kashmir, Madhya Pradesh, Manipur, Nagaland, Punjab, Rajasthan, Sikkim, Tamil Nadu, Tripura, Uttar Pradesh, West Bengal, Andaman & Nicobar Islands, Chandigarh, Delhi and Karaikal region of Pondicherry. The high school stage comprises Classes VIII to X in 13 States/UTs viz., Andhra Pradesh, Assam, Goa, Gujarat, Karnataka, Kerala, Maharashtra, Meghalaya, Mizoram, Orissa, Dadra & Nagar Haveli, Daman & Diu, Lakshadweep and Mahe and Yanam, regions of Pondicherry. However the Higher, Secondary/Senior Secondary stage of school comprising Classes XI-XII (10+2 pattern) is available in all the States and UTs though in some States/UTs these classes are attached to Universities/Colleges.[24]

Navodaya Vidyalaya Samiti

The National Policy on Education-1986 envisaged setting up of model schools, one in each District of the country. Accordingly, a scheme was formulated under which it was decided to set-up co-educational residential schools (now called Jawahar Navodaya Vidyalayas).

Navodaya Vidyalaya is fully residential co-educational institution providing education up to senior secondary stage. The scheme, which started with only two schools on experimental basis in 1985-86, has grown to 513 schools (as on 31st March 2008) covering as many districts in 34 States/UTs, with over 1.68 lakh students on rolls as on 31 March 2008. More than 30,000 new students are admitted every year.

The Vidyalaya envisaged a new style of growth with identification and development of talented, bright and gifted children predominantly from rural areas who may otherwise be denied good educational opportunities. Efforts are made to ensure that at least 33 per cent of the students enrolled are girls.

Migration is a unique feature of Navodaya Vidyalaya scheme whereby 30 per cent of students of Class IX from a Vidyalaya located in Hindi speaking area spend one academic year in a Vidyalaya located in Non-Hindi speaking area and vice-versa to promote national integration through understanding of the diversity and plurality of country's people, their language and culture.

Kendriya Vidyalaya Sangathan

The Government approved the scheme of Kendriya Vidyalaya Sangathan in 1962, on the recommendations of the Second Pay Commission. Initially, 20 regimental schools in different States were taken over as Central School. In 1965, an Autonomous Body called Kendriya Vidyalaya Sangathan was established with the primary objective of setting-up and monitoring Kendriya Vidyalaya to cater to the educational needs of the children of transferable Central Government Employees including Defence Personnel and Para-Military Force by providing common programme of education. At present, there are 931 Kendriya Vidyalaya (as on 17 June 2008) out of which three Kendriya Vidyalayas are abroad i.e., one each in Kathmandu, Moscow and Tehran. All Kendriya Vidyalaya follow a uniform syllabus.[25]

Educational Administration in India - In a Nutshell

Education is one of the largest human enterprises undertaken by most transitional as well as modern governments during present times. India had experienced a variety of circumstances in respect of promotion of education to its people. Looking from a historical perspective, it is a well-known fact that India under colonial domination received an indifferent attention from the Britishers in respect of education to natives. The conspicuous features of educational system before Independence in India was the divorce of the Central Government from education as it transferred the subject of education to Indian control as part of the system of Dyarchy introduced in the provinces in 1921 and Provincial Autonomy introduced in 1937. The local authorities were first placed in charge of primary education as a part of a programme of transferring powers to Indian people, and later on, they were permitted to develop other educational programmes at their discretion. The private educational institutions played an important role in British Indian Provinces especially in post-primary education.

After Independence

With Independence in 1947 a new chapter opened in educational administration in India. There could be no room for Central indifference to education. It was realized that in a vast country like India, with immense local diversities, education should largely be a responsibility of the State Government and Local Authorities. As such the subject of education was placed in State List and later it was brought to the Concurrent List as per 42nd Amendment in 1976. Article 282 of the Constitution enabled the Government of India to give grants-in-aid to the States, to develop their educational programmes. Entry 20 of List III in the Constitution provided economic and social planning as a concurrent responsibility of the centre and the states. It has been given the idea that there has to be healthy partnership the Central and State Government in the task of educational reconstruction.

Pertaining to primary and secondary education, the schools which are involved in this task were managed by three agencies viz., government, local bodies and voluntary organizations. The government schools form only one fifth of the total. The schools conducted by the local bodies are the largest in number. The schools run by private enterprises form about one third of the total. As far as finances are concerned, the State Government supports not only its own schools but also those of local bodies and voluntary organizations to some extent. In fact, it may be said that the bulk of expenditure on school education comes from State funds and feeses and that only a small and relatively less significant contribution is made by local bodies.[26]

Educational Administration at National Level

The agencies at the national level concerned with the development of primary and secondary education are the Ministry of Human Resource Development under which there is a Department of Education, and National Council of Educational Research and Training (NCERT).

Ministry of Human Resource Development (MHRD)

With the advent of Independence in 1947, a full-fledged Ministry of Education and Scientific Research was established. With the launching of Five Year Plans the policy was changed. The Centre allotted funds to the States, specially for the expression and development of universal primary education and social education of the adults. With the control of these grants the Centre started advising, guiding and supervising education in the States. At present the Department of Education is under the charge of a Minister of State which is a part and parcel of the Ministry of Human Resource Development under the charge of a Cabinet Minister which was created by the Congress (I) Government under the Prime Ministership of Rajiv Gandhi. Education, after becoming concurrent subject, the Government of India is now directly responsible for Secondary Education not only in the Union Territories, but also in all states. A Division in the Department of Education in the Union Ministry of Human Resource Development is entrusted with the responsibility of School Education.

The Minister for HRD controls the educational policies, directs, executes and ensures uniformity in the pattern of education in different states. He is the executive Head of the Ministry and responsible to the Parliament. He is assisted by a Minister of State and one or two Deputy Ministers according to need. The Educational Advisor is the administrative head of the Ministry. He is the Secretary to the Government of India and is the Principal Advisor to the Minister on all matters of policy and administration. The Union Ministry at present functions mainly through Five Bureaus dealing with the following heads:

1. School Education
2. Higher Education
3. Language; Literature and Fine Arts
4. Scholarships; and

5. Planning and Ancillary Educational Services

The Bureau of School Education deals with elementary, basic and secondary education and the Central School Unit. Each Bureau has been put in charge of a Joint Secretary or a Joint Educational Adviser. There are various advisory bodies to deal with special sectors of education and the important among them are 'All India Council' for Secondary Education constituted in the year 1955 and 'All India Council' for Elementary Education set up in the year 1957. These advisory bodies advise the Central and State Governments on issues which are of importance in formulating educational policies and programmes.[27]

National Council of Educational Research and Training

This Council was set up in September 1961 as an autonomous organization under the Ministry of Education, Government of India. The Union Minister for Education is its President and all state Education Ministers are its members, the Secretary to the Ministry of Education is the Director and an officer of the same Ministry is the Joint Director. The principal function of this Council is extension work with the state Education Departments centering round the development of school education.

Educational Administration at the State Level (Andhra Pradesh)

The state education system and its administrative structure in Andhra Pradesh is the synthesis of the different patterns that prevailed in the Nizam's dominion and the Andhra Regions before 1947. The synthesis came out effectively in 1956 when the Telangana and Andhra Regions were merged leading to the formation of the State of Andhra Pradesh.

In the Nizam's dominion there was an Education Department which was incharge of all educational matters. The key functionaries were the Education Secretary and Director of Public Instruction (DPI) assisted by a number of subordinate officers of each district who were inturn assisted by the Deputy Inspectors (DIs). The Revenue District was a co-terminus with the educational system.

The Andhra Region was governed by the pattern that was existing in the composite State of Madras. There was a Director of Public Instruction at the Headquarters and further there were

Regional Directors, the District Educational Officers and the Inspectors. The education districts did not synchronise with the revenue districts.[28]

Since 1956, after the emergence of the State of Andhra Pradesh, there was a Department of Education headed by a Minister who was a Cabinet Minister. Under the purview of this Department all branches of education i.e., Primary, Secondary, Higher, Technical and Social have been put together. The Minister was assisted by the Education Secretariat headed by a Secretary of the I.A.S. rank and supported by Deputy Secretaries and Assistant Secretaries. There were about 25 Sections which dealt with various educational matters.

In view of tremendous expansion of Primary, Secondary and Higher Education, in 1975 the Minister of Education was divided into two individual Ministries viz., Ministry of School Education and Ministry of Higher (Collegiate) Education. The Ministry of School Education is concerned with both Primary as well as Secondary Education in the state. Each Ministry is headed by one Minister who might be Cabinet rank sometimes.

In October, 1980 the Cabinet expansion took place under the Chief Ministership of T. Anjaiah and in order to accommodate as many of his followers as possible, he split the subjects into many independent branches and kept each branch under an independent minister. Consequently, the subject of education was also subjected to split and the technical education was separated from collegiate education and was put under the charge of one Cabinet Minister. In February, 1982 under the Chief Ministership of B.Venkatram, the primary, secondary and collegiate education was brought under one Cabinet Minister who was assisted by a Minister of State. However, the Technical Education continued to be under another Cabinet Minister. In August, 1982, under the Chief Ministership of Kotla Vijaya Bhaskara Reddy, the primary, secondary and collegiate education was put under the charge of Cabinet Minister and the technical education was brought under the charge of Minister of State. In 1983, January, the Telugu Desam Government under the Chief Ministership of N.T. Rama Rao, brought all branches of education including technical education under the charge of the Cabinet Minister. In August, 1984 under the Chief Ministership of Nadendla Bhaskar Rao, the Technical Education was separated and kept under the charge of State Minister and primary secondary and collegiate education was kept under the charge of Cabinet Minister. It was in 1993 under the Chief Ministership of Kotla Vijaya Bhaskara Reddy that primary and secondary education was brought under one Cabinet Minister and collegiate education which was renamed as Higher Education was kept under another Cabinet Minister and the technical education continued to be under State Minister. When N. Chandra Babu Naidu, assumed Chief Ministership after dethroning N.T. Rama Rao in August 1995 he kept school education (primary and secondary education) under the charge of Minister of State with independent charge. The same has been continued till the First term of Chief Ministership of Dr. Y.S. Rajasekhara Reddy from 2004 to 2009. In the year 2009 when Dr. Y.S. Rajasekhara Reddy was returned to power for his second term he merged the Intermediate Education to secondary education with 6th Class to Intermediate. He reduced Primary Education Ministry to 1st to 5th standards only and kept each under one Minister.

Administration of School Education (Primary and Secondary) in Andhra Pradesh

An attempt is made in this chapter to make an analytical and descriptive study of administrative structure of the Government which is responsible for the administration of primary as well as secondary education in Andhra Pradesh.

In Andhra Pradesh, the subject of education has been divided into Four specialized fields like *(a)* Primary Education *(b)* Secondary Education *(c)* Higher Education and *(d)* Technical Education. At present the subject of Higher Education is kept under the charge of Cabinet Minister and the Primary, Secondary and Technical Education are under the charge of State Ministers each.

Minister for Secondary Education

The Ministry for Secondary Education is headed by an elected Minister who is inturn answerable and accountable to State Legislature. He is responsible for continuing the educational policy and its execution. He administers his duties through the State Department of Secondary Education. The State Department of Secondary Education is organized at two focal points: policy making and co-ordination function at the Secretariat level and the direction, regulation and inspection functions at the Directorate level.

Secretariat Level

The Principal Secretary for Secondary Education is the administrative Head of the Secondary Education Secretariat who is directly responsible to the parent minister. He is assisted by one Additional Secretary, one Joint Secretary, one Deputy Secretary, five Assistant Secretaries and so on. The Secretary normally hails from Indian Administrative Service. The Secondary Education Secretariat is responsible for evolving general policies and plans, introducing legislative measures and serving as a liaison between the Secondary Education Minister and various Directorates that deal with executive aspects. By and large Secondary Education Secretariat is responsible for three types of activities viz., policy formulation, co-ordination and supervision.

It is the most important task of Secretariat Department to assist the Government in the formulation of educational policies and plans. Thus, in addition to providing Secretariat Assistance to the Minister, the Department advises the Government regarding the policy matters, it assists the Government in introducing new legislative measures, formulation of rules and regulations under the law.

In this context, special mention has to be made regarding the role of the Education Secretariat in framing the Budget. Acting in close liaison with the Department of Finance, the Education Secretariat finalises the budgetary proposals.

Secondly the Educational Secretariat is not only responsible for maintaining liaison with other departments of the State Secretariat but also with their Directorates respectively. This is also responsible for dealing with Government of India and other agencies like the University Grants Commission. For instance, all statistics concerning education are submitted to the Government of India by the Education Secretariat only.

Thirdly, the Education Secretariat is responsible for supervising and controlling the execution of the policies of the Government by the Directorate. Such supervision is carried out through their powers of approval and sanction and hearing of appeals. In addition to the budgetary control, Secretariat Department exercises such controls through personnel management also.

Directorate Level

While the Secretariat Department is chiefly responsible for the formulation of broad policies and general supervision over their implementation, the responsibility for the execution of the policies of the Government is entrusted to the Directorate. The education Directorate underwent several modifications since the formulation of the State in 1956. To begin with, there was a Director of Public Instruction, who administered education in the State with the assistance of four Deputy Directors, one Assistant Director, three Assistants and Special Officers.

There has been a major reorganization in the administrative structure of the Directorate during 1955. Accordingly, the monolithic character of the Director of Public Instruction came to an end when it was bifurcated into the Director of Public Instruction and Director of Higher Education. It may be said that this set up was necessary on account of fixation of priorities between Higher Education and School Education.[29] However, this reorganization did not last long. A couple of years later, the Government again amalgamated the Offices of Director of Public Instruction and the Director of Higher Education because of the failure of bifurcation.[30]

As the two-year Intermediate Course was introduced at that time, the Government wanted to give greater attention to the new management. Hence, all the functions of the Director of Public Instruction concerning Higher Education in the State were entrusted to the post of an Educational Adviser created in the Secretariat. An I.A.S. Officer took over as the education adviser and was also Ex-Officio Director of Higher Education-cum-Education Secretary to the Government.[31]

As the Educational Adviser, the Officer performed all functions relating to Higher Education. As Education Secretary he was to look after all other matters relating to education. However, this arrangement also came to an end during 1973-74 when the post of the Educational Adviser was abolished.

In 1975 the Government again bifurcated the Office of the Director of Public Instruction into two different Directorates, one each for Higher Education and School Education. It was said that the bifurcation had to be effected on account of tremendous expansion of Primary, Secondary and Higher Education.[32]

Thus, once again the executive administration relating to Higher Education was separated from the administration of the other aspects of administration such as primary and secondary education. As stated earlier, the responsibility for the administration of primary and secondary schools rested with the Directorate of School Education. At present after merging Intermediate Education with Secondary Education, a separate Directorate for Secondary Education has been created and kept under one Director who is of IAS Rank.

The Director of Secondary School Education is assisted by two Additional Directors, three Joint Directors, each one for Primary Education Services and for Vocational Education. These Joint Directors are assisted by one Deputy Director and Chief Accounts Officer. Now the Director of School Education was also assisted by a Director for APPEP, Director of SIET, Director of Public Libraries and some Special Officer for A.P. Open School Society and Member-Convener, A.P. State Literacy Mission Authority are kept under the Directorate of Primary Education.

Earlier directly under the control of the Director of School Education there was also State Council of Educational Research and Training (SCERT) at the State Level parallel to NCERT at Central level. The SCERT was headed by an Officer equal to the status of a Director of School Education. The Department of Education, Evaluation, Science Extension Services, Curriculum, Text Books, Psychological Studies, Educational Vocational Guidance, Teaching Aids and Audio Visual Education and Educational and Technological Cell are supplementary and complementary to each other. Now these are kept under the Directorate of Primary Education.

The Director of Secondary School Education, as Ex-Officio Commissioner for Government Examinations has to conduct all the examinations of secondary education. In this connection he is assisted by the following officers.

(a) Deputy Commissioner for Government Examinations.
(b) Secretary to the Commissioner for Government Examinations.
(c) Joint Secretary to the Commissioner for Government Examinations.

(*d*) Additional Joint Secretary to the Commissioner for Government Examinations.

(*e*) Assistant Commissioner for Government Examinations.

The Director of Secondary School Education occupies a very crucial position in the administrative hierarchy of educational administration in Andhra Pradesh. He exercises advisory, controlling, co-ordinating, development, financial and other functions. Thus, in the first place he has to advise the Government in respect of policy making pertaining to secondary education and secondly, as the Chief Executive Agency for Secondary Schools Administration in the State, he controls, guides and advises the District Educational Officers. He has to give necessary instructions to them for the proper implementation of the policies of the Government. The Director is responsible to conduct enquiries and dispose-off appeals submitted to him from the district level. Further, as part of his supervisory function, he not only inspects the offices of the District Educational Officers but also reviews the Inspection Reports of the District and other Officers. He is chiefly responsible for securing co-ordination among District Educational Officers in the State. Meetings of the District Educational Officers are convened regularly to achieve this end. He also acts like a liaison officer in bringing about co-ordination between the agencies like National Council for Educational Research and Training, State Council for Educational Research and Training, Scouts and Guides, Junior Red Cross, National Cadet Corps (NCC), Sports and Games in the State. Further, there are some developmental functions entrusted to the Director. He has to plan and sanction the opening of new schools or the upgrading of existing schools. He not only has to improve oriental education in the state but also manage education training schools. He is also responsible to prepare and submit budget estimates, revised estimates and other statements pertaining to secondary school education in the State.

He releases monthly grants and other payments to local bodies and local institutions. He has to dispose off the pension cases promptly. He has to make sure that all financial rules and regulations are properly followed by spending agencies in the full utilization of the budget proposals. He has to take care of supply of nationalized text books and other related matters.

Thus the success of Secondary Education in the State virtually depends on the role of the Director of Secondary Education. He should be a man of great vigour, vision and dynamism.

Regional Level

At the Regional Level, the Secondary Education Directorate was assisted by a number of subordinate officers in both Telangana and Andhra Regions upto the advent of Andhra Pradesh in 1956. Since 1956 to 1981 there were Regional Deputy Directors of Public Instruction one each at Kakinada, Guntur, Cuddapah, Anantapur, Warangal and Hyderabad. During 1981 the proposals of the Director of School Education for the establishment of Regional Officers of Joint Directors of School Education were approved by the Government of Andhra Pradesh. Accordingly Five Regional Joint Directors have been appointed to look after the needs of Seven Zones in the State as shown in Table 1.4.

Table—1.4
Zonal Headquarters of Regional Joint Directors

S.No.	*Office*	*Zone*	*Headquarters*
1.	Regional Joint Director	I & II	Kakinada
2.	Regional Joint Director	III	Guntur
3.	Regional Joint Director	IV	Cuddapah
4.	Regional Joint Director	V	Warangal
5.	Regional Joint Director	VI & VII	Hyderabad

Source: Office of the Regional Joint Director, Cuddapah.

District Level

At each district level there is one District Educational Officer who is the overall controlling officer in the district on educational matters. The District Educational Officer has to perform functions relating to Academic, Examinations, Administration, Planning and Organization and Budgetary and Financial matters. The District Educational Officer is assisted by Deputy Educational Officers and Parishad Educational Office at the district level in performing the above functions. These officers are inturn assisted by Inspectors of Schools and Deputy Inspectors of Schools who are incharge of schools in urban areas and Mandal Educational Officers in rural areas. At the district level there is a training institution namely

District Institution for Education and Training (DIET) which impart training to the teachers. This is an institution parallel to State Council of Education Research and Training at Hyderabad. This DIET is headed by one Principal and is under the direct control of one Joint Director who is incharge of Services at State Level.[33]

The Local Bodies

The local bodies in India in general and Andhra Pradesh in particular like Panchayat Raj Institutions in rural areas and Municipalities and Municipal Corporations in Urban areas also manage secondary educational institutions in their own way. Consequent upon the recommendations of the Hunter Commission of 1882 regarding the transfer of Secondary Schools to local bodies, the municipalities besides district local boards came into the lime light as agencies of secondary education which constituted the topic for present study.

An Overview

Education plays a vital role in giving human beings proper equipment to lead a gracious and harmonious life. Education in the widest sense is the context interaction between the individual and the Government. No good life is conceivable without education. Thus, education is purposeful and organized activity.

India adopted democratic system of Government whose success depends upon its educated citizens. It is with this view that free and compulsory education for children has been contemplated by the Indian Constitution with noble aims. The Constitution of India also placed Education subject in the Concurrent List and made both Central and State Governments as partners in enacting law in respect of education and its administration. The administration of education at national level as well as state, district, municipal, mandal and village levels is also linked in order to make both the Central and State Governments as partners in developing specifically primary and secondary education. Further the task of managing the schools and giving primary and secondary education to the people in rural and urban areas is taken up by the Local Self-Government bodies like Panchayat Raj, Municipalities and Municipal Corporations respectively. The Municipal Corporations in particular have made educational administration as part of their administration activities to impart secondary education to the people residing in their jurisdictions which is now a topic for the present study.

REFERENCES

1. Bhatia, K.K. *et al., Modern Indian Education and its Problems*, Ludhiana: Prakash Brothers, 1990.
2. Sharma, S.R., *Educational Development in India*, New Delhi: Anmol, 1990, p. 11.
3. Mohanty, J., *Indian Education in Emerging Society*, New Delhi: Sterling, 1994, p. 132.
4. Rai, B.C., *Sociological Foundation of Education*, Lucknow: Prakash Kendra, 1995, p. 5.
5. *Ibid*, p. 8.
6. *Macaulay was the Legal Member of Executive Council of the Governor General and Chairman of the Central Committee on Public Instruction, 1834 A.D.*
7. Dev, S.D., *Education and Career Year Book 1964-65*, New Delhi: Educational and Career Publishing House, 1966, p. 31.
8. *Alias Lord Halifex, He was the then President of the Board of Control of East India Company and Chairman of the Board of Control.*
9. Lakshmi, S., *Challenges in Indian Education*, New Delhi: Sterling, 1989, p. 12.
10. Saraya, R.N., *Development, Planning and Problems of Indian Education*, Jullandhar: Dhanpetrai & Sons, 1982, p. 203.
11. Bhatia, K.K., *Op.cit.*, p. 151.
12. Lakshmi, S., *Op.cit.*, p. 14.
13. Bhatia, K.K., *Op.cit.*, p. 152.
14. Safaya, R.N., *Op.cit.*, pp. 8-9.
15. Bhatia, K.K., *Op.cit.*, p. 153.
16. Lakshmi, S., *Op.cit.*, p. 20.
17. Sandeep, P. and Madhumati C., *Insights into Non-Formal and Adult Education*, Hyderabad: Gantami, 1992, p. 43.
18. Saxena, R.N., The Constitutional Law of India, Article 45, Part IV of Indian Constitution, Allahabad: Central Law Agency, 1979, p. 138.
19. *Ibid*, p. 124.
20. Saydian, P., *Problems of Educational Administration*, Bombay: Asia, 1957, p. 124.
21. Ministry of Information and Broadcasting, Government of India, *India-2006*, p. 218.
22. *Ibid*, p. 221.
23. Secondary Education, p. 2, http://education.nic.in/seced.asp
24. India-2006, *Op.cit.*, p. 682.
25. *Ibid.*, p. 240.

26. Kochhar, S.K., *Secondary School Administration*, New Delhi: Sterling, 1993, p. 13.
27. Chalapathi, B.V., *Rural Education Administration*, New Delhi: Deep & Deep, 1992, p. 2.
28. Dharmi, P. Sinha, Centre for Education Policy and Management *Descriptive Cum Critical Study of Education System in Andhra Pradesh*, Hyderabad: ASI, 1976, p. 10.
29. Government of Andhra Pradesh, G.O. Ms. No. 1771, GAD (SPL-A), dated 3.6.1966.
30. *Ibid.*, G.O.Ms. No. 860, GAD (SPL), dated 4.10.1967.
31. *Ibid.*, G.O.Ms. No. 2554, GAD (SPL), dated 21.9.1971.
32. Dharmi, P. Sinha, *Op. cit.*, p. 56.
33. Government of Andhra Pradesh, *Report on Public Instruction for the Year 1976-77*, Part I, p. 3.

2

Emergence of Municipal Government *vis-à-vis* Education

In India, Local Government is widely interpreted as Local Self-Government. The term originated when India was under British colonial administration and did not enjoy any provision of self-government either at the Central or State levels. When a decision was taken by the British Government to associate Indians in administering local affairs it meant a slice of self-government for the people. But today the term self-government has forfeited its significance as the country enjoys self-government both at the Central and State levels. In fact, in the Constitution of India the term used is Local Government.* The emergence of local government as a distinct governmental unit is a result of the interplay of several factors—historical, ideological and administrative. To that matter, every country contains large numbers of local governing bodies whose areas are too small, too sparsely populated and too poor to respond to the demands which are made upon them.[1]

Local Governments—From a Historical Perspective

Local self-government institutions are indispensable for the success of Democracy and it is here that the programmes of national development are put in action and people learn their first lesson of democratic rule. The institutions of local government are not new to India.

---

* Entry 4 in List II (State List) of the Seventh Schedule reads: 'Local Government, that is to say, the constitution and powers of Municipal Corporations, improvement trusts, district boards, mining settlement authorities and other local authorities for the purpose of local self-government or village administration.

Coming in particular, Municipal Government in India has its roots in pre-historic times.[2] The epoch-making excavations at Harappa and Mohanjodaro reveal that a highly developed urban civilization existed in the past. The cities had their councils which were elected bodies. In the words of Havell: "The administrative council of the city was modeled upon that of village communities and it may be assumed that like the latter, it was an elected body though certain matters were reserved for the council of imperial officials."[3]

Municipal Local Government: A British Creation

Though the existence of elective city councils in ancient India cannot be denied, yet there is no doubt that the foundations of modern system of Municipal Government were laid by the British which received representative character.[4] Thus, Local Government in India, as a representative organization was a creation of British, responsible to a body of electors, enjoying wide powers of administration and taxation and functioning both as a school for training in responsibility and as a vital link in the chain of organisms that make up the Government of the country.

A beginning of the Local Government may said to have been made in 1887 when for the first time a local governing body—a Municipal Corporation was set up for the city of Madras under the Order of the Court of Directors. Municipal Local Government is thus slightly less than three centuries old in India. Broadly, it may be divided into the following four periods and each period characterized by a definite aim and purpose.

Table-2.1
Growth of Local Government in India

Sl. No.	*Period From–To*	*Nature of Growth*
1.	1687–1881	Local Government was viewed to ease central and provincial finances and thus to subserve imperial needs.
2.	1882–1919	Local Government began to be viewed as Self-Government.
3.	1920–1947	Local Government came within the jurisdiction of provinces and further was transferred to popular control and Local Government was in a State of repair and reconstruction.
4.	1947–Present Day	Local Government has been keyed to the requirements of the constitution.

After the formation of Municipal Corporation, the next development was passing of Charter Act in 1793 which established Municipal Administration in the three presidency towns viz., Madras, Bombay and Calcutta. The Bengal Act of 1842 was extended to the district towns in Bengal empowering them to set up town committee for sanitary purposes upon applications made by two-thirds of house holders in a town.[5]

Lord Rippon's Resolution

Though considerable progress was made since 1870, both in the number and usefulness of municipalities, the progress was uneven. Hence, Lord Mayo's policy on local self-government was reviewed in 1881. On 18th of May, 1882 Lord Rippon who succeeded Lord Mayo as the Governor General of India who is acknowledged as the father of local self-government in India issued a historic resolution. To him local self-government was predominantly an instrument of political and popular education.[6] The resolution embodying this doctrine has been hailed as the Magna Carta. The underlying interaction of the Resolution was evidently to give the people a more real and meaningful share in the management of local affairs. An Indian Historian has rightly remarked.[7]

"Lord Rippon's reform of local self-government laid the basis of local and municipal self-government which soon took from root in India and became the ground work of democratic institutions in higher spheres".

Royal Commission on Decentralisation

Another significant stage in the history of Municipal Local Government was the publication of the Report of the Royal Commission on Decentralisation in 1909. The main recommendations made by the commission in respect of urban local self-governments and Municipalities are:

(*a*) Municipalities should be constituted in Urban areas.

(*b*) The responsibility of Primary Education should rest with the municipality and if it so desires and if resources permit, it may spend some amount on secondary schools also.[8]

The important recommendation made by the Royal Commission in respect of the role of municipalities relating to Education is that the responsibility of Primary Education should rest with the

Municipality and if it so desires and if resources permit, it may spend some amount on secondary schools also.[9]

Government of India Act of 1919

With the introduction of Dyarchy after the enactment of the Government of India Act of 1919, the Local Self-Government Department was transferred from bureaucratic hands to those of an elected minister in all provinces. As a result, the overall responsibility for the functioning of the local bodies was no longer to rest with the District Officers and they ceased to be the Chairmen, though they still retained general supervisory control over them. The popularly elected ministers established elected councils and gave executive authority to the elected Chairman. Thus the approach was more liberal and there was a deliberate attempt to give the local bodies greater freedom from outside control.[10]

Independence and After

With the dawn of Indian Independence and the consequent establishment of National Government new hopes were pinned on the Indian leadership for establishing popularly elected governments at the local level.[11]

The laudable landmark in the history of local government in India was in the year 1950 when the Constitution of India came into operation. It made local self-government as State subject. Most significant aspect in the progress of local self-government was as compared to the dramatic changes in this field, the rural areas have been involved in national planning and development but the urban areas have been kept out of the mainstream of the development process. In fact, the development of urban local government has been slow to the extent of being unimpressive. It is only of late that the urban local government has attracted to the attention of the government.

Some sporadic attempts have been made to reorganize the structure of urban local government institutions in the various States through laws.

- *(a)* adult franchise had replaced limited franchise in local bodies in all the States;
- *(b)* communal representation had been done away with and joint electorates had been substituted for separate electorates;

(c) there was an increasing tendency to make provisions of Municipal Acts for creating State cadres of municipal employees particularly for Executive Officers, Engineers, Accountants, Health Officers etc.[12]

Besides, a number of Central Committees and Commissions were set up from time to time to suggest ways for streamlining the local government structure in the country. These included *(a)* The Local Finance Enquiry Committee (1949); *(b)* The Taxation Enquiry Commission (1953); and *(c)* The Rural-Urban Relationship Committee (1963); In the States also various committees and commissions were appointed for looking into the problems of Municipal Administration and recommending measures for its improvement.

Another significant development was the separation of rural local government from urban local governments. The Government of India to this effect left necessary legislation to establish the above urban local bodies by the States for urban development.

Local Self-Government was one of the earliest fields thrown open to Indians by the British as a part of their philosophy to impart political education to Indians. In 1901, 'The Bombay District Municipalities Act' was passed which was followed by the Punjab Municipal Act of 1911, the United Provinces Municipalities Act of 1916, the Madras District Municipalities Act of 1920, the Bihar and Orissa Municipal Act of 1922, the Bombay Municipal Boroughs Act of 1925 and the Bengal Municipal Act of 1932. The period immediately following the reorganization of States in 1956 was characterized by enactments of Municipal Acts in several States. In view of this reorganization most of the States have reorganized their Acts. Prominent among them were Jammu and Kashmir (1951), Rajasthan (1959), Kerala (1956), Assam (1960), Karnataka (1964), Madhya Pradesh (1961), Gujarat (1963) and Maharashtra (1965). The State of Andhra Pradesh responded properly to the signals of the Government of India and enacted Andhra Pradesh Municipal Act in 1965* to establish Municipalities and Municipal Corporations in the State. The Constitution (Seventy-Fourth

* The Andhra Pradesh Municipalities Act, 1965 (Act No. 6 of 1965) reserved by the Governor on the 5th October 1964 and assets of the President received the assets of the President of India on 17th February 1965 and came into force from 2.4.1965.

Amendment) Act, 1992 was enacted by Parliament and came into force from June 1, 1993 and it reconstituted the Municipalities and Municipal Corporations in Andhra Pradesh with a provision of reservation of seats to women also besides Scheduled Castes and Scheduled Tribes and Backward Castes.

Generally speaking, study on local government either urban or rural may not be full-fledged and complete without a detailed description of its administrative structure at all levels. Specifically in the case of local self-governments in India, there is a notable feature that in most of the States the urban and local bodies such as Municipalities, Municipal Corporations, the Cantonment Boards and the Notified Area Committees are usually set up by an Act. But the provisions of these Acts are copied from a single source which spells out their administrative structure.[13]

The administrative structure of Municipal Government in India in general and in Andhra Pradesh in particular can be studied at three levels viz., National or Central, State and Local.

Structure at National/Central Level

Local Self-Government is the responsibility of respective States under the Constitution. Further they are created, sustained, regulated and even abolished by the States. The State administrative machinery for dealing with local government is thus of crucial significance for the progress of these democratic institutions at the grassroots level. While local government does not constitute the direct responsibility of the Central Government, still the latter provides financial assistance and consultancy services. Even otherwise, local government is too important an area of administration to be taken care of solely by the State Government or left solely to it.

At the outset, a question may be raised regarding the validity of a separate organization in the Central Government for dealing with subjects relating to local government when local government is not a direct responsibility of the Central Government under the Constitution, even under a federal system the Central Government has an important role to play in providing professional leadership, in setting up proper standards of services and in generally helping the states in solving day to day problems. More specifically the

Central Government is called upon to perform the following functions with regard to local self-government.

1. The Central Government has a responsibility for ensuring that information on important developments and activities of local self-government is made available to others.
2. It has to carryout a comparative study of the different systems of local self-governments prevalent in the country and communicate the findings to the states.
3. It has to ensure that the system of local self-governments – both in rural and urban as accepted at government conferences and committees is implemented by the states.[14]

Urban local government constitutes the charge of the Ministry of Urban Development. Historically speaking local government in India had its beginning in an urge to improve local sanitation and hence has continued as the responsibility of the Ministry of Health. The Ministry of Health was looking after both urban and rural local governments until 1958 when the latter was separated from it and came under the charge of the then Ministry of Community Development. In January 1966, a part of local self-government namely urban development was made the responsibility of the Ministry of Works and Housing which was renamed as the Ministry of Works, Housing and Urban Development. In 1967, the subject of urban development was transferred back to the Ministry of Health which carried a rather languish name, the Ministry of Health, Family Planning and Works, Housing and Urban Development. In February 1973, the subject of 'Urban Local Government' was transferred to the Ministry of Works and Housing. In 1985, a new Ministry, called the Ministry of Urban Development was created to deal with, among others, the urban local government.

Structure at States Level

Urban Local Government is the responsibility of the Department of Local Self-Government or Municipal Administration or Urban Development in any State in general. At the State level a number of departments deal with subjects which are the direct concern of the urban government. In addition to the Department of Local Self-Government or Municipal Administration and Urban Development the functional departments in the Secretariat administer the various components of the urban development. Thus, water supply, drainage and sewerage, road construction, land acquisition and development, housing and slum clearance, primary and secondary education etc., are being dealt with by respective functional departments. As is to be expected under such a fragmentary arrangement, the urban affairs do not get viewed as one integral function. Consequently there is a haphazard and piecemeal development bearing an imprint of lack of co-ordination. It is therefore, unusual to find the dwelling houses in a town fully completed yet remaining unoccupied for, want of electricity or water supply or even both.[15]

Administrative Structure of Municipalities in Andhra Pradesh

The need for an efficient, effective and democratic administrative structure for Municipalities in Andhra Pradesh was no doubt sincerely realized by the Government of Andhra Pradesh after the formation of Andhra Pradesh State in 1956. The legislative history of Municipalities in Andhra Pradesh could be traced back to the year 1965 when the Andhra Pradesh Municipalities Act was passed by the State Legislature. Which came into force from April 2, 1965.

Emergence of Andhra Pradesh Municipalities

The Municipalities of the Andhra Pradesh region were functioning in accordance with the Andhra Pradesh (Andhra area) District Municipalities Act of 1920 and that of Telangana followed the Andhra Pradesh (Telangana area) District Municipalities Act of 1956. With linguistic reorganization of States, the State of Andhra Pradesh came into existence during the year 1956, with the meager of the State of Andhra Pradesh and Telugu speaking districts of Hyderabad State. During the course of time it was found that the municipalities of the entire state need to be covered by an integrated Act to ensure uniformity. Hence, the Andhra Pradesh Municipalities Act of 1965 was enacted and all the Municipalities in Andhra Pradesh were administered under the provisions of this consolidated Act.[16]

The enactment of new Act namely The Andhra Pradesh Municipalities Act, 1965 by replacing the old plans in Andhra and Telangana Regions marked a new stage of development in the evolution of municipalities. Since, executive authority was distributed between the Council and the Executive Committee, the new system may be named as 'The Council Committee Plan'. Under this plan, the authorities charged with Municipal Administration were the Chairman, the Council, the Executive Committee and the Secretary. For the first time the Members of Legislative Assembly, Legislative Council were made as Executive members of the Municipal Council. The chief merit of this council committee plan was that it was highly democratic because the position of the elected Chairman was strengthened and the Council enjoyed wide powers. Thus the State had experienced of three different plans before the present Council, Chairman, Commissioner plan was introduced in 1977.[17]

The Integrated Act of Municipalities in Andhra Pradesh known as The Andhra Pradesh Municipalities Act, 1965 came into force from April 2, 1965 with due regard to saving the previous Rules and Acts herein force except that especially repealed. This Act of 1965 also dealt with various aspects like Municipal Authorities, hierarchy of officials commencing from the Chairman of Municipality who was later redesignated as Chairperson, the councilors who were later renamed as members.[18] Subsequently, this Act has tasted several Amendments from time to time to its account following the years 1971, 1976, 1978, 1979, 1981, 1986, 1990, 1992, 1994 and 1995. The major changes effected in the municipal system in Andhra Pradesh were though the Amendment Act of 1992 caused due to the 74th Amendment of Indian Constitution which came into force from June 1, 1993[19] and 1994 and 1995 under which the present structure of Municipalities is functioning.

The Andhra Pradesh Municipalities Act, 1965 which extended to whole of the State of Andhra Pradesh has empowered the State Government to constitute municipalities for 'Smaller Urban Areas'.[20]

After the emergence of Andhra Pradesh nearly a decade later the State Government not only enacted a comprehensive Act of Municipalities governing the entire Smaller Urban Areas in Andhra Pradesh but also framed the Rules by issuing notification in the official gazette in July 1965 which are known as Andhra Pradesh Municipalities Rules, 1965.[21] However these rules were also subjected to various changes in the light of the Amendments made to the Act from time to time. The major changes, additions and deletions were made to the Rules were in the light of the Amendment made to the Act 1992, 1994 and 1995.

These Rules spelt out the details regarding the configuration of Municipal Administrative structure only at municipalities level. With regard to Governments control over the municipalities no rules are found in the Andhra Pradesh Municipalities Rules, 1965 or in the later amended Rules. However, the Act specifically dealt about the controlling authorities and their powers over the municipalities.

Further, the Constitution 74th Amendment Act, 1992 passed by Indian Parliament has elevated the status of municipal bodies from statutory to constitutional. It is clearly evident that despite Directive in Article 40 of the Constitution, the municipal bodies as a whole continue to cling on to the respective State Governments both in administrative and financial matters, and remain as barren as ever. Now and new ideas evolved culminated in the passing of 74th Constitutional Amendment Act, 1992 which inserted Part IX A in the Constitution.[22]

Major Amendments to the Andhra Pradesh Municipalities Act[23] and Changes Effected in Municipal Administration

The Integrated Municipalities Act passed in 1965 had been divided into 7 parts with 30 sections. The important aspects in this Act were (1) Strengthening of the power of the Council (2) enhancing the powers and status of the Chairman (3) decreasing the powers and status of the Commissioner (4) Constitution of executive committee with Chairman and Vice-Chairman as members (5) Converting the status of the Commissioner into Secretary (6) Empowering the Secretary to levy taxes, removal of encroachments and Municipal Office management. With the enactment of this Act, certain changes were effected in municipalities. For the first time the Constitution of Alderman was introduced and all the executive authority under this system vested in an executive committee, an innovation in Andhra Pradesh which appears to be the first State to experiment with this arrangement and to abolish all other Committees of the Municipal Council.

The Andhra Pradesh Municipalities Act not only brought changes in the administration of municipalities, but also paved way for certain lapses. In view of this executive committee system the Municipal Administration weakened. Both the Chairman and Secretary felt that they lost hold on administration. As the Chairman is authorized to exercise supervision and control over the employees of municipality, the officials lost interest in administration. Hence, with a view to set right these lapses the 1965 Act was amended in the year 1971.

Amendments to Andhra Pradesh Municipalities Act Made in 1971[24]

The Amendments brought out in 1971 to the Andhra Pradesh Municipalities Act, 1965 are:

1. Abolition of Executive Committee in Municipalities and transfer of powers to the Municipal Commissioner.
2. Designing the Municipal Commissioner as the Chief Executive Officer of Municipality.
3. Abolition of Alderman System.
4. To bring all the employees of the municipality under the administrative control of the Commissioner.
5. Empowering the Chairman to suspend or transfer any of the employees.
6. Commissioner to operate the system under the authority of the Chairman and his control.

Amendments to A.P. Municipalities Act in the Year 1994[25]

The Andhra Pradesh Municipalities Act 1965 has been amended through Act No. 17 of 1994 to bring it in conformity with the provisions of Constitution 74th Amendment Act, 1992. The amended Act contains several important provisions aimed to strengthen the structure and finances of urban local bodies.

1. The designations of the Chairman, Councilor and Councilors of the municipalities have been redesignated as Chairperson, Member and Members respectively.
2. Constitution of Finance Commission by the Governor of Andhra Pradesh.
3. Constitution of Ward Committees to each ward in the municipality.
4. Provision of right to vote to the co-opted members from minorities.
5. Conduct of elections to all municipalities in the State by the State Election Commission.
6. Provision of one-third of the total number of offices to be filled by women by rotation in all categories like SC, ST, BC and Open Category.

7. The Commissioner empowered to exercise disciplinary control over the employees of the Municipal Council who shall be subordinate to him.
8. The practice relating to the appointment of Special Officer to the municipalities to exercise the powers and functions of the Council, Chairperson and Commissioner to be dispensed with.
9. Reservation of seats in the council to the Scheduled Castes and Scheduled Tribes based upon their population in the municipality.
10. One-third of total number of seats reserved for Backward Classes in the Council.
11. The offices of Chairpersons in the municipalities shall be reserved for the Scheduled Castes, Scheduled Tribes and women in such manner as the legislature of the state may provide upto the end of 2000 A.D.
12. Re-constitution of dissolved municipalities with in six months.

Forms of Urban Local Government

Keeping in view the local needs as well as importance of the local area there are six types of Urban Local Bodies:

1. Municipal Corporations
2. Municipalities
3. Notified Area Committees
4. Town Area Committees
5. Cantonment Boards
6. Improvement Trusts
7. Urban Development Authorities

Municipal Corporations in India

Municipal Corporation in India in the beginning was a State Government formed department that works for the development of a city, which has a population of more than two lakhs. The growing population and urbanization in various cities of India were in need of a local governing body that could work for providing necessary community services like health centres, educational institutes and matters related to housing and property tax.

Municipal Corporations in India formed under the Corporations Act of 1835 of Panchayati Raj System mainly dealt in providing essential services in every small town as well as village of a district/city. The aim behind its creation was to provide the convenient services to the people as it caters to their daily problems and holds a central importance in entire state departments.

Municipal Corporation is topmost of urban local government in the sense that the Municipal Corporation as an institution was more responsible and respectable and enjoys a greater measure of autonomy than other forms of local government.

In the American context, the Municipal Corporation is characterized as a body politic, created by the incorporation of the people of a prescribed locality and invested with subordinate powers of legislation, for the purpose of assisting in the civil government of the State and regulating and administering its local and internal affairs.[26] In the Indian context, the Municipal Corporations are established in big cities, under the Special Municipalities Acts passed by the State Legislatures, and in the case of a Union Territory, by Parliament. Adequacy of civic services and effective performance can hardly be ensured in towns, which do not command certain minimum resources.[27] The Rural Urban Relationship Committee (1966) has recommended that there should be Corporation form of Government only in those cities, which have a population of five lakhs and more and an annual income of Rupees one Crore and above.[28]

Major Developments in the Post-Independence Period

The Post-Independence period witnessed momentous developments in the field of local self-government. They may be studied under two broad heads.

The first relating to those which affected the structure and functioning of local bodies in rural areas and (Rural Local Government).

The second relating to those, which affected the urban local bodies (Urban Local Government).

There are many units of Local Government broadly classified into Rural Local Government and Urban Local Government. In Urban India, there are Municipalities and Municipal Corporations in towns and cities. Nagar Panchayats, which are created under the 74th Constitutional Amendment Act, 1992, are the new additions to the Urban Local Government. All these units in rural and Urban India differ very widely in area, population, membership, power, functions and finances within a State and from State to State. Besides these there are cantonment boards, notified area committees, town area committees and townships. They are partly elected and partly nominated. As such, they are said to be in semi-urban local bodies. And there is Metropolitan Government in the Indian Metropolis which is not different from the Municipal Government of a City. It is a Municipal Corporation on a longer canvass. In the very large cities like Kolkata, Mumbai, Chennai and New Delhi, one finds City Government with a Mayor and a Council in each having vast area and population. This is in no way different from any other City Government in India.

Major features of Urban Local Self-Government in India as per the constitutional framework are:

- Mention about Organisation of Panchayats under Article 40 but no specific mention about the creation of urban local bodies.
- Passing reference of urban local government in entry 5 of List II of 7th Schedule (State List) and entry 20 of the Concurrent List.
- Fivey Years Plan document highlighted the problems of municipal bodies and the inability of these bodies to meet the growing demands of urbanization.

Some important Committees relating to Urban Local Bodies are:

(a) The Local Finance Enquiry Committee (1949-51)
(b) The Taxation Enquiry Commission (1953-54)
(c) The Committee on the Training of Municipal Employees (1963)
(d) The Rural-Urban Relationship Committee (1963-66)
(e) The Committee on Ministers of Augmentation of Financial Resources of Urban Local Bodies (1963)
(f) The Committee on Service condition of Municipal Employees (1965-68)
(g) The National Commission on Urbanization (1988)

A Municipal Corporation is set up under a special statute passed by the State Legislature and is generally with a considerable measure of autonomy. Corporations were first established in the three Presidency towns of Bombay, Calcutta and Madras. They were established under special Acts of British Parliament. Later many Corporations were established either by an Act of Parliament or an Act of State Legislature. A Corporation was set up in Delhi by the Parliament in 1958.

The Corporation form of urban government is meant especially for bigger towns where civic problems acquire a high degree of complexity. As expected, Corporations vary considerably both in terms of population and the resources.[29] Broadly speaking, the following criteria may be considered sufficient for setting up a Municipal Corporation of a city:

1. Existence of a thickly populated area.
2. Existing development of the municipality and scope for its future development.
3. Financial position of the municipality-present and prospective.
4. Ability and willingness of the people to bear the burden of increased taxation.
5. Public opinion in favour of a Corporation.

The truth is that the State is the sole judge of which city should be converted into a Corporation, Town and when. Generally speaking, a sustained public opinion in favour of a Municipal Corporation and the bigness of a city induce the State Government to confer upon it the status of a Municipal Corporation.

The test of revenue-cum-population has an element of relevance only in the context of time and, so, loses meaning and validity as time changes.

Characteristics

Although Corporations vary both in population and revenue they all share some characteristics in common.

1. A Corporation is set up only as a result of a statute to be passed by the State Legislative Assembly.
2. A Corporation form of urban government is generally based on the separation of deliberative from executive functions.
3. The Mayor is the head of the Corporation and holds office for a renewable term of one year. What is more, the office of the Mayor is ceremonial in nature.

4. The State Government retains powers of control and supervision including even the power to dismiss the Council and take over administration.

In pursuance of the Acts passed by various state legislatures to create Municipal Corporations in their respective states, all these State Governments established Municipal Corporations in field urban areas. As for the latest statistics there are as many as 129 Municipal Corporations functioning in Indla.

The Constitution 65th Amendment Bill, 1989

The Constitution 65th Amendment Bill was introduced on 7th August, 1989 in the Parliament. The major provisions of the bill included:

1. To ensure Municipal Bodies being vested with necessary powers and removing their financial constraints to enable them to function effectively as units of Local Government.
2. Three types of Nagarpalikas were envisaged. Nagar Panchayats for a population between 10,000 and 20,000 Municipal Council for urban areas with a population between 20,000 and 3,00,000 and Municipal Corporation for urban areas with a population exceeding 3,00,000.
3. Provision for elected Ward Committees.
4. Adequate representation for SC, ST and women in urban bodies.
5. Setting up of Finance Commission in the States to ensure flow of finances to local bodies.
6. Audit of accounts by Comptroller and Auditor General.
7. Granting constitutional status to urban local bodies.

Salient Features of 74th Constitutional Amendment Act (1992) in Relation to Finances and Organization

The National Front Government reviewed the provisions of 65th Constitutional Amendment Bill and introduced as a fresh bill in Lok Sabha in September 1990. This bill was lapsed on account of the dissolution of the Lok Sabha. The Congress (I) Government headed by P.V. Narasimha Rao, introduced a Constitutional Amendment Bill (74th) in the Lok Sabha on 16th September, 1991.

The bill was based on 65th Constitutional Amendment Bill. Both the houses of Parliament passed it in December 1992. More than a half of the State Legislatures have ratified the bill. The bill received the Presidential assent on 20th April 1993. The bill discusses about financial decentralization. In this context, it may be stated that the 74th Constitutional Amendment Act 1992 provides 18 functions to the list of obligatory and discretionary functions. However, the Andhra Pradesh Municipal Corporations Act, 1994 has not incorporated these to be discharged by the Corporations in the State.

The Twelfth Schedule under Article 243(W) contains the following conditions.

- Urban planning including town planning.
- Regulation of land use and construction of buildings.
- Planning for economic and social development.
- Roads and Bridges.
- Water supply for domestic, industrial and commercial purposes.
- Public health, sanitation and conservancy and solid waste management.
- Fire services.
- Urban forestry, protection of the environment and promotion of ecological aspect.
- Safeguarding the interests of weaker sections of society including handicapped and mentally retarded.
- Slum improvement and upgradation.
- Urban poverty alleviation.
- Provision of urban amenities and facilities such as parks, gardens and playgrounds.
- Promotion of cultural, educational and aesthetic aspects.
- Burials and burial grounds, cremations and cremation grounds and electric cremations.
- Cattle ponds, prevention of cruelty to animals.
- Vital statistics including registration of births and deaths.
- Public amenities like street lighting, parking lots, bus stops and public conveniences and
- Regulation of slaughter houses and tanneries.

Though most of the Indian Municipal Corporations due to lack of adequate funds, have not been able to discharge their functions both obligatory, the 74th Constitutional Amendment Act 1992, provided for a Schedule of 18 functions. As such they find it very difficult to take up these.

Municipal Corporations in Andhra Pradesh – From a Historical Perspective

The Municipal Administration in Andhra Pradesh was under two Acts governed by Madras Presidency in Andhra Region and Nizam in Telangana Area. In Telangana in 1869, for the first time the Kotwal-e-Baldia, the City Police Commissioner used to look after the Municipal Administration. In the year 1869, Sir Salar Jung - I the then Nizam has constituted the Department of Municipal and Road Maintenance and a Municipal Commissioner was appointed for Hyderabad Board and Chadarghat Board. In 1886, Chadarghat had become Chadarghat. These two boards were amalgamated in the year 1933 into a Corporation and given statutory status under the Hyderabad Municipal Act. In 1945 Secunderabad Municipality was formed. In 1951, it became Corporation. In 1950, two separate Corporations were created under the Hyderabad Corporation Act 1950. These two Corporations were again merged into a single Corporation by The Hyderabad Municipal Corporation Act 1955 on August 3rd 1960. In 1956, Hyderabad became capital of Andhra Pradesh after the state was formed. In 1965, the State Legislature passed the A.P. Municipal Corporations Act and the erstwhile Municipalities which have fulfilled the requirements for elevation as Municipal Corporations were elevated and became Municipal Corporations. As today there are as many as 15 Municipal Corporations in Andhra Pradesh and Kurnool Municipal Corporation is one such.

Structure of Municipal Administration in Andhra Pradesh

State Legislature

|

Minister for Municipal Administration
(Cabinet Rank)

|

Department of Municipal Administration

|

Commissioner/Director of Municipal Administration

The structure of Municipal Administration in Andhra Pradesh commences from the State Legislature at the apex followed by the Minister for Municipal Administration and Commissioner/Director of Municipal Administration. The Minister occupies an intermediate position between the State Legislature and the Director.

Concept of Urban Development in Andhra Pradesh

Though urban development has been taking place for the last three decades in Andhra Pradesh, it appears that the concept of urban development is not clear since it is viewed by different thinkers in different ways. For instance, planners view urban development as the preparation of master planning, sociologists assume it to be the measures taken for rehabilitation of slums; political scientists view it as one connected with elections and the plans of city government. Whereas public administrators may view it from a different angle of the organizational arrangements and the civic amenities to be provided in urban areas.[30]

Out of various objectives the Municipal Corporations are also taking care of education particularly at secondary levels and looking after their administration with in its geographical area which stands prominent in view of the importance of education in a contemporary society, especially a developing society like India.

Municipal Corporations and Education

As stated earlier in Chapter I the history of secondary education was invariably connected with the growth of local self-government. Commencing from Hunter's Commission of Education in 1882 added with Lord Rippon's Resolution of the same year local bodies were put incharge of primary education for effective administration. Since then local bodies were administering primary education and were also levying taxes for educational purposes. In due course education was transferred to the Municipal Administration too in urban areas and were permitted to assign funds for educational purpose.

The concept of secondary education under the control of local bodies has been viewed differently by different sections in the society. How for these local bodies in urban areas are successful in managing the secondary education through the institutions under their control is a question to be dealt with. Specifically, the Municipal Corporations in urban areas are brought to the field of management of secondary education ever since the British period in India and how far these Municipal Corporations could win the hearts of their local people in respect of their performance in managing secondary education is a topic to be studied in the light of the case study done on Kurnool Municipal Corporation in Andhra Pradesh.

An Overview

The novel feature of urban local governments in India after the attainment of Independence has been one of formulating public policies in general and policies in respect of educational administration in particular at urban local levels. These local governments witnessed a series of vicissitudes and ups and downs in their progress and finally reached to this present stage but still striving to secure additional fillip to raise to the expectations of the people in making public policies. It is laudable to note that secondary education in urban areas is being administered by Municipal Corporations to contribute for social, economic, political and cultural development of its people. If education at the secondary level is to be strengthened in urban areas, there is every need to strengthen the urban local bodies in general and Municipal Corporations in particular in all states.

Andhra Pradesh is one of the Premier States in India which also geared to the needs of primary and secondary education to its people in urban areas and has entrusted this responsibility to its Municipalities and Municipal Corporations also. The administrative system of Municipal Corporations in Andhra Pradesh is designed in such a way that it should respond to the needs of urban local people in respect of various other demands including the demand for good and standard education at secondary levels. The organizational structure of Kurnool Municipal Corporation is dealt in succeeding chapter.

REFERENCES

1. Encyclopaedia of the Social Sciences, Vol. IX-X, p. 583.
2. Calder Ritchie, *The Inheritors* (London: 1961), p. 99.
3. Havell, E.B., *The History of Aryan Rule in India* (London: 1918), pp. 77-78.
4. Nigam, S.R., *Local Government* (New Delhi: S. Chand, 1982), p. 170.
5. *The Imperial Gazetteer of India*, Vol. IV (Oxford: Clarendon Press: 1909), p. 286.
6. *Quoted from Report of the Indian Statutory Commission*: emd 3568; Vol. I, (London: H.M.S.O. 1930), pp. 299-300, L.G. 2.
7. Panikkar, K.M., *A Survey of Indian History* (Bombay: 1957), p. 211.
8. Maheswari, S.R., *Local Government in India*, Agra: Lakshmi Narain, 1984, pp. 18-19.
9. Vishnoo Bhagwan, *Municipal Government and Politics in Haryana*, New Delhi: S. Chand, 1974, p. 15.

10. *Report of the Rural Urban Relationship Committee*, Vol. 1, p. 10.
11. Nigam, S.R., *Local Government* (New Delhi: S. Chand and Co., 1982), p. 173.
12. *Report of the Rural Urban Relationship, op. cit.*, p. 12.
13. Kistaiah, M., (Ed.), *Public Policy and Administration* (New Delhi: Sterling, 1986), p. 68.
14. Maheswari, S.R., *Local Government in India* (Agra: Lakshmi Narain, 1984), p. 28.
15. *Ibid*, p. 39.
16. Mohit Bhattacharya, *State Directorate of Municipal Administration* (New Delhi: Centre for Training and Research in Municipal Administration, IIPA).
17. Andhra Pradesh Municipalities Act, 1965.
18. Andhra Pradesh Municipalities Act, 1994.
19. Gazette of India (Ext. Part II, Section I, dated 20-4-1993 and vide S.O. 346 (E), dated 1-6-1993).
20. Andhra Pradesh Municipalities Act, 1994 Section 2, Clause, 42(a), Read: Having regard to population of the area, the density of population there in and so on the Governor may deem fit to specify an area as a municipality.
21. Government of Andhra Pradesh, G.O. Ms. No. 938, M.A., dated 28.7.1965.
22. A.P. Municipalities Manual, 1995, (Hyderabad: Panchayat Publication, 1995), p. 1.
23. Andhra Pradesh Municipalities Act, 1965.
24. Andhra Pradesh Municipalities Act, Act 5 of 1971.
25. Andhra Pradesh Municipalities Act, Act 17 of 1994.
26. Tooke, C.W., *Municipal Corporation*, Encyclopaedia of Social Sciences, New York: Macmillan, 1985, p. 86.
27. Maheswari, S.R., *Op. cit.*, pp. 169-170.
28. Government of India, *Report of the Rural-Urban Relationship Committee, Ministry of Health and Family Planning*, New Delhi: 1966, Vol. I, Para 4.11.
29. Nayak Prasad Kumar, *Indian Administration*, New Delhi: Unique, p. 649.
30. Kistaiah, M. (ed.), *Public Policy and Administration* (New Delhi: Sterling, 1986), p. 64.

3

Organisational Structure of Municipal Corporation (A Case Study)

Kurnool is one of the Four districts of Rayalaseema Region of Andhra Pradesh in India. Kurnool district derived its name from Kurnool its headquarters town. Etymologically, Kurnool is a corruption of Kandenavolu, a Telugu name by which it is referred to in the literature of the past. This place developed round the Jaghir of the Nawabs of Kurnool in course of the last century and half. Kurnool district is situated between the northern latitudes of 14^0 54′ and 16^0 18′ and eastern latitudes of 76^0 58′ and 79^0 34′. The latitude of the district varies from 100 ft. above the Mean Sea Level. This district is bounded on the North by the Tungabhadra and the Krishna rivers as well as Mahaboobnagar district, on the East by Guntur and Prakasam districts on the West by the Karnataka and on the South by Anantapur and Kadapa districts.[1] The district ranks tenth in population with 35.29 lakhs people accounting for 4.63 per cent of the total population of the State as per 2001 population census. While in area it occupies the third place with 17,658 sq. kms which account for 6.41 per cent of the total area of the State. Kurnool district consists of 3 Revenue Divisions, 54 Revenue Mandals, 53 Mandal Praja Parishads, 928 revenue villages, one Municipal Corporation, 4 Municipalities, 898 Gram Panchayats and 647 hamlet villages.[2]

The History of the District as an Administrative Unit and Changes in its Component Parts

Kurnool district was for a long time not a complete unit as its component parts were ruled at different periods of time by various dynasties. The dynasties that held away over this district include the Nandas, Mauryas, Satavahanas, Pallavas, Kakatiyas, Rayas of Vijayanagara, Bahmanis, Adil Shahis of Bijapur, Qutub Shahis of Golkonda, Moghuls and Asaf Jahis, besides the local rulers namely the Nalas, Kadambas, Telugu Cholas of Bedinenipalli, Velanadu Cholas, Kayasthau, Velugodu Chiefs, Nandyal Chiefs, Owk Chiefs, Kandenavolu Chiefs, Kurnool Nawabs, Banaganapalle Nawabs and Palegars.

Kurnool, originally a Jaghir under the Nawabs of Kurnool, was ceded to the British in A.D. 1800. In A.D. 1807 the taluks of Koilkuntla, Chennampalle and Nossam alongwith 21 others constituted the division of the Principal Collector. Of these, Adoni, Nagaladinne, Gulyam and Panchapalliem formed the Adoni division: Cumbum, Dupadu, Giddalur and Budvel (now in Kadapa*) represented the Cumbum division; and remaining five taluks, now in the Bellary district of Mysore State, constituted the Harpanahalli division. The Government later deemed it inexpedient to continue the post of the Principal Collector and directed that the area be divided into three separate divisions or Collectorates of Bellary, Cuddapah and Kodikonda (now in Hindupur taluk of Anantapur district). Even this was shortlined, for in A.D. 1808 the Kodikonda division was abolished and merged with the other two districts of Bellary and Cuddapah. In A.D. 1810 the taluk of Nagaladinne was amalgamated with that of Adoni, while Chennampalle was merged with Panchapalliem in A.D. 1821. Sometime later, the taluks of Nossam and Giddalur were absorbed in Koilkuntla and Cumbum taluks respectively. Thus about the middle of the nineteenth century A.D., Adoni taluk consisted of 214 villages, Gulyam taluk (with headquarters at Alur) had 106 villages and the taluk of Panchapalliem (with headquarters at Pattikonda) had 196 villages. Similarly the taluk of Koilkuntla covered 100 villages, while Cumbum and Dupadu (with headquarters at Markapur) included 172 and 313 villages respectively. In A.D. 1858, Cumbum, Dupadu, Koilkuntla and Panchapalliem taluks were merged in Kurnool district. While Adoni and Gulyam remained in Bellary district. In A.D. 1859, the name of Gulyam taluk was changed to Alur with Alur as the headquarters.

In A.D. 1860, the district consisted of eight taluks, namely (1) Chagalamarri (then in Siruvel or Sirvel taluk), (2) Siruvel,

* Earlier it was named as Cuddapah.

(3) Nandyal, (4) Panyam or Panem (now in Nandyal taluk), (5) Nandikotkur, (6) Atmakur, (7) Dhone and (8) Guduru or Gudur (now in Kurnool). The composition of these taluks underwent a series of changes during A.D. 1860-61. The taluks of Chagalamarri, Panyam, Dhone, Gudur, Atmakur and Dupadu were abolished. Ninety-nine villages of Dupadu taluk including Kanigiri and the villages of Venkatagiri Samsthanam were transferred to Nellore district and ten villages from Bellary (i.e., Adoni taluk) and five from Cuddapah were shifted to this district. Chagalamarri was merged with Siruvel A substantial portion each of Panyam and Atmakur was merged with Nandyal and Nandikotkur respectively. Dhone and Gudur were constituted into Ramallakota taluk. Thus the district finally emerged with eight taluks namely Pattikonda, Nandyal, Koilkuntla, Siruvel, Cumbum, Dupadu, Ramallakota and Nandikotkur. All the new taluks were named after their respective headquarters towns. On the first of October 1860, ten villages of Cuddapah district (Duvur or Duvvur taluk) were transferred to Chagalamarri taluk. This resulted in the merger of Siruvel taluk with Chagalamarri to facilitate boundary adjustments between Cuddapah and Kurnool districts. In February 1861, the name of Dupadu taluk was changed into Markapur after the name of its Cusbah. In A.D. 1873, Nagalapur (Nagalapuram) was shifted from Bellary to Adoni and during the next year Kalagotla and the hamlets of Parlapalle and Halsungutty (attached to Peddamariveedu or Pedda Maravadi and Bailoo Pattikonda respectively in Pattikonda taluk) were made over to Adoni taluk. Adoni and Alur appreciably affected subsequently by Meyer's scheme of constitution of new districts, divisions and taluks in the presidency. In A.D. 1878, Siruvel taluk gained Chintalacheruvu from Proddatur taluk of Cuddapah district. About the same period, the villages of Magaturu, Ganepalle and Velagalapaya were transferred from Markapur to Cumbum taluk owing to their difficult accessibility from Markapur and by A.D. 1886, the headquarters of Cumbum was shifted to Mundlapadu, a centrally located place.

About the beginning of 20th Century, the headquarters of Siruvel taluk was shifted from Chagalamarri to Allagadda while Giddalur became the headquarters of Cumbum. In 1909, Vengamapalle in Jammalamadugu taluk of Cuddapah district was added to Koilkuntla taluk of this district. As the result of the reorganization of taluks named Kurnool and Dhone were carved out of the portioning of Nandikotkur, Ramallakota, Pattikonda, Peapully (Pyapili) and Nandyal. Thus increasing the number of taluks in the district to nine. In April 1923, Siruguppa taluk was abolished and the villages in its jurisdiction were distributed among Bellary, Adoni and Alur. This in turn led with the reconstitution of Siruguppa taluk on the 15th of April, 1929. Adoni lost thirty three villages lying to its north-west. Seven villages from Alur taluk were also transferred to Siruguppa. No further territorial changes were effected in the district till February 1949, when the small Banaganapalli state with an area of about 583 sq.kms., was merged with the district and assigned the status of an independent sub-taluk. In August, 1951, certain readjustments between the villages of Banaganapalle, sub-taluk and Koilkuntla taluk led to their reconstitution. Banaganapalle taluk included Banaganapalle, Nandavaram and Owk (Avuku) firkas. While Koilkuntla taluk comprised Koilkuntla, Dornipadu, Akumalla, Kolimigundla and Sanjamala (Sanjamula) firkas. In 1952, Owk firka was shifted from Koilkuntla to Banaganapalle taluk and Sanjamala firka from Banaganapalle to Koilkuntla. The next and the most important accession to the district was the transfer of Alur and Adoni taluks from Bellary district under sub-section 3(2) of the Andhra State Act, 1953. In 1954, Atmakur sub-taluk comprising 38 villages was separated from Nandikotkur taluk and given an independent status. Since then, there have been practically no changes in the composition of the district. In 1957, however, the headquarters of Cumbum and Siruvel taluks were changed to Giddalur and Allagadda respectively. In this connection, it may be mentioned that consequent on the formation of Andhra State on the 1st of October 1953, Kurnool became its capital and continued to be so till the 1st November 1956, when Hyderabad became the capital of Andhra Pradesh State.[3] During this period some of the district offices including of the District Collector and the Superintendent of Police functioned at Nandyal.

Kurnool Municipality and Corporation

The Kurnool Municipality was established under the Madras Towns Improvement Act of 1865 and it began functioning from A.D. 1866. Of the achievements of the Chase Bazaar, the extension of water channel to the fort, the provision of lights and the installation of protected water supply system in A.D. 1897. Under the Act of 1884, the municipality came to have its first elected Chairman while all the councilors were appointed by the Government. In spite of sustained interest evinced by the councilors, the financial position of the municipality was unsatisfactory as could be evidenced from an observation made by the Acting Collector in 1920-21. Popular enthusiasm in civic affairs was, however, fairly high and the elections to the municipality, conducted in 1929, recorded a seventy per cent exercise of franchise by the voters. The council came to have its first elected Vice-Chairman in 1921. After having travelled a long journey of its performance this Municipality crossing its various grades of status finally took the elevation as Municipal Corporation in August 1994.[4]

The area of the Municipal Corporation as per old master plan was 15.02 sq. kms while the strength of its council was 36. After upgrading into Municipal Corporation in 1994 and the inclusion of major Gram Panchayat namely Kallur into the Corporation in 2002, the Municipal Corporation area has increased to 49.73 sq.kms.

Kurnool District and its Municipalities

The urban area of Kurnool district is divided into four Municipalities and one Municipal Corporation. They are:

1. Kurnool (Municipal Corporation)
2. Adoni Municipality
3. Dhone Municipality
4. Nandyal Municipality
5. Yemmiganur Municipality

Municipal Corporation Structure in Kurnool

An analysis of the administrative structure, organizational set up in the field of Public Administration in general and Municipal Administration in particular is a very complex process. Generally the issues and problems confronted in the setting up of these two areas do not receive adequate attention sometimes. The organizations are usually set up after a legislative enactment. Although the need and the policy to set up an organization may receive adequate attention but it is unfortunate that the spelling out of details of its administrative structure and organizational set up are generally done in haste.

The Municipal Administrative system in Andhra Pradesh in general (as discussed in Chapter II) and Kurnool in particular is acclaimed to be one of the earliest in the country. With a notable objective of providing urban development and municipal services to the people in Kurnool, the Government of Andhra Pradesh has provided an organizational structure just below the Director, and followed by the Regional Directors of Municipalities under whose supervision and control there are municipalities of all grades including the Kurnool Municipal Corporation as shown below:

Commissioner and Director of Municipalities
(State Level)
↓
6 Regional Directors
(Regional Level)
↓
(Local Level)
↓

Municipal Corporation	Selection Grade Mun-icipalities	Special Grade Mun-icipalities	Municipalities Grade–I	Municipalities Grade–II	Munici-palities Grade–III

Upgradation of Municipality to Municipal Corporation[5]

An area covered by a smaller urban area (Municipality) including adjacent Gram Panchayats if any considered suitable for inclusion may be declared as larger urban area under Section 2(d) of the Andhra Pradesh Municipal Corporations Act, 1994 (Act No. 25 of 1994) provided the following criteria is satisfied:

(a) *Population:* 4 lakhs provided that a Municipality with lesser population may also be considered if it is of regional importance has to play a significant role in regional development by virtue of its strategic location.

(b) *Density of population per sq.km.:* 10,000 provided that a Municipality with a lesser density of population may also be considered if it is of regional importance or has to play a significant role in regional development by virtue of its strategic location.

(c) *Revenue:* Rs. 4 crores and above.

(d) *Percentage of population engaged in non-agricultural activities:* Not less than 85 per cent.

(e) *Economic importance:* Established industries, potential for growth of industries, commerce, higher education, medical facilities and adequate infrastructure necessary for economic and industrial growth.

(*f*) *Other factors:* The number of peripheral villages whose growth and expansion are towards the proposed larger urban area.

An area satisfying the criteria specified in Rule 2 may be declared as a larger urban area by the Government under clause (d) of Section 2 of the Act.

The pattern of organizational structure adopted by Municipalities and Municipal Corporations in Andhra Pradesh as provided by the Andhra Pradesh Municipalities Act, 1965 and A.P. Municipal Corporation Act 1994 respectively is a mid-way between centralization and decentralization. In certain respects the organization and the authority is decentralized where as in some other important essential aspects it is centralized.

In Andhra Pradesh the urban local bodies are not organically linked with other kinds of urban local bodies established in the state. Though there are Urban Development Authorities, Municipal Corporations, different graded municipalities, each of them is separate and exclusive in dealing with each other. Thus, due to this absence of organical linkages the higher graded body has no administrative authority or control over each other. All these bodies are grouped and placed under the control of one government authority. For instance, the municipalities of Grade I, II, III, Special Grade and Selection Grade which are headed by Municipal Commissioners and who do not belong to I.A.S. are placed under their respective Regional Directors of Municipalities. In the same way the Municipal Corporations and Urban Development Authorities which are under the control of Commissioners of I.A.S. rank are placed under the control of Principal Secretary to Government, Department of Municipal Administration and Urban Development, Government of Andhra Pradesh. In view of this, the Kurnool Municipal Corporation has come under the jurisdiction of Regional Director of Municipalities, Kadapa.

The overall structure of the Kurnool Municipal Corporation can be studied from three angles viz., administrative structure, organizational set up and working as analysed hereunder:

Municipal Corporation Authorities

The Municipal Corporation Authorities charged with carrying out the various provisions of the Andhra Pradesh Municipal Corporation Act, 1994 in respect of Kurnool Municipal Corporation comprise the administrative structure.

The administrative structure of Kurnool Municipal Corporation as per Section 4 of Andhra Pradesh Municipal Corporation Act, 1994 consists of the following Municipal Authorities namely;

(a) a Corporation;
(b) a Standing Committee;
(c) a Commissioner; and
(d) the Wards Committee

Corporation

The Municipal Corporation is the people's assembly and makes laws, which are called bye-laws, within the framework of the Municipal Corporation Act for the civic governance of the city. Section 3 of the Andhra Pradesh Municipal Corporations Act, 1994 states 'that by a notification issued by the Governor specifying an area as a larger urban area under clause (d) Section 2, a Corporation shall be constituted for such area. Thus the Kurnool Municipal Corporation was formed in this way in 1994. Thus, this Corporation, as the Act says 'be a body corporate, having perpetual succession and a common seal with power to acquire, hold and dispose of property and to enter into contracts and may by its corporate name, sue and be sued.

The Municipal Corporation of Kurnool Consists of the Following Categories of Members[6]

(a) Such number of elected members as may be notified from time to time by Government of Andhra Pradesh.
(b) Every member of Legislative Assembly of the state representing a constituency of which a Municipal Corporation or portion thereof forms part.
(c) Every member of House of People representing a constituency of which a Municipal Corporation or a portion thereof forms part as ex-officio members, who have the right to speak and participate in proceedings of any meeting/ but have right to vote in the meetings.

(*d*) Every member of the Council of States registered as an elected within the larger urban area is an ex-officio member.

(*e*) Five members co-opted by the Municipal Corporation from among the persons having special knowledge and experience in Municipal Administration.

(*f*) Two persons belonging to minorities to be co-opted from among the persons who are registered voters in the Municipal Corporation larger area. They have right to speak and participate in the proceedings of the meetings without right to vote.

As per the Municipal Corporation Rules, 1994 the number of elected members for each Municipal Corporation is fixed in accordance with the population of that Municipal Corporation as shown in Table 3.1 excluding the ex-officio members.

Table–3.1

Fixation of Strength of Municipal Corporation

S.No.	*Population of Municipality*	*No. of Elected Members*
1.	Population not exceeding 40,000	21
2.	Exceeding 40,000 but not exceeding 1,00,000	21 + for every 10,000 population above 40,000 one additional member
3.	Exceeding 1,00,000 but not exceeding 2,00,000	27 + and for every 15,000 population above one lakh one additional member
4.	Population exceeds 2,00,000	27 + and for every 20,000 population above 2 lakh one additional member and total not exceeding 45

Source: Government of Andhra Pradesh, G.O. Ms. No. 42 M.A. and U.D. (Ele.II), dated 4.2.1995.

Thus the Municipal Corporation is a deliberative wing consisting of members elected on adult franchise.[7] For purpose of election to the members, the Municipal Corporation territorial area is divided into wards and the residents who have attained the age of eighteen years and registered as voters in that ward elect one member who is called as 'Corporator'.

Reservation of Seats

The Andhra Pradesh Municipal Corporations Act, in conformity with the constitutional provisions, provided for reservation of seats for members of Scheduled Castes, Scheduled Tribes and Backward Classes and for Women in every municipality out of the total strength of elected members subject to the following rules:[8]

1. Reservation of seats for Scheduled Castes and Scheduled Tribes in proportion to the population of these categories to the total population of the Municipal Corporation concerned and also by rotation to different wards.
2. One-third of the total number of seats to be reserved for Backward Classes and seats to be allotted by rotation to different wards.
3. One-third of the seats reserved for Scheduled Caste, Scheduled Tribe and Backward Castes to be reserved for Women belonging to these categories.
4. Not less than one-third of total number of seats (including those reserved for SC, ST, BC Women) to be reserved for Women.

Prior to the Andhra Pradesh Municipal Corporation Act as amended in 1994, the facility of reservation was also in vogue in respect of electing the Corporators of Municipal Corporations but in a different manner unlike at present. The reservation of seats allocated to Scheduled Castes, Scheduled Tribes, Backward Castes and Women was at the strength of 15 per cent, 6 per cent, 25 per cent and 9 per cent respectively out of the total strength.[9]

Co-opted Members

As per the Andhra Pradesh Municipal Corporation Act, 1965 as amended in 1994, representation has been given to two categories of persons through co-option. The first category is those persons who have experience and knowledge in municipal as well as local administration and the second category is those persons belonging to the minorities. In respect of municipalities having less than one lakh population two members, and in respect of those Municipal Corporations having more than 3 lakh population three members are co-opted under the category of members having special knowledge or experience. The persons eligible under this category must possess the following qualifications.[10]

(*a*) A registered voter in that Municipal Corporation.

(*b*) A person who held office of Chairperson/Sarpanch/ Member of the Municipal Council/Gram Panchayat or

Combination of these offices for a total period of not less than ten years; or

(c) An advocate who has served as Municipal Corporation Standing Committee for a term of 3 years.

(d) A retired officer who has worked in the Municipality/ Municipal Corporation/Municipal Administration Department; or

(e) Person having special knowledge in Roads and Buildings/ Water Works/Town Planning/Public Health.

In respect of co-option of members belonging to minorities i.e., the communities like *(a)* Muslims, *(b)* Christians, *(c)* Sikhs, *(d)* Buddhists, *(e)* Zorastrains (Parsis) as notified by the Government of India. The Municipal Corporation can co-opt one member from among these minority communities. The co-opted member must be a registered voter in the Municipal Corporation and shall not be less than 21 years of age.

An analysis of the present composition of Kurnool Municipal Corporation reveals that as per the provisions of the Act, it possesses all elected, co-opted and ex-officio members. Including the Chairperson there are 57 persons in the Municipal Corporation as shown in Table 3.2.

Table-3.2
Distribution of Memberships among Various Categories

S.No.	*Category*	*No. of Persons*
1.	Mayor (Elected)	1
2.	Deputy Mayor (Elected)	1
3.	Corporators (Elected)	48
4.	Co-opted	5
5.	Ex-officio	2
	Total	57

Source: Office of the Commissioner, Municipal Corporation, Kurnool.

After formation of Kurnool Municipal Corporation in 1994, the elections were held first time in March 1995 and the Corporation was having 44 wards. For which Corporators were elected for each ward. The Mayor was elected directly by the voters along with their Corporators. The MLA and MPs of the Corporation area became ex-officio members and two members were drawn as co-opted members from Minority Muslims. The total strength stood at 49.

During 2002-03 also the Municipal Corporation area continued to have 44 wards with 44 Councilors out of which 7 seats were reserved for Scheduled Castes one seat for Scheduled Tribes and 15 seats for Women.[11] With the Amendment of the Act in 1994, in conformity with 74th Amendment of the Constitution the reservation of seats in Municipal Corporation was altered taking into consideration the population of SCs, STs in the Municipal Corporation area and effecting the provision of 1/3 seats reservation to women of all categories. Thus with the Government Order issued in February, 1995 the wards in Kurnool Municipal Corporation have been set according to the reservation rules as shown hereunder.[12] At present the Kurnool is divided into 50 wards with fifty Corporators elected one from each Ward including the Mayor, who is one of the Corporators from among the elected Corporators who is indirectly elected by the Corporators in turn on party basis.

Table–3.3
Existing Pattern of Reservation to Various Categories in Kurnool Municipal Corporation

S.No.	*Category*	*General*	*Women Reservation*	*Total*
1.	General	16	08	24
2.	Scheduled Castes	05	03	08
3.	Scheduled Tribes	01	00	01
4.	Backward Classes	11	06	17
	Total	**33**	**17**	**50**

Source: Office of the Commissioner, Municipal Corporation, Kurnool.

An analysis of Table 3.3 reveals that the rule of reservation prescribed as per the Act in respect of Kurnool Municipal Corporation has been followed in allocating the seats to Scheduled Castes, Scheduled Tribes, Backward Classes and Women. Out of 50 wards, 16 wards left for general and 8 for general women category. Five Scheduled Caste general and three Scheduled Caste Women, one seat for Scheduled Tribes general, and eleven for Backward Classes general and six for Backward Classes women. Overall, 24 wards are left to general (open) category, eight wards to

Scheduled Castes one ward to Scheduled Tribe and 17 wards to Backward Classes.

Table-3.4
Kurnool Municipal Corporation
List of Hon'ble Mayor, Deputy Mayor and Corporators

Sl.No.	*Name of the Corporator*	*Desig-nation*	*Ward No.*	*Party*	*Reservation of Ward*
1.	S. Raghurami Reddy	Hon'ble Mayor	47	Congress	Unreserved
2.	S. Abdul Razack	Deputy Mayor	15	Congress	Unreserved
3.	N. Sreeramulu	Corporator	1	Congress	BC (General)
4.	K.V. Ramani	Corporator	2	Congress	Women (General)
5.	B. Chinnamma	Corporator	3	T.D.P.	Women (General)
6.	B. Adenna	Corporator	4	Congress	Unreserved
7.	S. Salam	Corporator	5	Independent	Unreserved
8.	S. Krishna Kumari	Corporator	6	B.J.P.	BC (Women)
9.	M. Naseerunnisa Begum	Corporator	7	Congress	Women (General)
10.	P. Babu	Corporator	8	Congress	BC (General)
11.	P. Sreenivasulu	Corporator	9	Congress	BC (General)
12.	Saleem Basha	Corporator	10	Congress	Unreserved
13.	M. Vittal Setty	Corporator	11	Congress	Unreserved
14.	Jayanthi Venkateswarlu	Corporator	12	Congress	Unreserved
15.	J. Muralidhar Goud	Corporator	13	T.D.P.	BC (General)
16.	U. Lakshmi Devi	Corporator	14	Congress	BC (Women)
17.	Md. Shareef	Corporator	16	Congress	BC (General)
18.	N. Sreeramulu	Corporator	17	CPI (M)	Unreserved
19.	Salkapuram Prabhavati	Corporator	18	Independent	SC (Women)
20.	G. Venkata Swamy	Corporator	19	Congress	ST (General)

Contd...

Sl.No.	Name of the Corporator	Designation	Ward No.	Party	Reservation of Ward
21.	Venkataiah	Corporator	20	Congress	SC (General)
22.	Y. Sudha	Corporator	21	Congress	Women (Gen)
23.	K. Sukanya Devi	Corporator	22	Congress	Women (Gen)
24.	P. Purushothama Reddy	Corporator	23	Congress	Unreserved
25.	M.J. Baburaju	Corporator	24	Congress	Unreserved
26.	D. Prabhudas	Corporator	25	Congress	SC (General)
27.	E. Madhusudhan	Corporator	26	Congress	Unreserved
28.	S. Satyana-rayanamma	Corporator	27	Independent	BC (Women)
29.	G.M. Meena	Corporator	28	Congress	BC (Women)
30.	T. Venkata Krishna Reddy	Corporator	29	T.D.P.	Unreserved
31.	G. Ramamohana Reddy	Corporator	30	Independent	Unreserved
32.	Lakshmi Devi	Corporator	31	CPI (M)	SC (Women)
33.	P.D. Hussain	Corporator	32	Congress	BC (General)
34.	B. Somanna	Corporator	33	CPI (M)	BC (General)
35.	M. Chinna Narasimhulu	Corporator	34	Independent	SC (General)
36.	Krishna Murthy	Corporator	35	Congress	BC (General)
37.	N. Alivelu	Corporator	36	CPI (M)	BC (Women)
38.	C. Chalapathi	Corporator	37	CPI (M)	BC (General)
39.	B. Sunkanna	Corporator	38	Congress	SC (General)
40.	P. Nirmala	Corporator	39	CPI (M)	Unreserved
41.	T. Ramudu	Corporator	40	CPI (M)	BC General
42.	S. Naseem Khatoon	Corporator	41	Congress	General (W)
43.	E. Pulla Reddy	Corporator	42	CPI (M)	Unreserved
44.	P. Vimala Devi	Corporator	43	Independent	General (W)

Contd...

Sl.No.	*Name of the Corporator*	*Desig-nation*	*Ward No.*	*Party*	*Reservation of Ward*
45.	Meharunnisa Begum	Corporator	44	Independent	General (W)
46.	Sandyapogu Giddamma	Corporator	45	CPI	SC (Women)
47.	P.G. Padmavathi	Corporator	46	Congress	BC (Women)
48.	P.G. Narasimhulu Yadav	Corporator	48	Congress	Unreserved
49.	Adoni Balaraju	Corporator	49	Congress	SC (General)
50.	Sidhar Mahesh	Corporator	50	Congress	SC (General)
51.	P. Girija Reddy	Cooption	Persons of experience and knowledge in Municipal Admn.		
52.	G.L.V. Seshaiah	Cooption	Persons of experience and knowledge in Municipal Admn.		
53.	M.P. Thippanna	Cooption	Persons of experience and knowledge in Municipal Admn.		
54.	S.K. Ramija Bi	Cooption	Muslim Minority		
55.	G. Abdul Kalam	Cooption	Muslim Minority		
56.	K. Jaya Surya Prakash Reddy	Ex-officio	Hon'ble Member of Parliament Ex-officio Member		
57.	M.A. Gaffoor	Ex-officio	Hon'ble Member of Legislative Assembly Ex-Officio Member		

Source: Office of the Commissioner, Kurnool Municipal Corporation, Kurnool.

An analysis of Table 3.4 (elected ward members of Kurnool Municipal Corporation) reveals that out of 50 members elected, as many as 17 women got elected belonging to all categories of which Backward Classes women are 6. Scheduled Castes women 3 and no women from Scheduled Tribe category. Out of the remaining 33 members 16 members are from open general category, 11 members from Backward Classes general category, and five from Scheduled Castes general and one from Scheduled Tribes general categories. It is also interesting to note that two woman two men members belonging to Muslim minority category got elected from women general and general wards respectively. Two Scheduled Castes candidates got elected under open category. No Christian, Buddhist or Parsi got elected under open general category. It is also interesting to note that none of the members from any ward got elected uncontested.

In respect of the co-opted members, as per the provisions of the Act and the Rules, the Kurnool Municipal Corporation had to co-opt three members from the categories of persons of experience and knowledge in Municipal as well as local administration and two persons from minorities. Accordingly, Kurnool Municipal Corporation had co-opted three members from the first category as per the Act as the total population of Kurnool Municipal Corporation is 3.43 lakhs as per 2001 census. They are P. Girija Reddy, G.L.V. Seshaiah and M.P. Thippanna under persons of Experience and Knowledge in Municipal Administration and from minority community, S.K. Ramija Bi and G. Abdul Kalam representing from Muslim Minority had been co-opted. As the rules also prescribe that any person having special knowledge in water works also be co-opted. Accordingly G.L.V. Seshaiah has been co-opted as he was a geologist with M.Sc. Post-Graduate degree with Geology and has been engaged in groundwater works. The second person M.P. Thippanna is a person hailing from weaker sections served the Kurnool Municipal Corporation as Corporator for more than five years.

The present analysis of the representation through election as well as co-option reveals that certain communities with considerable magnitude of strength in their population in Kurnool city like Christians have no representation in the council. As the Muslim representation is already there with good strength of four elected members in the Corporation, it would have been better if one person from Christian community is co-opted. In fact, the Kurnool Municipal Corporation has no strength of Buddhist or Parsi voters to reckon with.

Ex-Officio Members

When the Municipal Councils were constituted after the adoption of the Act in 1965, there was no provision for the category of ex-officio members though there was a provision for Alderman. In 1971 when the Act was amended the post of Alderman was abolished. Instead, the MLAs and MLCs (representing the constituencies of which the municipality forms part) were made as ex-officio councilors. Again in 1981, the Member of the House of the People representing the constituency of which the municipality forms a part was made as an ex-officio member.[13] In 1994 the Rajya Sabha Member registered as electors within the Municipality were also made as ex-officio members with voting rights.[14]

The Kurnool Municipal Corporation provided accommodation for ex-officio members with two persons, one representing Legislative Assembly Constituency and the other from Parliamentary Constituency following part of the Corporation vide Table 3.5.

Table-3.5
Ex-officio Members of Kurnool Municipal Corporation

Year	*MLCs*	*MLAs*	*MPs*	*Total*
1994-1995	–	1	1	2
1995-1996	–	1	1	2
1996-1997	–	1	1	2
1997-1998	–	1	1	2
1998-1999	–	1	1	2
1999-2000	–	1	1	2
2000-2001	–	1	1	2
2001-2002	–	1	1	2
2002-2003	–	1	1	2
2003-2004	–	1	1	2
2004-2005	–	1	1	2
2005-2006	–	1	1	2
2006-2007	–	1	1	2
2007-2008	–	1	1	2
2008-2009	–	1	1	2

Source: Annual Administration reports of Kurnool Municipal Corporation 1994-95 to 2008-09.

During the 1994-95 the Kurnool Municipal Corporation was having two ex-officio members representing Kurnool Legislative Assembly, and Kurnool Lok Sabha one from each. The present ex-officio member representing Legislative Assembly is T.G. Venkatesh got elected on Communist Party of India (Marxist) ticket which had an election alliance with Congress Party. The Lok Sabha Member Kotla Jaya Surya Prakash Reddy got elected on Congress (I) Ticket from Kurnool Parliamentary Constituency. The tenure of last Kurnool Municipal Council ended by 18.8.1994 and the first Kurnool Municipal Corporation was constituted on 19.8.1994. The elections for the First Kurnool Municipal Corporation were conducted and the body was constituted on 30.3.1995. During the intermittent period the District Collector acted as the Special Officer of Kurnool Municipal Corporation.[15]

The basic objective in making Members of Legislative Assembly or Lok Sabha or Rajya Sabha as ex-officio members is to ensure that their counsel and guidance is available to the Municipal Corporation and the members are also made to keep in touch with the affairs of the Municipal Corporation. However, the inclusion of ex-officio members provided considerable sway over the Municipal Administration by the Government. The elected member of Lok Sabha or Legislative Assembly however has to undertake the oath as ex-officio member, though this ritual of oath taking is only directory and not mandatory.

Term of Office

The term of the Chairperson as well as the Corporation has significant importance in the composition of Municipal Corporation in the State. The term of office of the body is to be determined judiciously. A considerable length of period is necessary to provide a long range point of view to the members to allow them to show their worth and make their impact felt on the working of the Municipal Corporation as a whole.

The term of office of elected members of the Municipal Corporation including the Chairperson is Five years.[16] The ex-officio member of the Corporation holds his office as he continues to be the Member of the Legislative Assembly or Member of Parliament. The ordinary vacancies in the office shall be filled at ordinary elections which shall be completed before the expiry of the term of office.[17] The Act also speaks that the term of office of the Municipal Corporation and Chairpersons of the newly constituted Municipal Corporation shall be co-terminus with the elected Corporators and the Chairpersons of the Municipal Corporation in the State elected in the last preceding ordinary elections.[18]

Any member, the Vice-Chairperson (Deputy Mayor) or Chairperson (Mayor) may by writing under his hand addressed to the Commissioner resign his office which is to be placed on the table of the Corporation and if the Corporation satisfy itself as to its genuineness from the concerned person accept the resignation which shall take effect on and from the date on which the notice was received.

Thus, the Kurnool Municipal Corporation constituted under Section 2 of the Act is a body corporate with perpetual succession and a common seal and subject to any restriction and qualification imposed by this Act or any other law and vested with the capacity of suing and being sued in its corporate name, acquire, hold and transfer of property, enter into contracts and do all things necessary for the purposes of the Act.[19]

Mayor—The Chairperson

The office of the Mayor who is the Chairperson for each Municipal Corporation in the State is envisaged by the Andhra Pradesh Municipalities Act. The Kurnool Municipal Corporation is headed by a Mayor who also acts as the Chairperson who is an indirectly elected non-official. The Chairperson occupies the key position in any Municipal Corporation. He is the head of the Municipal Corporation. The term 'Chairman' has been substituted by the term 'Chairperson' by the Andhra Pradesh Municipal Corporations Act of 1994. The office of the Chairperson in Kurnool Municipal Corporation is of considerable importance because the Chairperson's powers, functions, position, prestige and the role he has to play in the power game at the Municipal Corporation level all made this post very crucial one. The importance of this post was either upgraded or down graded in accordance with the policy shifts of the higher level government.

As per the existing provisions of the Andhra Pradesh Municipal Corporations Act 1994 the Chairperson elected directly by the voters of the Municipal Corporation from among themselves in the manner prescribed by the Act[20], upto the year 2006 the Mayor was elected directly by the voters of the Corporation. But later the present Congress Government introduced indirect election of the Mayor through getting elected directly by the elected Corporators one from among themselves.

The Mayor must have attained the age of twenty one years. There was no restriction for the ex-officio members contesting for the post of the Chairperson. In the event of MLA or MP who are ex-officio members get elected as Chairperson they should cease to be members of State Legislature or Parliament within 15 days.[21] From 1981 onwards 15 per cent, 6 per cent, 9 per cent and 21 per cent of the total number of Chairmen posts were reserved for Scheduled Castes, Scheduled Tribes, women, and Backward Castes by rotation respectively in the State. As per the Andhra Pradesh Municipal Corporation (Reservation of offices of Chairpersons in Municipal Corporation Rules 1995 the State Government declares the offices of Chairpersons of Municipal Corporations to be reserved in the State for Scheduled Tribes, Scheduled Castes and Backward Classes and women on rotation basis taking into consideration the largest percentage of population of the said category.[22]

The Mayor of Kurnool Municipal Corporation presides over the meetings of the General Body and Standing Committees and possess general control over all the affairs of the Municipal Corporation.

Table–3.6
Incumbents to the Post of Mayor/Chairperson of Kurnool Municipal Corporation

S.No.	*Name of the Incumbent*	*Tenure From*	*Tenure To*	*Total Period*
1.	B. Ananthaiah	1995	2000	5 years
2.	L. Feroz Begum	2000	2005	5 years
3.	S. Raghurami Reddy	2005	Till to date	3 years

Source: 1. Office of the Commissioner, Municipal Corporation, Kurnool.
2. Annual Administration Reports 1995-96 to 2008-09.

Table–3.7
Background of the Incumbents Served as Chairman/ Chairperson of Kurnool Municipal Corporation

S.No.	*Name*	*Qualifications*	*Caste*	*Profession*
1.	B. Ananthaiah	S.S.C.	Mala (SC)	Business
2.	L. Feroz Begum	B.A.	Muslim	Business
3.	S. Raghurami Reddy	Intermediate	Kapu	Agriculture

Source: Office of the Commissioner, Kurnool Municipal Corporation.

Powers and Functions of the Mayor/Chairperson

One of the important developments in the recent years has been that the Mayor who is the Chairperson had emerged as a very powerful functionary. He enjoys legislative, administrative, financial and emergency powers. Section 154 of the Act lays down the powers and functions of the Chairperson. The powers of Chairperson in a nutshell are as follows:

The Mayor/Chairperson shall:

(a) Make arrangements for the election of the Vice-Chairperson.

(b) Refer any resolution of the Corporation for its consideration which in his opinion is in excess of the powers of the Corporation or inconsistent with any law.

(c) Convene meetings of the Corporation and of the executive committee.

(d) All official correspondence between the Corporation and the governments or the Heads of the departments has to be conducted in the name of the Chairperson.

(e) He can incur in each case contingent expenditure incidental to the Municipal Administration and report the expenditure so incurred and the reasons thereof to the Corporation at its next meeting.

(f) The Chairperson may in case of emergency direct the execution of any work or the doing of any Act of which ordinarily require the sanction of the Corporation the doing of which in his opinion is necessary for public safety.

(g) Every meeting of the Corporation and executive committee shall be prescribed over by the Chairperson and in his absence by the Vice-Chairperson.

The Chairperson shall present order and shall decide all points of order arising at or in connection with meetings. When the conduct of a meeting of the Corporation or a member of the executive committee is, in the opinion by the Chairperson disorderly, he may direct that such a member shall withdraw from the meeting.

Powers of the Corporators

Any Corporator shall call the attention of the Chairperson to any neglect in the execution of Municipal Corporation work, to waste any Municipal Corporation property or to the needs of any locality and may suggest any improvements which may appear desirable.

Every Corporator have the right to move resolutions and have the access during office hours to the records of the Municipal Corporation after giving a reasonable notice to the Chairperson.

Vice-Chairperson/Deputy Mayor

Section 91(1) to (2) of the Andhra Pradesh Municipal Corporation Act of 1994 provides for the post of Vice-Chairperson, next to the Chairperson. He is also known as Deputy Mayor. The Vice-Chairperson holds the office of the Chairperson in the absence of the former and performs the functions of the Chairperson until a new Chairperson is elected. Every Corporation shall elect one of its elected members to be its Vice-Chairperson within fifteen days from the date of the election of the Chairperson. The Chairperson by an order in writing may delegate any of its functions to the Vice-Chairperson.

Special Officer

The Andhra Pradesh Municipal Corporation Act of 1994 provided for the facility of appointment of Special Officer by the Government to exercise the powers, discharge the duties and perform the functions of the Corporation where a Municipal Corporation is constituted for the first time. He has to cause arrangement for election to be made so that the Chairperson and the elected members may come into office. He exercises the powers of the Chairperson, the Wards Committees till they are elected as well as the Commissioner till he is appointed by the government. An insight into the working of Kurnool Municipal Corporation shows that in its history only one time a Special Officer was appointed where the District Collector acted as Special Officer from 19.8.1994 to 29.3.1995 for a period of seven months only till the first Kurnool Municipal Corporation got elected and assumed office on 30.3.1995.

Standing Committee

Section 93(i) of the Act provides a Standing Committee instituted immediately after general elections to the Corporation. The Government of Andhra Pradesh constitutes a Standing Committee for each Municipal Corporation. This Committee is composed of 5 members who are the elected Chairpersons of Wards Committees constituted. The term of Standing Committee is one year and the Chairpersons of Ward Committees are provided an opportunity to become the members of Standing Committee on rotation basis. The

Chairperson is elected from among the Chairpersons of Ward Committees. The Kurnool Municipal Corporation at present has got 5 members for the Standing Committee as shown in the Table 3.8.

Table-3.8
Members of Standing Committee in Kurnool Municipal Corporation

S.No.	*Name*	*Ward Committee*	*Status*
1.	P. Sreenivasulu	1	Chairperson
2.	M.D. Shareef	2	Member
3.	G. Ramamohan Reddy	3	Member
4.	T. Ramudu	4	Member
5.	P. Vimala Devi	5	Member

Source: Office of Municipal Corporation, Kurnool.

The Standing Committee exercises the powers and perform such functions as entrusted by the Act. This Committee meets once in a week or at such other times as shall be found necessary to scrutiny the Municipal accounts as they think fit. The number of meetings held from 1996 to 2008 and the number of issues discussed and the Chairpersons chaired the meetings are shown in Table 3.4.

Municipal Commissioner

The Municipal Commissioner is the Administrative Head of the Kurnool Municipal Corporation. Section 104 of the Andhra Pradesh Municipal Corporation Act, 1994 provides for the appointment of Municipal Commissioner for every Municipal Corporation in the State including Kurnool Municipal Corporation. Section 104 of the Act says that the Government shall be the executive authority of that Municipal Corporation. In case of any Municipal Corporation where it is considered necessary to do so the government may also appoint a Deputy Commissioner to assist the Commissioner.

The Commissioner is a full time officer appointed or deputed by the State Government to manage the affairs of the Municipal Corporation and to ensure smooth functioning and administration of the Municipal Corporation. He belongs to the State Government Service called Andhra Pradesh Municipal Commissioners Subordinate Service. As the head of the executive branch of Municipal

Table-3.9
Standing Committees Meetings

Year	*No. of Meetings*	*Issues*	*Chairpersons*
1996	13	36	Jaleel Ahmed
1997	15	41	Abdul Rahiman
1998	18	47	Vijay Kumar
1999	12	34	Laxman Goud
2000	11	39	L. Viswanatham
2001	13	54	Narasimhulu Yadav
2002	21	82	L. Ravi Kumar
2003	26	151	P. Jacob
2004	18	68	Y. Nagaraju
2005	7	21	S. Salam
2006	4	27	S. Raghurami Reddy (Mayor) Chairman
2007	4	37	S. Raghurami Reddy
2008	8	66	Sreenivasulu
Total	**170**	**703**	

Source: Office of Municipal Corporation, Kurnool.

Government, the Commissioner has been vested with adequate powers to carry out his duties and responsibilities. He is also the ex-officio Secretary of Municipal Corporation.

The salaries, allowances, leave allowances, pension and contributions towards the provident fund of the Commissioner are paid from the consolidated fund of the State.

Control of Chairperson over Commissioner of Municipal Corporation

The Andhra Pradesh Municipal Corporation Rules 1994 empowers the Chairperson to exercise administrative control over the Commissioner of Municipal Corporation. The Chairperson may in the interest of the Municipal Administration give any lawful institutions to the Commissioner in writing. In respect of transfer of the staff of Municipal Corporation connected with collection of taxes, the Commissioner has to pass orders only with the concurrence of the Chairperson and Municipal Corporation.

Table-3.10
Incumbents to the Post of Commissioner in Kurnool Municipal Corporation

S.No.	Name	From D M Y	To D M Y	Total Period D M Y
1.	K. Anjaneyulu	21-08-94	21-09-95	00-01-01
2.	Satish Chandra (IAS) JC (FAC)	02-10-95	25-11-95	25-01-00
3.	C. Sivasankara	26-11-95	15-03-96	20-03-00
4.	Dr. M. Nageswara Rao	16-03-96	30-07-96	15-04-00
5.	Harpreeth Singh (IAS) JC (FAC)	31-07-96	06-09-96	07-01-00
6.	M. Prasada Rao (IAS)	07-09-96	10-01-97	04-04-00
7.	Harpreeth Singh	11-01-97	24-07-98	15-06-01
8.	A. Ajay Jain (IAS) JC (FAC)	25-07-98	20-08-98	27-00-00
9.	G. Ramanarayana Reddy	21-08-98	15-05-00	25-08-01
10.	C. Nagaraja Rao (FAC)	16-05-00	06-12-00	22-06-00
11.	G. Jayalaxmi (IAS)	07-12-00	10-03-01	05-03-00
12.	Vikas Raj (IAS) JC (FAC)	11-03-01	02-06-01	23-02-00
13.	K. Venkatarami Reddy	03-06-01	05-05-04	03-10-02
14.	Vijayalakshmi (FAC)	06-05-04	30-05-04	25-00-00
15.	K. Venkatarami Reddy	31-05-04	14-06-04	15-00-00
16.	K. Vijayalakshmi	15-06-04	05-08-04	21-01-00
17.	K. Venkateswarlu	06-08-04	01-06-06	27-09-01
18.	N. Somi Reddy	02-06-06	28-05-07	26-11-00
19.	Srimannarayana	29-05-07	19-06-07	22-00-00
20.	L. Vandana Kumar	20-06-07	05-03-08	16-08-00
21.	S. Suresh Rao (FAC)	06-03-08	01-04-08	25-00-00
22.	P. Dhanunjaya	02-04-08	Till date	

Note: D: Days, M: Months, Y: Years.
Source: Annual Administrative Reports of Kurnool Municipal Corporation 1994-95 to 2008-09.

It is quite distressing to observe from Table 3.10 that the post of Commissioner in Kurnool Municipal Corporation has been subjected to frequent change of incumbents which had hampered the administrative as well as operational works.

It is generally recognized that the effective functioning of any organization like Municipal Corporation depends upon to a greater extent in the direction, guidance of the Commissioner who is the Chief Executive Officer to the total organization. Surely it takes some time for him to acquire intimate knowledge of the problems and activities of the individual municipality. Frequent changes of incumbents to this post is therefore not desirable as it amounts to an enormous waste of precious knowledge and experience of individual incumbents. Hence, continuity of service in this post is very necessary.

Meetings

In order to transact its business activities the ordinary meetings of Kurnool Municipal Corporation are generally held once in every month. Emergency and special meetings can also be convened. The meetings are presided over by the Chairperson and in his absence the Vice-Chairperson. All the orders and decisions are authenticated by the signature of the Chairperson.

The quantum of work turned out by the council is reflected through the number of meetings held and items discussed and disposed. The number of meetings held since 1994 is shown in Table 3.11.

Table-3.11
Meetings of the Kurnool Municipal Corporation

Year	*G.B.*	*E.M.*	*Spl.M.*	*Total*	*No. of Items Discussed*
1994	4	-	-	4	27
1995	8	4	1	13	18
1996	7	-	4	11	24
1997	6	-	1	7	18
1998	8	-	1	9	18
1999	4	-	1	5	12
2000	3	1	-	4	28
2001	2	-	2	4	19

Contd...

Year	*G.B.*	*E.M.*	*Spl.M.*	*Total*	*No. of Items Discussed*
2002	7	3	1	11	35
2003	5	-	1	6	47
2004	2	-	1	3	6
2005	6	1	1	8	34
2006	4	-	1	5	41
2007	6	-	2	8	34
2008	4	2	-	6	37
Total	**76**	**11**	**17**	**104**	**398**

Source: Annual Administration Reports of Kurnool Municipal Corporation, Office of the Kurnool Municipal Corporation, Kurnool.

An analysis of Table 3.11 shows that as many as 104 meetings were held during the period from 1994 to 2008, of which 76 were General Body, 11 Emergency and 17 were Special Meetings. The number of items discussed were 398 i.e., in a period of 14 years with an average of 21 per year. The highest number of meetings held was 47 in the year 2003 and the lowest number of meetings held in the year 2004 was 6.

Allowances

The Chairperson, Vice-Chairperson, the Council members and the ex-officio members are entitled to draw the following Travelling Allowances and Daily Allowances for their journeys made to perform the functions of Municipal Corporation under the Rules.[23]

Table-3.12
Honorarium and Allowances of Mayor/Deputy Mayor and Corporators of Kurnool Municipal Corporation

S.No.	*Category*	*Nature of Allowance*	*Per Month in Rs.*
1.	Mayor	Honorarium including compensatory, conveyance and special allowance	14,000.00
2.	Deputy Mayor	Honorarium including compensatory, conveyance and special allowance	8,000.00
3.	Corporators	Conveyance allowance	4,000.00

Source: G.O. Ms. No. 126 Municipal Administration and Urban Development (Elec. II) Department, dated 6.2.2008.

Ward Committees

Section 10 of the Andhra Pradesh Municipal Corporations Act, 1994 provides for constitution of Wards Committees by the Commissioner and Director of Municipal Administration in all Municipal Corporations. The Act says that:

1. There shall be constituted by the Government, by order, such number of Wards Committees to the Corporation as may be determined by them, so however, that each Wards Committee shall consist of not less than ten wards:
   Provided that in constituting Wards Committees the Government maintaining geographical continuity as for as possible.
2. Each Wards Committee consists of the members elected from the wards for which the Wards Committee is constituted.
3. The Chairperson of the Wards Committee is elected by the Members thereof from among themselves in the prescribed manner. He is holds office for a period of one year from the date of election and is eligible for re-election.
4. The Chairperson shall cease to hold office if he ceases to be a member of the Wards Committee. Any casual vacancy in the office of the Chairperson shall be filled by election of another Chairperson from among the elected members of the Wards Committee, as soon as may be, after the occurrence of the vacancy.
5. The powers and functions of the Wards Committee and the manner of conduct of business at its meetings shall be such as may be prescribed.

Powers and Functions of Chairperson of Wards Committee

1. The Chairperson of the Wards Committee shall convene the meetings of Wards Committee. Every meeting of the Wards Committee shall be presided over by the Chairperson.
2. At the first meeting in every year of the Wards Committee the Chairperson may nominate from among the members, a panel of not more than two temporary Chairpersons, anyone of whom presides at any meeting of the Wards Committee in the absence of Chairperson in the order in which they are nominated in the panel.

3. The Chairperson shall preside over and shall decide all points of orders arising at or in connection with the meeting. There shall be no discussion on any point of order and the decisions of Chairperson on any point of order shall be final.
4. When the conduct of a member in the opinion of the Chairperson is disorderly, he may direct that such member shall withdraw from the meeting of Wards Committee and such member shall thereupon withdraw and shall not be allowed to attend for the remainder of the day's meeting.
5. If any member who has been ordered to withdraw continues to remain in the meeting, the Chairperson may take steps to cause him to be removed.
6. The Chairperson shall refer any resolution of the Wards Committee to the Standing Committee or the Corporation, as the case may be, for its consideration which in his opinion is in excess of the powers of the Wards Committee.
7. All Official correspondence between the Wards Committee and the Standing Committee, Corporation shall be conducted in the name of the Chairperson.
8. The Chairperson may occur in each case contingent expenditure incidental to the office administration of Wards Committee an amount not exceeding Rs. 200.
9. The Chairperson if he so chooses to resign may send his letter of resignation in writing to the Secretary of Wards Committee. The Secretary shall on receipt of such resignation place it before the next meeting of the Wards Committee which shall accept the resignation after satisfying the genuineness of the resignation. Before the resignation is accepted by the Wards Committee, it shall be open to the Chairperson to withdraw such resignation by writing a letter under his hand addressed to the Secretary.
10. In case the Chairperson is incapacitated due to any reason or a vacancy arises due to death or resignation, the Wards Committee shall elect another member from among themselves for the remaining team of the Office of the Chairperson within fifteen (15) days from the date of occurrence of vacancy in accordance with the procedure prescribed in these rules.

Powers of the Members of Wards Committees

Section 22 and 23 of the Act provide for the powers of the Members of Kurnool Municipal Corporation Wards Committees:

1. No member shall vote or take part in discussion of any question coming up for consideration at a meeting of the Wards Committee, if the question is one in which apart from its general application to the public be has personal interest or he or his partner has any direct or indirect pecuniary interest.
2. The Chairperson may prohibit any member from voting or taking part in the discussion of any matter in which he for reasons to be recorded in writing, believes such member to have such interest, or he may require such member to absent himself during the discussions.
3. Such member may challenge the decision of the Chairperson who shall, thereupon, put the question to the meeting and the decision of the meeting shall be final.
4. If any member present at the meeting believes that the Chairperson has any such personal or pecuniary interest in any matter under discussions, the Chairperson shall, if a motion to that effect is carried absent himself from the meeting during discussion.
5. The member concerned shall not be entitled to vote on the question referred to in sub-rule (3) and the Chairperson concerned shall not be entitled to vote on the motion referred to in sub-rule (4).
6. Every member shall have the right to move resolutions and to interpolate the Chairperson on matters connected with the Municipal Administration.
7. Every member shall have access during office hours to the records of the Wards Committee after giving a reasonable notice to the Chairperson.

Provided that the member shall not have access to such records of the Wards Committees, if they are considered as confidential or secret by the Chairperson.

The Kurnool Municipal Corporation at present is having Five Wards Committees, each with ten members. As there are 50 wards in the Corporation every year five Wards Committees are constituted with a provision of re-election of Corporators as Wards Committee members.

Organizational Set up of Kurnool Municipal Corporation

The organizational set up of Kurnool Municipal Corporation is divided into seven sections on the basis of functions performed by the various heads. Table 3.13 provides the organizational set up.

Table-3.13
Organizational Set up of Municipal Administration in Andhra Pradesh

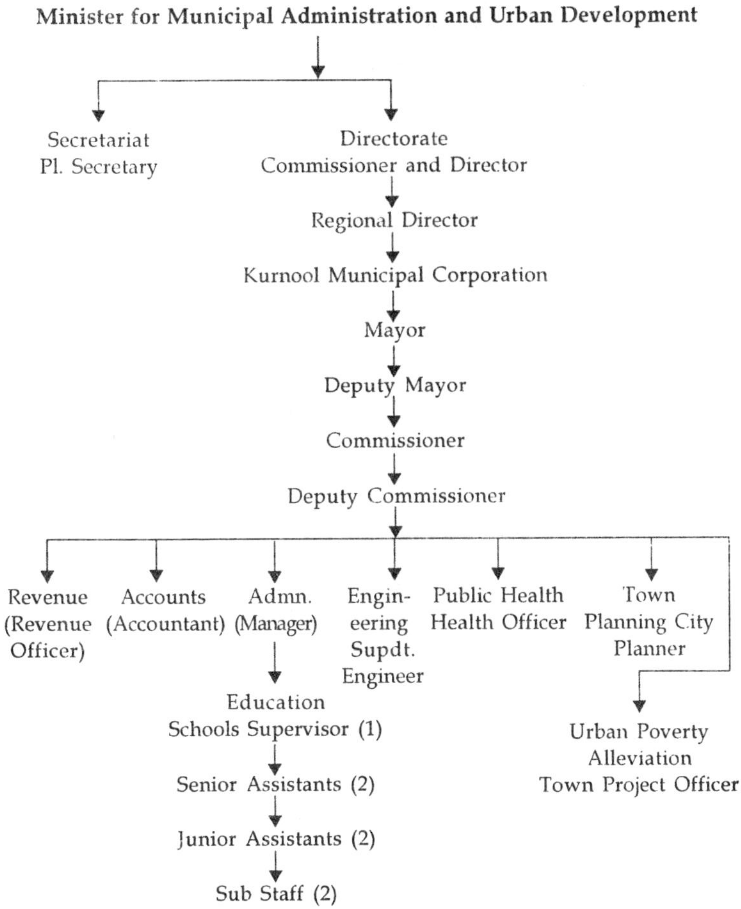

Source: Office of Kurnool Municipal Corporation, Kurnool.

The Commissioner of Kurnool Municipal Corporation is assisted by seven Heads of Departments to look after Revenue, Accounts, Administration, Engineering, Public Health, Town Planning and Urban Poverty Alleviation. These Departments are headed by Revenue Officer, Accountant, Manager, Superintendent Engineer, Health Officer, City Planner, and Town Project Officers respectively. The Education subject is kept under the Headship of Commissioner assisted by Manager of Administrative Wing.

Functions of Kurnool Municipal Corporation

The Kurnool Municipal Corporation like any other Municipal Corporation in the State perform several functions which are intended to meet the civic needs of the citizens of the Anantapur Town. The major functions performed by the Municipality are Five fold. They are:

1. *Engineering and Communication* – which looks after matters relating to Roads, Bridges, Ferries and Buildings, Causeways, Lighting, Water Works, Vehicles Maintenance and so on.
2. *Public Health* – which relates to birth and maternity relief, sanitation, food adulteration, water supply, family planning, prevention of epidemics and so on.
3. *Town Planning* – which relates to General Town Planning Scheme, Detailed Town Planning Scheme, Slum Area Development Programme, Prevention of Encroachments and so on.
4. *Revenue Collection* – which includes collection of poverty tax including general cess, water and drainage tax, scavenging cess, education tax, lighting tax, library cess etc. It also includes vehicle tax, animal tax and professional tax.
5. *Education* – which includes provision of elementary and secondary education.

A detailed study of educational administration in Kurnool Municipal Corporation is dealt in the subsequent chapters.

Finance

The efficiency of any organization depends to a greater extent on its financial position. The better the financial resources of an organization are the better the amenities and services provided by the organization. Therefore, in order to evaluate the performance of the Kurnool Municipal Corporation it is necessary to consider the sources of its revenue and how effectively the various municipal taxes are collected and spent.

However, inspite of these limitations imposed by nature, the Kurnool Municipal Corporation has done somewhat well in exploiting the limited resources available to it to an optimum extent and utilized them for providing amenities and services to its citizens at a reasonable level of satisfaction.

As in the case of other Municipal Corporations in Andhra Pradesh, the Kurnool Municipal Corporation also gets its revenue through the following resources; (1) Tax Resources; (2) Non-Tax Resources (3) Grants-in-aid and loans.

Today, the taxation is regulated by the Act of State Legislation passed from time to time. According to the provision of Andhra Pradesh Municipal Corporation, the Kurnool Municipal Corporation is levying the following taxes.

Property Tax, Water Tax, Title Transfer Tax, Rents from Shopping Complexes, Market Cess, Cess from Slaughter Houses, Vacant Land Taxes, Advertisement Taxes, Entertainment Taxes, Registration Taxes, Professional Taxes, etc., and Grants from Government.

Budget

The Kurnool Municipal Corporation frames a budget showing the probable receipts and expenditure which is proposed to incur during the following years and submits a copy of the same to the State Government.

An Overview

The historical base of Kurnool district has laid strong foundation for its organization and working of municipal set up which inturn also reflected in its working in Kurnool. The Andhra Pradesh Municipal Corporation Act, 1994 though designed the administrative structure for its policy making and internal organizational structure for its effective working, still there are various lapses in it which requires thorough overhauling. The entire system of Kurnool Municipal Corporation is more concentrated on revenue raising and surplus balances but not much interested in spending for civic amenities. Various interviews and group discussions held with various civilians of the Municipal

Corporation brought this into light. The most important aspect like education found no suitable place in the organizational structure and received unfair treatment. Therefore, the way how the Kurnool Municipal Corporation is dealing the subject of education, its administrative procedures and its attention towards secondary schools is dealt in forthcoming chapters.

REFERENCES

1. *Andhra Pradesh District Gazetteers*, Kurnool, 1974, pp. 1-2.
2. *Census of India, 2001*, Census of Kurnool District, Director of Census Operations, Hyderabad.
3. *Andhra Pradesh District Gazetteers*, Kurnool, 1976, pp. 1-4.
4. Government of A.P. G.O. Ms. No. 450 MA, dated 19.8.1994.
5. Government of A.P. G.O. Ms. No. 449 M.A. & U.D. (Elecs-I) (MA), dated 18.8.1994.
6. Government of Andhra Pradesh, G.O. Ms. No. 42 M.A. & U.D. (Elec-II) Department, dated 4-2-1995.
7. Section 5 (3) of Andhra Pradesh Municipalities Act, 1965, p. 35.
8. *Ibid.*, Sec. 8 (a) as amended by Act 17 of 1994.
9. Section 8 of Andhra Pradesh Municipalities Act, 1965.
10. Section 9 of Andhra Pradesh Municipalities (Amended) Act, 1990.
11. Government of Andhra Pradesh, G.O. Ms. No. 319, M.A., dated 15.4.1981.
12. Government of Andhra Pradesh, G.O. Ms. No. 117, MA, HMA & UD Department, dated 7.2.1987.
13. Section 5 (2) of Andhra Pradesh Municipalities Act, 1965, as amended by Act 5 of 1982.
14. Government of Andhra Pradesh, G.O. Ms. No. 298, M.A., dated 31.5.1994.
15. *Annual Administration Reports 1993-94 to 1995-96* of Kurnool Municipal Corporation.
16. Section 20 of Andhra Pradesh Municipalities Act as amended in 1986.
17. Section 21 (2) of Andhra Pradesh Municipalities Act, 1994.
18. *Ibid*, Sec. 7 (5).
19. *Ibid*, Sec. 5.
20. Government of Andhra Pradesh G.O. Ms. No. 40, M.A., dated 3.2.1995.
21. Sec. 23 (b) of Andhra Pradesh Municipalities Act, 1986.
22. Government of Andhra Pradesh G.O. Ms. No. 36 M.A. & U.D., dated 3.2.1995 and Kurnool Municipal Council Rc. No. 41818/94, Elections 1-2, dated 6.2.1995.

4

Educational Administration in Municipal Corporation (A Case Study)

Education is the most significant sector in development process and this is equivalent to saying that entire future of the country would largely depend upon the development of Indian education. The progress of a nation is decided and determined not in the legislatures where passions and prejudices warp judgement and vitiate the laws that may be framed, not in courts where punishments more often harden than reform offenders, not in factories where men become mechanized and think of their individual interests instead of the common, but in schools where the minds of the future citizens are moulded, where the habits, attitudes and outlook of those that are to shape and preside over the destinies of the nation are formed.[1]

The framers of the Indian Education Commission Report (1964-66), while discussing 'Education as Instrument of Change' stated "The realization of the country's aspirations involves changes in the knowledge, skills, interests and values of the people as a whole. This is basic to every programme of social and economic betterment of which India stands in need. If this 'change on a grand scale' is to be achieved without violent revolution, there is one instrument only that can be used: Education......It is a sure and tried instrument".[2]

Keeping these noble aims in mind the governments at all levels have contemplated various forms of agencies both formal and informal to impart education to begin with pre-primary to advanced studies. Especially in Andhra Pradesh there are good number of elementary schools, secondary schools, colleges and universities as formal agencies of education run by various authorities like Local

Bodies, State Government, University Grants Commission and other private managements. Much in particular, the local bodies at rural and urban levels, in addition to their avowed responsibilities to provide amenities to the people in their respective jurisdiction are also concentrating on expansion and administration of pre-primary, primary and secondary education. Specifically in this context, the Municipalities and Municipal Corporations in the state are very much involved in the programme of education through management of primary and secondary schools and Kurnool Municipal Corporation is also a case in point. Educational administration thus emerged as a part of Municipal Administration in Kurnool Municipal Corporation to undertake the task of imparting secondary education to its citizens.

Administration has been defined by Ordway Tead as a comprehensive effort to direct, guide and integrate associating human strivings which are focused towards some specific ends or aims. Educational administration is also a comprehensive effort intended to achieve some specific educational objectives and it deals with the educational practices, where as educational philosophy sets the goal, educational psychology explains the principles, educational administration tells the do-how of educational objectives and principles. It infact, is the dynamic side of education. Educational administration deals with educational institutions right from the schools to the secretariat. It is concerned with both human and material resources. The human elements include *(i)* Children *(ii)* Parents *(iii)* Teachers and *(iv)* Other employees in general. On the material side there are *(i)* money *(ii)* building, and grounds *(iii)* equipment and instructional supplies. Beyond these two elements and ideas, laws and regulations, community needs and so on. All of these have a bearing on the educational process. The integration of these 'parts' in to a 'whole' is educational administration.

French, Hull and Dodds compare educational administration to a lens as it brings everything about the school into focus for community, faculty and students. If it (educational administration) is a poor lens, the image is blurred and obscure and no one in the school or community gets a clear picture of what the school is trying to do. If it is a good lens, the school becomes a clear cut and vivid projection of the ideals and ideas we hope to bring into being.[3]

Educational Administration – Meaning

Education is one of the largest human enterprises undertaken by modern government. The objectives, procedures and machinery together constitute educational administration. In the words of I.C. Kandel;

"Fundamentally, the purpose of educational administration is to bring pupils and teachers together under such conditions as well as successfully promote the end of education".[4]

Sir Graham Balfour writes very aptly, "the purpose of educational administration is to enable the right pupils to receive the right education from the right teachers, at a cost within the means of the state, which will enable pupils to profit by their learning".[5]

In a democratic country like ours, educational administration is a necessity. Some suitable, stable element properly motivated and organized in the machinery becomes necessary to withstand and survive the changes and upheavals caused because of change of governments. Superior educational administration, in fact, is so basic to the satisfactory functioning of democracy. Errors of judgement can be retrieved in a farm or factory but these can be fatal when we are concerned with the moulding of ideas and values of society. An efficient and sound system of educational administration is, in fact, the basis of a good democracy.

Besides, with crores of children being educated in educational institutions, with thousands of teaching and other personnel working in them, with huge sums of money being spent on education, it is absolutely necessary to evolve an efficient system of educational administration at all levels - national, state, local and institutional. So that light of education penetrates in every nook and corner of this country to make the dream of a democratic, socialistic state a reality as early as possible.

In common parlance, educational administration means the organizational set-up for the governance of educational institutions. It is also associated with many synonymous words such as supervision, direction, guidance and control. It involves such major facts as personnel administration, institutional administration and financial administration and so on. Educational Administration is to enable the right pupils to receive the right education from the right teachers at a cost within the means of the other conditions which will enable the pupils best to profit by their training.[6] This is possible through systematic educational administration.

Educational Administration – Public Administration

At present the sphere and scope of public administration have been extended to a very large extent because the multifarious activities of any national governments are no longer limited to the national boundaries alone, but they have a long range impact from local to the international level. Along with it, educational administration has also grown enormously, with the State's acceptance of responsibility for the public education one hand, and with consequent proliferation of the educational institutions in an unprecedented proportion on the other.[7]

School as a Formal Agency of Education in Kurnool Municipal Corporation

Among formal agencies as discussed in Chapter I, schools are the most important formal agencies of education recognized and run by Kurnool Municipal Corporation and are rather planned and supervised by trained and related personnel. No doubt they have more or less fixed routine job and with a certain code of discipline and perform their functions.

Schools are to be the first class nurseries for the education of children in democratic citizenship which India needs to make its democracy permanently viable. Efficient school administration is crucial to the success of democracy. Some theory and philosophy will have to be evolved for guiding the educational administration process at all levels and to be clear about the objectives so that we do not miss the targets.[8]

Scope of School Administration

The following may be considered as necessary components of school administration.

1. Providing the human equipment – headmaster, teaching staff, ministerial staff and menial staff.
2. Providing the material equipment such as building, furniture, farms, laboratories, library, museum, art gallery etc.
3. Preparing the curriculum for the different classes.

4. Organization of a systematic co-curricular programme.
5. Preparing time-table.
6. Maintaining discipline.
7. Organization of library, museum, hostel etc.
8. Organization of health and physical education.
9. Organization of exhibitions and museums.
10. Organization of guidance service.
11. Maintaining the school records.
12. Providing various auxiliary services like mid-day meals, school uniform, text books etc.
13. Coordinating the work of home, school and community.
14. Supervision of school work.
15. Evaluation of pupil achievement.
16. Financing and budgeting.
17. Co-operating with departmental authorities and implementing the orders of the higher educational authorities.

In short, anything and everything having to do something with the education of the child through the agency of the school, will be included in school administration.

Characteristics of Successful School Administration

There are some essential features in a good school administration:

(i) *Flexibility:* One of the essential characteristics of successful schools administration is its flexible character. The administration should be dynamic, not static: it should provide enough scope for additions and alterations. The rules and regulations should act as a means to an end and not an end in themselves.

(ii) *Practicability:* The school administration must not be a bundle of theoretical principles, but must provide practical measures to achieve the desired objectives. Whatever objective is decided it must be achievable and practicable to avoid frustration.

(iii) *Conformity to the social and political philosophy of the country:* There must be close connection between school administration and the social and political philosophy of a country. It must adjust itself to the impact of new ideals, new patterns and new mores of the society.

(*iv*) *Efficiency:* Successful administration is that which results in maximum efficiency. This will be possible only when human and material resources are properly utilized – right man at the right place; right work at the right time, every activity and project is well planned and well executed.

(*v*) *Successful achievement of desired objectives:* Successful administration is one which leads to the successful achievement of desired objectives of education in a particular community e.g., healthy social living, development of good physical, social, moral, intellectual and aesthetic qualities and healthy democratic living.

School administration must facilitate education. It exists for the pupil and its efficiency has to be measured by the extent to which it contributes to teaching and learning.

Realising the importance of education the various formal agencies of education have devoted their efforts to give primary as well as secondary education to the people of Kurnool district of which Kurnool Municipal Corporation is a part benefited by them.

Education in Kurnool District

Though Kurnool district is one of the drought prone districts of Andhra Pradesh, still this district is lucky to be endowed with good educational institutions. As per 2001 census this district has a total population of 35.29 lakhs of which 17.96 lakhs are males and 17.33 lakhs are females and it stands tenth among the 23 districts of the State. The proportion of rural and urban population to the total population of the district works out 77 per cent and 23 per cent respectively with a clear rural base and bias. The Scheduled Castes from 6.29 lakhs (17.82%) and the Scheduled Tribes are 0.70 lakhs (1.98%) lakhs in the district.

Literacy and Educational Scenario

The literacy percentage of Kurnool district is 53.22 per cent which is lower than that in the State (60.47%) as a whole.

The Kurnool district educational scenario is reflected through the working of various educational institutions as shown in Table 4.1. Table 4.1 shows that there are as many as 3564 educational institutions all over the district comprising of institutions managed by Central, State Government, local bodies and private managements. Of these primary schools comprise 2000, upper primary schools 992 and High Schools 572. Primary schools under State Government are 81, under Mandal Parishad 1505, under Municipality 96, under Private Aided 106, and under private un-aided 212, with a total student strength of 1,32,913 boys and 1,26,559 girls. The Upper Primary Schools under State Government are 8, under Mandal Parishad 657, under Municipality 28 under private aided 27 and under private unaided 272 with a students strength of 1,19,811 boys and 1,05,202 girls. Secondary schools under State Government 54, under Mandal Parishad 260, under Municipality 5, under Municipal Corporation 8, under private aided 59 and private unaided 195. With a total student strength of 1,14,548 boys and 86,302 girls. The total number of teachers employed in all the above schools are 18,582 of which 10,546 are male and 8,036 female.

The higher education needs in the district are met by various institutions like one University, 8 P.G. Colleges, 41 Degree Colleges, 47 exclusive Junior Colleges, 10 Engineering Colleges and 6 Polytechnic Colleges, 15 Colleges of Education

Realising the need and urgency of distance education and to keep educational facilities at the doorsteps of each individual and to satisfy the needs of every citizen whoever is desirous of furthering studies, Dr. B.R. Ambedkar Open University had started five study centres in the Degree Colleges in the District.

Table-4.1

Primary and Secondary Education in Kurnool District

S.No.		*No. of Institutions*	*Teachers*			*Students Enrolled*		*Total*
			Male	*Female*	*Total*	*Boys*	*Girls*	
1.	Primary Schools	2000	3395	3254	6649	132913	126559	259472
2.	Upper Primary Schools	992	3535	2599	6134	119811	105202	225013
3.	High Schools	572	3616	2183	5799	114548	86302	200850
	Total	**3564**	**10546**	**8036**	**18582**	**367272**	**318063**	**685335**

Source: Hand Book of Statistics, Kurnool District, 2006-07, pp. 200-206.

Educational Administration under Kurnool Municipal Corporation

As discussed in the III Chapter, Kurnool Municipal Corporation is one of the Fifteen Municipal Corporations constituted in Andhra Pradesh.

Kurnool Municipal Corporation's contribution to the field of primary as well as secondary education is considerable. This Municipal Corporation maintains 64 schools of which 49 are Primary schools, 7 are Upper primary schools and 8 are High schools. Of the Primary schools 32 are Telugu medium and 17 are Urdu medium schools. Of the Upper primary schools 5 are Telugu medium and two are Urdu medium. Seven High schools are Telugu Medium schools and there is one Urdu medium high school.

In addition to above there are good number of government aided management Primary Schools and High Schools and also private management primary as well as High Schools in Kurnool Municipal Corporation jurisdiction.

The educational administration in Kurnool Municipal Corporation is carried out more by general administrators than specialists in education. The Mayor who is the Chairperson of the Municipal Corporation and the Municipal Commissioner are the only two authorities, of whom the former is an elected un-official who needs no prescribed educational qualifications to be elected as Chairperson and the latter is a government official with no specialized knowledge in the field of primary and secondary education. The organizational structure of secondary education system however reveals the lapse of absence of any specialized officer of education put in the municipal system to supervise and administer the secondary schools under Kurnool Municipal Corporation. The State Government Officers like the District Educational Officer and his subordinate officers are involved in the supervision of academic activities of the Municipal Corporation schools. Thus, these government officers only are brought into the organizational structure of secondary education in Kurnool Municipal Corporation.

Organisational Structure of Secondary Education in Kurnool Municipal Corporation

It is evident that organization is the formal structure of authority which is well defined and coordinated towards the attainment of specific objectives. These objectives are achieved by combined efforts of different specialists belonging to the organization. An insight into the organizational structure of Kurnool Municipal Corporation reveals that the pattern of organizational structure of secondary education is not well planned and not equipped with specialized functionaries in the municipal organization. Except trained teachers and non-teaching staff there are no other officers in the municipal organization who could fully devote their time and energies for the effective functioning of the educational administration.

Table 4.2 gives a detailed picture about the organizational structure of Educational Branch in Kurnool Municipal Corporation. As usual the Kurnool Municipal Corporation is headed by an elected body known as Municipal Corporation as discussed in the Chapter III. The Corporation is headed by the Mayor as the Chairperson and under him there is Municipal Commissioner who is the Chief Executive Officer appointed by the State Government.

Immediately below the Municipal Commissioner there are two Junior Assistants who look after matters relating High Schools and the other is a Junior Assistant to look after affairs relating to Primary and Upper primary schools matters relating to teachers' salary bills, leaves etc.

Municipal Corporation Commissioner *vis-à-vis* Education

As discussed earlier, the Municipal Corporation Commissioner is a multi-functionary and who has to look after both primary and secondary education along with other functions in the municipality directly. Regarding his concern for education he is responsible for smooth functioning of Secondary Schools. He exercises two types of supervision over the schools. One is institutional supervision exercised over the movable and immovable properties of educational institutions in the Municipal Corporation. Second is the academic supervision, in which he exercises administrative control over all academic aspects of the teaching and non-teaching staff of the schools. He makes visits and inspects the schools and makes suitable suggestions for the enhancement of students strength and attendance, to keep the premises clean and tidy and to enhance good discipline among the staff and students. He is the Authority who is empowered to take disciplinary action against the employees of the schools on the grounds of irregularities and misbehaviour

Table–4.2

Organisation of Education Wing in Kurnool Municipal Corporation State Government

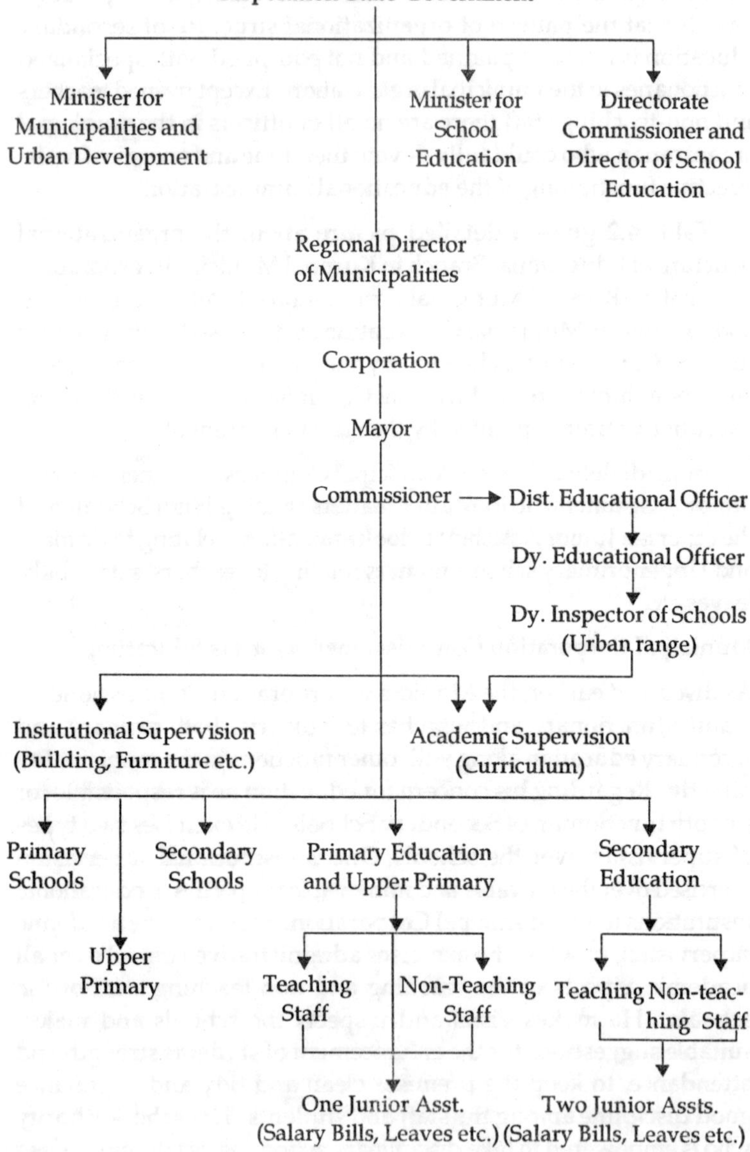

found by him through personal visits to schools, through enquiries based on the complaints received by him and on the advises of the District Educational Officer who is a parallel officer of education who is also authorized to exercise academic control over the Municipal Corporation schools.[11]

District Educational Officer (DEO)

The District Educational Officer in Kurnool is an officer of the State Government who has to look after the administration of primary as well as secondary education at the district level imparted by the government schools, and also holds supervisory as well as inspecting authority over other schools run by local bodies like Municipalities and Municipal Corporations which enjoy government grant-in-aid. He also exercises academic supervision (Curriculum) over all the Primary and Secondary Schools in the district including the schools under Kurnool Municipal Corporation. As already pointed out that the Municipal Commissioner in Kurnool Municipal Corporation directly exercises control over the secondary schools managed by it in parallel to the District Educational Officer but enjoys the power of taking disciplinary action against the teaching as well as non-teaching and subordinate staff of the schools. There is a Schools Supervisor in the cadre of a Secondary Grade Teacher in the Kurnool Municipal Corporation who assists the Municipal Commissioner in this aspect. It is a great lapse on the side of Municipal Administration in not having atleast one officer in the cadre of Municipal Educational Officer in its organizational system to look into the working of educational institutions run by Kurnool Municipal Corporation.

The District Educational Officer in Kurnool is assisted by Four Deputy Educational Officers in carrying on inspection and administration of secondary education in the district. These Deputy Educational Officers are assisted by Mandal Educational Officers. One Mandal Education Officer is incharge of urban range and he inspects and studies the performance of the Municipal Corporation schools in Kurnool taking the assistance of the Schools Supervisor of Kurnool Municipal Corporation and report the same to the District Educational Officer through their immediate officers who inturn report the same to the Municipal Commissioner of Kurnool Municipal Corporation. The District Educational Officer and the Municipal Commissioner of Kurnool Municipal Corporation also make surprise visits to all these schools and make on-the-spot study of the functioning of these schools. Instructional and curricular aspects are generally supervised by the District Educational Officer.[12]

Powers and Functions of District Educational Officer *vis-à-vis* Municipal Corporation Schools in Kurnool Municipal Corporation

The powers and functions of the District Educational Officer in respect of Municipal Corporation schools are three fold. They are:

(a) Academic

1. He visits Secondary Schools and submits the visit reports in the Director of School Education as well as to the Municipal Commissioner.
2. He reviews the Inspection Reports of Deputy Educational Officers and other Inspectors and follow-up work.
3. He organizes academic courses for Teachers, Headmasters and Inspectors of Schools.
4. Conduct of Science Fairs, Sports and Games meet etc., and
5. Improving the quality of education in the district.

(b) Examinations

1. Constitution of Common Examination Boards.
2. Plenary examinations for class other than X (SSC) in accordance with the common examination Board Constitution.
3. Advance action for the conduct of X class (SSC) public examinations like consultation of examination centres, appointment of departmental officers and custodians of question papers.
4. Conduct of SSC examinations and the provision of required vigilance work.
5. Organization and conduct of spot valuation of answer scripts of the SSC examinations.
6. Supervision in connection with Headmasters Accounts Tests.

(c) Administration

1. Writes confidential reports on teachers of Municipal Schools to the Municipal Commissioner.
2. Prompt sanction and disbursement of various kinds of scholarships.

3. Submission of educational statistical return to the government received from the Municipal Corporation, and
4. Conducting enquiries on academic matters.

Deputy Educational Officers *vis-à-vis* Municipal Corporation Schools in Kurnool Municipal Corporation[13]

In Kurnool district there are four Deputy Educational Officers of which one is incharge of Schools in Kurnool division. He is assisted by one Deputy Inspector of Schools who is incharge of urban range and who covers all schools under Kurnool Municipal Corporation. The Deputy Educational Officer is required to inspect the Municipal Corporation Schools at the rate of one regular inspection, one follow-up visit and a surprise visit of each school. The Inspection Reports are prepared at every time and copies will be submitted to the District Educational Officer as well as to the Municipal Commissioner for proper action.

Powers and Functions

(i) Conducting annual inspection of the schools and prompt submission of T.I.Rs to the D.E.O. He should give a demonstration lesson followed by discussion with the teachers. A brief resume of the discussion should be appended to the T.I.Rs.

(ii) Making follow-up visits to the schools.

(iii) Making surprise visits to secondary schools.

(iv) Organising centres of school complex professionally so as to ensure that each school gets the benefit of the school complex.

(v) Supervising and guiding the organization of subject clubs in the schools and programmes of supervised study.

(vi) Providing guidance in preparation and implementation of institutional and instructional plans.

(vii) Encouraging teachers to undertake action research programmes.

(viii) Organising conference, seminars and workshops of subject teachers with a view to improving their professional competence.

(ix) Giving demonstration lessons by competent subject teachers adopting modern techniques of teaching.

(x) Adopting atleast one high school to develop it as a model

school. The selected institution for adoption should not have been adopted by any of his predecessors.

(xi) Trying out innovations in selected schools.

(xii) Scrutinising evaluation tools and procedures adopted and ensuring their quality.

(xiii) Assessing schools on the basis of their performance in curricular, co-curricular activities and bestowing more attention on these schools below the minimum level as a priority.

(xiv) Helping in the organization of Book Banks.

(xv) Organising and conducting panel inspection of High schools.

(xvi) Improving the quality of secondary education.

Ancillary Functions

(i) Planning programmes of annual inspection and obtaining approval of the District Educational Officer before the beginning of the academic year.

(ii) Issuing instructions and ensuring that all the institutions draw up institutional plans before the commencement of the academic year.

(iii) Review of the Inspection Reports of the Primary and Upper Primary Schools conducted by the Mandal Education Officers.

(iv) Providing guidance in the functioning of parent-teacher associations at the school as well as Municipal Corporation level for the promotion of school improvement programme.

(v) Assisting the District Educational Officer, in;

- *(a)* the conduct of common examinations and public examinations.
- *(b)* Organizing District School Fairs, sports meet, scout rallies and educational week; and
- *(c)* Proper distribution of nationalized text books.

(vi) Maintaining essential educational statistics.

(vii) Conducting enquiries on academic matters.

(viii) Enlightens public co-operation in utilizing community resources for improvement of schools.

Headmasters

As stated earlier, directly under the control of the Municipal Commissioner, there are Primary, Upper-primary and Secondary

Schools under Kurnool Municipal Corporation. Each school is headed by one Headmaster. In respect of Headmasters of Secondary schools, these posts are filed by those who are holding the seniority as School Assistants working in Secondary Schools. In the absence of the Headmaster of a particular school, the next senior will act as Incharge Headmaster. The duties of Headmaster of primary schools vary from the duties of Secondary School Headmasters in respect of academic matters but same in respect of supervision and administration of school work. The only difference is that the primary school Headmaster will be incharge of generally V standard and acts as its class teacher. He teaches all the subjects to the V class students. But the secondary school Headmasters teach preferably one or two subjects teaching prescribed periods per week. The upper primary school Headmaster also fall in line with Secondary School Headmasters. The duties of Headmasters of the Secondary Schools are given here under.

Duties of Headmasters of the Secondary Schools[14]

1. *Academic*

- *(a)* Teaching of eight periods a week. Preferably one subject completely in general;
- *(b)* Guiding teachers of his own subjects in particular and others in general;
- *(c)* Arranging for professional guidance from his own and also from local experts, if available, in other subject areas;
- *(d)* Informing the departmental inspecting officers for the guidance he requires in specific areas;
- *(e)* Formulating minimum academic programme and institutional plan with the help of his assistants and implement it;
- *(f)* Arranging demonstration lessons in all the subject areas by competent subject teachers;
- *(g)* Undertaking action research programmes;
- *(h)* Arranging conferences, workshops, seminars etc.;
- *(i)* Organising innovative activities.

2. *Supervision*

- *(a)* Periodical (monthly) check-up of the lesson plans and year plans prepared by the assistant teachers of his own school;
- *(b)* Preparation of time table and their proper implementations;

(c) Observation of classroom teaching of Assistants to the extent of one period during a working day (preferably X class) and recording it with suggestions for improvement;

(d) Proper organization of activity areas, namely, physical education, health education, creating activity and Socially Useful Productive Work (SUPW) and moral education;

(e) Introduction of Scouting and Guiding as co-curricular activities and their proper supervision;

(f) Preparing the school for participation in science fairs and in games and sports;

(g) Completion of syllabus as per the plan of School Education Department;

(h) Organise Book Banks, Sanchayika School Bank, Co-operative Stores etc., wherever possible;

(i) Maintain a watch register to the academic and para-academic work turned out by Assistants.

3. ***Administration***

(a) Observation of classroom teaching of every Assistant to the extent of one period for each term;

(b) Maintain all the registers prescribed, if supplied by the management;

(c) Collect, utilize and maintain the accounts relating to special fee funds;

(d) Supervise work of office staff;

(e) Submit pay bills etc., promptly.

The Assistants who are in-charge of school in the absence of the Headmaster are expected to do the following duties. They are:

1. When the Headmasters proceed a Casual Leave they should place invariably the First Assistant of the in-charge of the post of Headmaster to attend current duties of the post of Headmaster.
2. The First Assistants so kept in-charge of the post of the Headmaster should attend to the correspondence like issue of T.C's, Marks and sanctioning casual leaves and attesting true copies. He is also not expected to be sent by the regular Headmaster alone. During the in-charge period, he should not make any purchases which involve monetary commitments.

3. The Assistant in-charge can attend to the above functions only when he is kept in-charge of the post of the Headmaster may sanction casual leave to the staff of the school in deserving cases and all such cases should be brought to the notice of the Headmaster when he joins duty after availing casual leave.

What the Assistant In-charge not to Do

It is irregular for the Assistant to submit Pay Bills etc., when the Headmaster is on casual leave on or Other Duty attending a conference or is under invigilation or correction work in connection with any government examination.

Teachers

Each Headmaster in every school under Kurnool Municipal Corporation is assisted by teachers. In each Municipal High School having 6th to 10th classes, the following staffing pattern is provided by the Government. There are various categories working in secondary schools. They are:

Table-4.3
Staffing Pattern in High Schools
(As Per A.P.E.Rs)

1. Headmasters	–	1
2. School Assistant (Subject wise)		
Mathematics	–	1
English	–	1
Physical Science	–	1
Biological Science	–	1
Social Studies	–	1
Telugu	–	1
Hindi	–	1
Physical Education	–	1
3. Ministerial Staff: (each)		
(a) Junior Assistant		
(b) Record Assistant		
(c) Office Attender		
(d) Laboratory cum Library Attender		
(e) Night Watchman		
(f) Sweeper cum Watchman		

Source: Government of A.P. G.O. Ms. No. 103 Education, dated 5.08.2005.

(N + 1) formula is applicable in the case of full-fledged High Schools. One teacher for each section in addition to Panel Headmaster. If the number of sections in each school is more than 5, additional teaching staff is provided in the following priority basis as shown below:

1. School Assistant (Mathematics)
2. School Assistant (English)
3. School Assistant (Physical Science)
4. School Assistant (Biological Sciences)
5. School Assistant (Social Sciences)

If the work load per week is more than 30 periods an additional post of School Assistant (Language) is sanctioned and if it increases more than 30 two School Assistant posts are permitted. If the pupil's strength in each school is more than 400, one additional School Assistant (Physical Education) and if it increases more than 800, two School Assistants (Physical Education) are permitted. In co-education schools, if there are two School Assistants (Physical Education) posts are available, of these one must be a Lady School Assistant. If the school is exclusively for Girls, all the School Assistants (Physical Education) must be women. If the total workload is 30 periods per week one post of Art/Music/Dance/Craft Teacher will be permitted.*15

Allocation of Workload**

The Government of Andhra Pradesh have made lot of changes in respect of workload subject periods, staff strength and allocation of workload: Vide G.O. Ms. No.103 (Education) dated 5.8.2005 all the teaching posts in the High Schools including Languages, Physical Education have been re-designated as School Assistants. Accordingly the subject-wise workload has been reallocated and fixed to each post defending upon the strength of the school. The following is the subject-wise workload as shown in Table 4.4.

An analysis of Table 4.4 shows that the workload per week in each High School is fixed to 48 periods of which 37 periods are allotted to teaching subjects and 11 periods are allotted to teaching non-subjects. The teaching subjects are First language Telugu, Second language Hindi, Third language English, Mathematics, Physical Science, Biological Science and Social Studies. The First language Telugu is taught for 6 periods, the Second language Hindi

Table-4.3 (A)

Present Teaching Staff in Secondary Schools in Kurnool Municipal Corporation

S. No.	Name of the School	H. M. S.	School Assistants T	H	E	M	PS	Posts Sanctioned and Working Cadre Wise NS	SS	SGT	TP Gr. II	Urdu Gr. II	HP Gr. II	Skt. Pt.	Tai-loring	PET	PD	Drg.	Craft	PVI	Mu-sic	Wo-rk	Va-cant	To-tal
1.	Damodaram Sanjeevaiah Memorial Municipal Corporation High School	1	2	1	2	4	2	2	3	-	1	-	1	1		2	-	1	-	-	1	23	1	24
2.	Nehru Memorial Municipal Corporation High School	*	2	-	1	2	2	2	1	-	-	-	1	-	-	1	-	-	*	-	-	12	2	14
3.	Cattamanchi Ramalinga Reddy Memorial Municipal Corporation High School	1	2	1	4	4	4	4	2	-	2	-	1	-	-	2	1	-	-	-	-	26	3	29
4.	Indira Gandhi Memorial Municipal Corporation High School	-	1	1	2	2	3	2	3	-	-	-	-	-	-	1	-	-	-	-	-	16	3	19

Contd...

S. No.	Name of the School	H. M. S.	School Assistants T	H	E	M	PS	Posts Sanctioned and Working Cadre Wise NS	SS	SGT	TP Gr. II	Urdu Gr. II	HP Gr. II	Skt. Pt.	Tai-loring	PET	PD	Drg.	Craft	PVI	Mu-sic	Wo-rk	Va-cant	To-tal
5.	Sri Potti Sreeramulu Memorial Municipal Corporation High School	-	1	-	1	3	2	1	-	-	-	-	1	-	1	-	-	-	-	-	-	10	2	12
6.	Dr. B.R. Ambedkar Memorial Municipal Corporation High School	-	-	1	1	1	1	1	1	1	-	-	-	-	-	-	-	-	-	-	-	7	2	9
7.	Sri Tanguturu Prakasam Pantulu Memorial Municipal Corporation High School	-	1	-	1	3	-	-	1	2	-	-	1	-	-	-	-	-	-	-	-	9	2	11
8.	Municipal Corporation High School (Urdu)	-	-	1	1	-	1	1	1	2	-	-	-	-	-	1	-	-	-	-	-	8	3	11
	Total	**3**	**10**	**5**	**13**	**20**	**15**	**13**	**12**	**5**	**6**	**1**	**6**	**1**	**1**	**10**	**1**	**2**	**2**	**1**	**1**	**111**	**18**	**129**

Noie: * Indicates sanctioned and vacant.
Source: Office of the Commissioner, Kurnool Municipal Corporation, Kurnool.

Table-4.4
Allocation of Subject-wise Workload Per Week

S.No.	*Subject*	*No. of Periods*
1.	First Language (Telugu)	6
2.	Second Language (Hindi)	3
3.	Third Language (English)	6
4.	Mathematics	8
5.	Physical Science	4
6.	Biological Science	4
7.	Social Studies	6
	Total Periods	**37**
	Non-Subjects	*No. of Periods*
8.	Health & Physical Education	2
9.	Environmental Education	2
10.	Work Experience/Vocational Education/ Computer Education	2
11.	Art/Music/Dance Education	2
12.	Games/Debates/Essay Writing/Quiz	3
	Total	**11**
	Grand Total	**48**

Source: Government of A.P. DSE Rc. No. 90/E1-2/02, dated 7.6.2002.

is taught for 3 periods, the Third language English taught for 6 periods, Mathematics taught for 8 periods, Physical Science is taught for 4 periods, Biological Science is taught for 4 periods and Social Studies is taught 6 periods in a week.

The non-subject items taught in the school are (1) Health and Physical Education/Environmental Education (2) Work experience/ Vocational education/Computer education (3) Art/Music/Dance education (4) Moral education (5) Games/Debates/Essay Writing/ Quiz etc. For Games/Debates/Essay Writing/Quiz three periods allotted and the rest of the items two periods each is allotted.

Allotment of Work to Teachers

The Headmaster of the High School teaches 8 periods (each period may range from 40 to 45 minutes) per week and must teach at least one subject full for X class. The respective School Assistants trained in their specialized subjects should teach VIII, IX and X classes. The School Assistants of Physical Science should teach Mathematics to VI and VII classes and the School Assistants of Biological Sciences should teach Science to VI and VII classes. For VI and VII classes except Telugu and Hindi subjects the rest of the subjects will be taught by School Assistants/S.G.T. as allotted by the Headmaster. Every teacher should teach minimum of 24 periods, and maximum of 30 periods except on certain special occasions. The Physical Education School Assistant must be present from 8/9 A.M. to 11/12 noon in the morning in the afternoon 2/3 P.M. to 4.30/5.30 P.M.

The total number of working days for each school is fixed at 220 days per an academic year. The academic calendar is prepared by the Government and the details are supplied to each school. The working hours of the schools may also be slightly changed with the consent of School Committee.

Table-4.5
Sanctioned Posts of Teaching Staff in Secondary Schools of Kurnool Municipal Corporation

S.No.	*Name of the Post*	*No. of Posts Sanctioned*	*Working*	*Vacant*
1.	Headmasters	3	2	1
2.	School Assistants			
	(*a*) Telugu	15	11	4
	(*b*) Hindi	10	7	3
	(*c*) English	13	13	0
	(*d*) Mathematics	20	19	1
	(*e*) Physical Science	15	15	0
	(*f*) Natural Science	13	13	0
	(*g*) Social Studies	12	12	0
3.	Secondary Grade Teachers	3	3	0
4.	Urdu	1	0	1
5.	Sanskrit	1	1	0
6.	Tailoring Instructors	1	1	0
7.	Physical Director/P.E.T.	10	5	5
8.	Drawing Instructor	2	1	1
9.	Craft Instructors	2	0	2
10.	P.V.I.	2	0	2
11.	Music Instructor	1	0	1
		124	**103**	**21**

Source: Office of the Commissioner, Municipal Corporation, Kurnool.

As per Rule 7(2) of Andhra Pradesh Education Rules the allotment of class work to the teachers is as follows:

Duties of the Teachers

1. *Academic*

- *(a)* To teach the allotted subjects during the allotted periods;
- *(b)* Guiding subject to junior teacher, if any;
- *(c)* Correction of written work of the pupils regularly;
- *(d)* Correction of answer scripts relating to all unit tests and terminal examinations;
- *(e)* Developing aptitude for professional advanced participation;
- *(f)* Implementation of minimum academic programme chalked out in his subjects;
- *(g)* Diagnosing pupils deficiencies and conducting remedial teaching;
- *(h)* Proper use of teaching materials and aids available in the schools;
- *(i)* Improving black-board work;
- *(j)* Undertaking action, research and innovative practices.

2. *Classroom Administration*

- *(a)* Maintenance of classroom discipline;
- *(b)* Maintenance of attendance register;
- *(c)* Encouraging pupils in maintaining personal hygienic and classroom cleanliness;
- *(d)* Attending the classes regularly;
- *(e)* Assisting the Headmaster in the distribution of text-books. Teachers' Day flags, etc.
- *(f)* Participation and organization of National Festivals in the school;
- *(g)* Arrangement and organization of co-curricular and extra-curricular activities;
- *(h)* Encouraging pupils to follow dress restrictions and general discipline in school; (i) adhering to the duties and responsibilities specifically designed to the subject departments;
- *(i)* Any other duties and responsibilities assigned to him by the Headmaster under order of his superiors.

The Headmasters of Secondary Schools are also assisted by Non-teaching staff like Junior Assistants, Typists, Laboratory Assistants, Library Assistants, Record Assistants and the Attenders and Sweepers. The duties of non-teaching staff are as follows:

Categories of Non-Teaching Staff

The following categories of employees come under non-teaching staff.

1. Senior Assistants
2. Junior Assistants
3. Typists
4. Laboratory Attenders
5. Library Assistants
6. Record Assistants
7. Watchman/Sweeper/Attender

The Duties of Senior Assistant/Junior Assistant

(a) The Junior Assistant shall register the letters received from the Government or Head of the Department and put up to the Head of the Institution for necessary orders;

(b) He shall preserve all the record of the managements such as T.C. Books, Cash-Registers, Attendance Registers, Acquittance Register, leave accounts etc.

(c) He shall prepare the monthly pay bills of the teaching and non-teaching staff of the institution.

(d) He shall maintain the leave accounts of the teaching and non-teaching staff of the institutions and submit them to the Head of the Institution.

(e) He shall collect the fee such as special and tuition fee and post in the daily book and also obtain the signature of the Head of the Institution.

(f) He shall also maintain the ledger account to be carried out for scrutiny and audit;

(g) He shall maintain the stamp account, service postage account and accounts relating to special fee and other fees and vouchers safely;

(h) He shall maintain the Service Register entries upto date.

The Duties of the Lab Assistants

(a) He shall keep the laboratory clean and tidy;

(*b*) He shall be responsible for dusting of equipment and apparatus and should be done carefully at least once in three days;
(*c*) He shall see that the apparatus is kept at the proper place after use either by the teacher or by the pupil;
(*d*) He shall see that the students do not take away the apparatus or the material from the laboratory;
(*e*) He shall also see that the students do not touch the acids and other dangerous chemicals;
(*f*) He shall arrange the apparatus for conducting experiments.

The Duties of Library Assistant

(*a*) He shall prepare the indent of the books subject-wise;
(*b*) He shall see that the books are not eaten away by the white ants etc.;
(*c*) He shall prepare the catalogue of the books subject-wise;
(*d*) He shall issue books to the students and see that they are circulated and returned in time;
(*e*) He shall maintain the account of periodicals and their circulation among the staff members and students of the institution;
(*f*) He shall maintain the stock-register upto date with full details of books purchased.

The Duties of Attender/Sweepers

They shall maintain the unkeep of the institution and its premises namely laboratory, library, staff rooms, toilets and playground etc. The existing staffing pattern of non-teaching staff in Secondary Schools of Kurnool Municipal Corporation is shown in Table 4.6.

An Overview

The schools have become the most important formal agencies of promoting literacy and mostly the local bodies like Municipalities and Municipal Corporations in urban areas have taken up the task of managing the schools as a part of their Municipal Administration under the name of educational administration. In particular, no doubt, the Kurnool Municipal Corporation has taken up the task of strengthening secondary education by managing as many as eight high schools. It is also employing number of teaching and non-teaching staff to meet the goals. But an insight into the Educational

Table-4.6
Particulars of Non-Teaching Staff in Kurnool Municipal Corporation

S.No.	Name of the School	Sr. Asst.	Jr. Asst.	Record Asst.	Librarian	Watchman	Office Subordinate	Sweeper	Total
1.	Damodaram Sanjeevaiah Memorial Municipal Corporation High School	1	2	4	1	2	2	2	14
2.	Nehru Memorial Municipal Corporation High School	-	-	2	-	1	2	1	6
3.	Cattamanchi Ramalinga Reddy Memorial Municipal Corporation High School	-	1	2	-	1	1	-	5
4.	Indira Gandhi Memorial Municipal Corporation High School	-	-	-	-	-	-	-	-
5.	Sri Potti Sreeramulu Memorial Municipal Corporation High School	-	-	-	-	-	-	-	-
6.	Dr. B.R. Ambedkar Memorial Municipal Corporation High School	-	-	-	-	-	-	-	-
7.	Sri Tanguturu Prakasam Pantulu Memorial Municipal Corporation High School	-	-	-	-	-	-	-	-
8.	Municipal Corporation High School (Urdu)	-	-	-	-	-	-	-	-
	Total	1	3	8	1	4	5	3	25

Source: Office of the Commissioner, Kurnool Municipal Corporation, Kurnool.

Administration performed by Kurnool Municipal Corporation reveals that there are various problem areas and trouble spots which require lot of attention both at the Municipal Corporation as well as State Government levels. The problem infact faced by the educational institutions and the weaknesses found in the educational administration of Kurnool Municipal Corporation need suitable remedial measures. Especially the absence of a full time and full-fledged officer with a designation of Municipal Educational Officer is absent in the Municipal organizational system in Kurnool. The Municipal Commissioner who is a generalist is the only line officer found in the system and under his direct control as many as sixty four Headmasters both for Elementary and Secondary Schools are brought to report him in addition to various other officers and office staff working under him which yielded too much span of control. The authority of the District Educational Officer now and then comes in conflict with that of the authority of Municipal Commissioner in dealing with things relating to academic matters. The organizational structure and the administrative arrangements should always be conducive to the effective functioning of the primary and secondary schools under the system and yield good results. This kind of result-oriented performance of the schools is much essential in any system and from the perspective how the secondary schools under Kurnool Municipal Corporation are working is studied in the successive chapter.

REFERENCES

1. Aggarwal, J.C., *Theory and Principles of Education*, New Delhi: Vikas, 1995, p. 104.
2. *Ibid*, p. 80.
3. Kochhar, S.K., *Secondary School Administration*, New Delhi: Sterling, 1997, p. 3.
4. Bhatia, K.K., and others, *Modern Indian Education and its Problems* (Ludhiana: Prakash Brothers, 1990), p. 75.
5. Kochhar, S.K., *Op.cit.*, p. 4.
6. Government of Andhra Pradesh, G.O. Ms. No. 1199, Education dated 29.12.1978 and Anantapur Municipal Council Res. No. 665, dated 11.1.1979.
7. *Interview with S. Ranganayakulu, a student of X standard Damodaram Sanjeevaiah Municipal Corporation High School, Kurnool on 5.1.2009.*
8. Kochhar, S.K., *Op. cit.*, p. 8.
9. *Hand Book of Statistics 2006-07*, Kurnool District Chief Planning Officer, Kurnool, p. VI.
10. *Ibid*, pp. 199-215.

11. *Interview with Sri. P. Dhanunjaya, Municipal Commissioner,* Kurnool Municipal Corporation on 11.10.2008.
12. *Interview with Sri. K. Krishna Rao, DEO, Kurnool on 9.1.2008.*
13. *Interview with Smt. Ghousia Begum, Deputy Educational Officer (Retd.), Kurnool on 16.2.2008.*
14. Government of A.P., G.O. Ms. No. 13, Education (Rules), dated 8.1.1986.
15. Government of A.P., G.O. Ms. No. 103 Education, dated 5.8.2005.
16. Government of A.P., DSE Rc. No. 90/E1-2/02, dated 7.6.2002.

5

Kurnool Municipal Corporation Secondary Schools–At Work

Secondary Education serves as a bridge between Elementary Education and Higher Education to prepare young persons of the age group of 10 to 14 years. The secondary education begins where the primary education ends. The secondary education is a connecting link between primary stage and university stage and seeks to provide future leadership to the society in the various walks of life. Secondary education is essential for training the young pupils to be effective members of the society. The individuals potentialities are developed, his ability, aptitude and attitudes, interest and character are shaped at this stage. After secondary education the individual enters life knowledgeably and keeps himself mentally alert.[1]

As a nation building endeavour, quality education at these two levels namely primary and secondary stages is essential. Teachers for primary schools are drawn from secondary schools. Strong primary education should be provided to enable pupils to enter the high school with the expected entry behaviour. The effective terminal behaviour resulting from secondary education alone will help the student either to opt for higher education or choose a job for satisfying his 'bread and butter aim'.

Realising the importance of school education, the urban local bodies like, Municipalities and Municipal Corporations in Andhra Pradesh in general and Kurnool Municipal Corporation in particular has taken up the task of primary as well as secondary education by establishing and managing as many as 64 schools in Kurnool city area of which the schools earmarked for imparting secondary education are eight in number as given in Chapter IV.

School as a Basal Unit of Educational Administration

School is the basal unit of the big hierarchy of educational administration. Today, as never before, India needs educational institutions not only to guard its past but also to advance its future. "The density of India is now being in the classrooms" – this is the assessment of the situation by the first ever comprehensive Commission (1964-66) of Indian Education. Schools are to be the first nurseries for the education of children in democratic citizenship which India needs to make its democracy. Permanently viable efficient school administration is crucial to the success of democracy. Some theory and philosophy will have to be evolved for guiding the educational administration process at all levels and to be clear about the objectives so that we do not miss the targets.[2]

The Kurnool Municipal Corporation in line with other managements like Central, State Governments, local bodies and private managements has recognized the 'school' as a basal unit of educational administration and established primary and secondary schools under its management in Kurnool city.

Secondary Education

The Kurnool Municipal Corporation paid prominent attention towards secondary (High school) education. While the strength of elementary education lies on an effective secondary education system, equally the roots of secondary education rests on a strong elementary education system. This is rightly realized by Kurnool Municipal Corporation and had taken up the management of secondary schools alongwith primary schools in its Municipal Corporation area.

Within the Municipal Corporation limits of Kurnool city, there are 100 secondary (High) schools out of which Eight Secondary Schools are run by Kurnool Municipal Corporation. Nine are run by the State Government and the remaining 83 are run by Private Managements.

Table-5.1
School Education Scenario in Kurnool Mandal-2007-08

S.No.	Category of Schools	Numbers	Total Strength
1.	Pre-Primary Schools*	3	74
2.	Primary Schools*	179	34,649
3.	Upper Primary Schools*	75	16,696
4.	High Schools*	86	32,014

* Includes schools under all managements.

Source: Hand Book of Statistics 2007-08, Kurnool District, Office of Chief Planning Officer, Kurnool.

An analysis of Table 5.1 shows the school educational scenario of Kurnool Mandal during 2007-08. There are 3 Pre-Primary Schools with a total strength of 74, 179 primary schools with a total strength of 34,649, 75 Upper Primary Schools with a total strength of 16,696 and 86 High Schools with a total strength of 32,014 run by various managements like State Government, Mandal Parishad, Zilla Parishad, Municipal Corporation and private aided and unaided managements. Of these 86 High Schools eight are run by Kurnool Municipal Corporation as shown in Table 5.2.

An analysis of Table 5.2 shows the number of High Schools and their names run under the management of Kurnool Municipal Corporation. As stated in the analysis of Table 5.1, the eight schools under Kurnool Municipal Corporation are 1. Damodaram Sanjeevaiah Memorial Municipal Corporation High School established in the year 1859 as a Board School offered upto VIII Standard which was later upgraded as High School in the year 1890. The second one is Indira Gandhi Memorial Municipal Corporation High School which was also started as a Board School in the year 1948 which was later upgraded as High School in the year 1990. The third one is Municipal Corporation High School which was started as a Urdu Medium Primary School in the year 1952 which was later elevated as High School in the year 1997. The fourth one is Sri Potti Sreeramulu Municipal Corporation High School started as a Primary School in the year 1954 which was later upgraded as High School in the year 1987. The fifth one is Nehru Memorial Municipal Corporation High School started as a Primary School in 1965 which was later upgraded as High School in 1968. The sixth one is Cattamanchi Ramalinga Reddy Memorial Municipal

Table-5.2
Number of Secondary (High) Schools under the Management of Kurnool Municipal Corporation

S.No.	*Name of the School*	*Year of Establishment*	*Year of Upgradation as High School*
1.	Damodaram Sanjeevaiah Memorial Municipal Corporation High School	1859	1890
2.	Nehru Memorial Municipal Corporation High School	1965	1968
3.	Cattamanchi Ramalinga Reddy Memorial Municipal Corporation High School	1965	1968
4.	Indira Gandhi Memorial Municipal Corporation High School	1948	1990
5.	Sri Potti Sreeramulu Memorial Municipal Corporation High School	1954	1987
6.	Dr. B.R. Ambedkar Memorial Municipal Corporation High School	1972	1997
7.	Sri Tanguturu Prakasam Pantulu Memorial Municipal Corporation High School	1978	1998
8.	Municipal Corporation High School (Urdu)	1952	1997

Source: Official Records of above Schools, Kurnool.

Corporation High School which was also started as Primary School in 1965 and upgraded as High School in 1968. The seventh one is Dr. B.R. Ambedkar Memorial Municipal Corporation High School started as Primary School in 1972 which was upgraded as High School in 1997. And the eighth one is Sri Tanguturu Prakasam Pantulu Memorial Municipal Corporation High School started as Primary School in the year 1978 and elevated as High School in the year 1998. Of all these schools the oldest school is Damodaram Sanjeevaiah Memorial Municipal Corporation High School and the latest High School is Sri Tanguturu Prakasam Pantulu Memorial Municipal Corporation High School. Before the upgradation of Kurnool Municipality as Municipal Corporation all these High Schools were managed by Kurnool Municipality prior to 1994. The medium of instruction is Telugu in all High Schools except in Municipal Corporation High School (Urdu). However, English Medium curriculum is also offered in 2 Schools namely, Damodaram

Sanjeevaiah Memorial Municipal Corporation High School and Cattamanchi Ramalinga Reddy Memorial Municipal Corporation High School. The admission is open to all categories irrespective of caste, religion, region etc., in these high schools.

Strength of the Students

The backbone of any high school is its numerical strength of the students. Further, the strength of the students also always depends upon the reputation of that particular high school gained in respect of its curriculum, coaching, guidance, results, discipline, establishment, facilities, location, environment and above all the parental treatment of the teachers. In otherwords, the reputation of the school has direct correlation with the strength.

An analysis of Table 5.3 gives the details about the strength of the students in Kurnool Municipal Corporation High Schools from 1999-2000 to 2008-09. The total strength of the students in 1999-2000 was 2881 which was on an increasing trend till to 2005-06, which stood at 40.94. In 2006-07 there was a fall in the strength and continued till the next year also. In 2008-09 the strength raised to 4002. In 1999-2000 the highest strength was maintained by Cattamanchi Ramalinga Reddy Memorial Municipal Corporation High School with 835 and the least strength was with Municipal Corporation High School (Urdu) 94. This school continued to maintain the highest strength over all the other schools till 2006-07, whereas in 2007-08 the Indira Gandhi Memorial Municipal Corporation High School over took the Cattamanchi Ramalinga Reddy Memorial Municipal Corporation High School and continued to maintain the lead till today.

The Municipal Corporation High School (Urdu) though continued to increase in its strength upto 2004-05, from its next year it continued to show a down trend. Of all these eight schools this Urdu school maintained lower strength all through the years of the study period. The increase in the trend of the strength of enrolment in the above said High Schools may be attributed to the establishment of social welfare hostels run by the government nearby these schools.

An analysis of Table 5.4 gives details about class-wise enrolment of the 8 Municipal Corporation High Schools during the years from 1999-2000 to 2008-09. The trend of enrolment in VI class in the

Table–5.3
Strength of the Students in Kurnool Municipal Corporation High Schools From 1999-2000 to 2008-09

S. No.	Name of the School	1999-2000	2000-2001	2001-2002	2002-2003	2003-2004	2004-2005	2005-2006	2006-2007	2007-2008	2008-2009	Average Attendance
1.	Damodaram Sanjeevaiah Memorial Municipal Corporation High School	438 (79)	591 (83)	734 (88)	810 (84)	829 (82)	804 (81)	812 (78)	779 (78)	743 (83)	734 (88)	7274 (82.4)
2.	Nehru Memorial Municipal Corporation High School	300 (78)	353 (76)	395 (81)	359 (80)	343 (84)	347 (78)	381 (88)	383 (86)	383 (88)	411 (86)	3360 (80.50)
3.	Cattamanchi Ramalinga Reddy Memorial Municipal Corporation High School	835 (88)	908 (86)	919 (91)	894 (90)	900 (88)	918 (85)	923 (87)	879 (88)	832 (86)	758 (85)	8766 (87.60)
4.	Indira Gandhi Memorial Municipal Corporation High School	570 (89)	615 (87)	592 (92)	579 (91)	735 (89)	825 (89)	843 (90)	876 (92)	970 (90)	1080 (89)	7685 (89.80)
5.	Sri Potti Sreeramulu Memorial Municipal Corporation High School	235 (91)	260 (92)	268 (86)	260 (88)	258 (89)	266 (83)	308 (84)	281 (89)	225 (83)	276 (89)	2637 (87.40)
6.	Dr. B.R. Ambedkar Memorial Municipal Corporation High School	203 (90)	195 (88)	225 (87)	209 (89)	254 (91)	259 (90)	298 (89)	268 (91)	285 (90)	285 (92)	2481 (89.70)

Contd...

S. No.	Name of the School	1999-2000	2000-2001	2001-2002	2002-2003	2003-2004	2004-2005	2005-2006	2006-2007	2007-2008	2008-2009	Average Attendance
7.	Sri Tanguturu Prakasam Pantulu Memorial Municipal Corporation High School	365 (88)	256 (89)	348 (87)	334 (84)	324 (89)	379 (86)	282 (91)	244 (90)	232 (89)	264 (90)	3020 (88.30)
8.	Municipal Corporation High School (Urdu)	94 (83)	149 (82)	182 (84)	219 (84)	250 (86)	285 (88)	247 (87)	213 (89)	193 (88)	179 (87)	2011 (85.80)
	Total No. of Pupils Present	**2607 (85.75)**	**2841 (85.38)**	**3187 (87.00)**	**3160 (86.25)**	**3397 (87.25)**	**3471 (85.00)**	**3552 (86.75)**	**3448 (87.88)**	**3366 (87.13)**	**3523 (88.25)**	– –

Source: Consolidated Attendance Registers of High Schools under Kurnool Municipal Corporation.
Note: Figures in parenthesis denote percentage of Attendance.

Table-5.4
Class-wise Enrolment of Pupils From 1999-2000 to 2008-09

S.No.	*Year*	*No. of Schools*	*Classes*					*Total*
			VI	*VII*	*VIII*	*IX*	*X*	
1.	1999-2000	8	655	661	695	558	471	3040
2.	2000-2001	8	823	601	704	613	586	3327
3.	2001-2002	8	898	703	782	693	587	3663
4.	2002-2003	8	806	739	734	691	694	3664
5.	2003-2004	8	803	758	977	711	644	3893
6.	2004-2005	8	849	715	967	875	677	4083
7.	2005-2006	8	748	721	953	867	805	4094
8.	2006-2007	8	769	677	945	809	723	3923
9.	2007-2008	8	837	699	890	763	674	3863
10.	2008-2009	8	868	859	910	690	665	3992
Total for a decade period			**8056**	**7133**	**8557**	**7270**	**6526**	**37542**

Source: Official Records of Kurnool Municipal Corporation Secondary Schools from 1999-2000 to 2008-09.

year 1999-2000 starting with 655 reached to 868 during 2008-09 with ups and downs during the study period. Same is the case in all classes from VII to X. But the trend of enrolment although the years shows that the enrolment in VI class was with a higher number and the enrolment in X class was in a declining number except in the year 2005-06. This shows the habit of dropouts due to various causes or leaving the Municipal Schools intermittently and joining in other private schools.

An analysis of Table 5.5 and Table 5.6 reveal the ranking of High Schools based on the pupil strength in on every academic year starting from 1999-2000 to 2008-09. The Cattamanchi Ramalinga Reddy Memorial Municipal Corporation High School stood in first rank continuously for 8 years from 1999-2000 to 2006-07 and then obtained 2nd rank in the next two academic years. The Indira Gandhi Memorial Municipal Corporation High School got twice first rank and five times 2nd rank and 3 times third rank. The Damodaram Sanjeevaiah Memorial Municipal Corporation

Table-5.5

Ranking of High Schools According to their Pupils Strength

Year	*Damodaram Sanjeevaiah Memorial Municipal Corporation High School*	*Nehru Memorial Municipal Corporation High School*	*Cattamanchi Ramalinga Reddy Memorial Municipal Corporation High School*	*Indira Gandhi Memorial Municipal Corporation High School*	*Sri Potti Sreeramulu Memorial Municipal Corporation High School*	*Dr. B.R. Ambedkar Memorial Municipal Corporation High School*	*Sri Tanguturu Prakasam Pantulu Memorial Municipal Corporation High School*	*Municipal Corporation High School (Urdu)*
1999-2000	3	5	1	2	6	7	4	8
2000-2001	3	4	1	2	5	7	6	8
2001-2002	2	4	1	3	6	7	5	8
2002-2003	2	4	1	3	6	8	5	7
2003-2004	2	4	1	3	6	7	5	8
2004-2005	3	5	1	2	7	8	4	6
2005-2006	3	4	1	2	5	6	7	8
2006-2007	3	4	1	2	5	6	7	8
2007-2008	3	4	2	1	7	5	6	8
2008-2009	3	4	2	1	6	5	7	8

Source: Consolidated attendance registers of concerned schools from 1999-2000 to 2008-09.

Table-5.6
Calculated Ranks of High Schools Based on their Pupils Strength

S.No.	Name of the High School	No. of Ranks Secured Based on Pupils Strength							
		Rank I	Rank II	Rank III	Rank IV	Rank V	Rank VI	Rank VII	Rank VIII
1.	Damodaram Sanjeevaiah Memorial Municipal Corporation High School	-	3	7	-	-	-	-	-
2.	Nehru Memorial Municipal Corporation High School	-	-	-	8	2	-	-	-
3.	Cattamanchi Ramalinga Reddy Memorial Municipal Corporation High School	8	2	-	-	-	-	-	-
4.	Indira Gandhi Memorial Municipal Corporation High School	2	5	3	-	-	-	-	-
5.	Sri Potti Sreeramulu Memorial Municipal Corporation High School	-	-	-	-	3	5	2	-
6.	Dr. B.R. Ambedkar Memorial Municipal Corporation High School	-	-	-	-	2	2	4	2
7.	Sri Tanguturu Prakasam Pantulu Memorial Municipal Corporation High School	-	-	-	2	3	2	3	-
8.	Municipal Corporation High School (Urdu)	-	-	-	-	-	1	1	8

Source: Consolidated attendance registers of concerned schools from 1999-2000 to 2008-09.

High School stood thrice in 2nd rank. It stood 7 times in third rank and the Indira Gandhi Memorial Municipal Corporation High School stood thrice in the third rank. The Nehru Memorial Municipal Corporation High School stood eight times in fourth rank and twice in fifth rank. The Sri Tanguturu Prakasam Pantulu Memorial Municipal Corporation High School stood twice in fourth and sixth ranks, thrice in fifth and seventh ranks. The Sri Potti Sreeramulu

Memorial Municipal Corporation High School stood thrice in fifth rank, five times in sixth rank and twice in seventh rank. The Dr. B.R. Ambedkar Memorial Municipal Corporation High School stood twice in fifth, sixth and eighth ranks and four times in seventh rank. The Municipal Corporation High School (Urdu) stood one time each in sixth and seventh rank and eight times in eighth rank.

Attendance

Attendance in any secondary school is the responsiveness of the students to the coaching and discipline that offered and also the responsibility of the individual teacher on one side and the encouragement and awareness of the parents on the other side. In other words, the teachers, the parents and the concerned students are responsible and important in boosting up the rate of attendance in the High Schools. It is very much a fact in respect of secondary schools managed by Kurnool Municipal Corporation.

An analysis of Table 5.3 also reveals the fact that the percentage of attendance in respect of individual as well as total High Schools under Kurnool Municipal Corporation was not cent per cent in any year. The highest rate of percentage of attendance was 88.25 in the year 2008-09 and the least was 85 per cent in the year 2004-05. The highest percentage of attendance was 92 scored by Indira Gandhi Memorial Municipal Corporation High School in 2001-02 and 2006-07, Sri Potti Sreeramulu Memorial Municipal Corporation High School in 2000-01 and Dr. B.R. Ambedkar Memorial Municipal Corporation High School in 2008-09. The least percentage of attendance scored was 76 per cent scored by Nehru Memorial Municipal Corporation High School in the year 2000-01. The highest percentage on an average scored by individual school for the whole period was 89.80 per cent by Indira Gandhi Memorial Municipal Corporation High School and the least percentage was 82.40 per cent scored by Damodaram Sanjeevaiah Memorial Municipal Corporation High School.

Various reasons are attributed to this problem. Firstly many of the students get admission in municipal schools and as no good teaching is available, they attend to tutorial schools and other private tuitions. Only on rolls they are found and not in the classrooms. There is also no proper guidance from the teachers to the students about regularity to the school, their every time presence in the classroom and the consequences of absenteeism and its impact on their preparations and performance in the examinations and so on. Some students as they come from low income group, they join in the schools and regularly get promotion to next class as there is no detention system, but daily attend to some kind of wage earning, to supplement their parents income.

Public Examination Results

The performance evaluation of any High School can be spelt out through its output in the form of the percentage of successful candidates in the public examinations conducted by the competent bodies. Earlier the public examinations are conducted in secondary school level in two stages. They were one at the end of VII standard and the other at the end of X standard which are called as VII Standard District Common Examination conducted by District Educational Officer of the concerned district and Secondary School Certificate (SSC) Public Examination conducted by Board of Secondary Education, Government of Andhra Pradesh, Hyderabad respectively. But the District Common Examination was dispensed with from the year 2006-07 and the seventh standard also came under non-detention pattern. However the SSC Public Examinations are being conducted regularly every year and all the Eight High Schools under Kurnool Municipal Corporation came under this pattern.

An analysis of Table 5.7 and Table 5.8 reveals that the percentage of results in SSC Public Examinations achieved by all the eight schools under Kurnool Municipal Corporation were quite unsatisfactory and never crossed 55 per cent. The overall highest percentage of results in SSC examinations was 55 per cent achieved in the year 2005-06 and the least was 28 per cent in the year 1999-2000. The highest per cent achieved by Damodaram Sanjeevaiah Memorial Municipal Corporation High School was 58 per cent in 2005-06 and the least was 28 per cent in 2000-01. In respect of Nehru Memorial Municipal Corporation High School, the highest percentage of results was 68 per cent in the year 2007-08 and the least was 30 per cent in 1998-99 and 1999-2000. In respect of Cattamanchi Ramalinga Reddy Memorial Municipal Corporation High School, the highest percentage of results was 56 per cent in the year 2005-06 and the least was 19 per cent in the year 2001-02.

Table–5.7

Percentage of SSC Public Examination Results in Kurnool Municipal Corporation High Schools From 1998-99 to 2007-08

S. No.	*Name of the School*		*Years* 1998-1999	1999-2000	2000-2001	2001-2002	2002-2003	2003-2004	2004-2005	2005-2006	2006-2007	2007-2008
1.	Damodaram Sanjeevaiah	Appeared	92	62	106	81	150	131	166	181	145	164
	Memorial Municipal	Passed	31	21	29	29	57	47	89	104	62	74
	Corporation High School	percentage	34	34	28	36	38	36	54	58	43	45
2.	Nehru Memorial Municipal	Appeared	61	61	82	61	53	53	58	60	68	50
	Corporation High School	Passed	18	18	34	22	19	31	27	40	29	34
		percentage	30	30	43	36	36	58.5	46.55	67	42.5	68
3.	Cattamanchi Ramalinga	Appeared	131	97	129	131	155	142	151	164	173	169
	Reddy Memorial Municipal	Passed	34	26	42	26	48	45	68	92	85	51
	Corporation High School	percentage	35	27	33	19	31	32	45	56	49	30
4.	Indira Gandhi Memorial	Appeared	81	96	117	130	108	103	116	120	139	134
	Municipal Corporation	Passed	38	42	54	62	46	53	62	61	69	73
	High School	percentage	47	46	46	48	43	51	54	51	45	54
5.	Sri Potti Sreeramulu	Appeared	44	39	52	45	62	48	40	70	48	56
	Memorial Municipal	Passed	13	11	14	23	19	27	28	40	31	26
	Corporation High School	percentage	43.5	28	28	51	31	56	70	58	63	46.5

Contd...

S. No.	Name of the School		Years									
			1998-1999	1999-2000	2000-2001	2001-2002	2002-2003	2003-2004	2004-2005	2005-2006	2006-2007	2007-2008
6.	Dr. B.R. Ambedkar Memorial Municipal Corporation High School	Appeared	33	35	35	35	36	32	17	75	40	34
		Passed	10	9	13	14	19	27	14	52	33	30
		percentage	30	25.7	37	40	53	84	82	73	82.5	88
7.	Sri Tanguturu Prakasam Pantulu Memorial Municipal Corporation High School	Appeared	42	52	50	50	50	61	56	56	52	41
		Passed	4	3	4	20	16	20	21	14	26	23
		percentage	18	17	19	39	32	30	39	25	50	53
8.	Municipal Corporation High School (Urdu)	Appeared	–	14	18	18	29	27	36	50	33	38
		Passed		2	7	12	12	20	18	18	11	16
		percentage		22	39	66	42	74	50	40	33	42
		Appeared	**470**	**452**	**583**	**540**	**649**	**594**	**640**	**773**	**694**	**696**
		Passed	**135**	**126**	**182**	**181**	**238**	**258**	**329**	**424**	**335**	**352**
		percentage	**28.72**	**31.23**	**31.23**	**33.52**	**36.67**	**43.43**	**51.41**	**54.85**	**48.27**	**50.57**

Source: Official Records of respective schools of Kurnool Municipal Corporation.

Table-5.8
Performance of High Schools in Kurnool Municipal Corporation in SSC Public Examinations

Year	*No. Appeared*	*No. Passed*	*Pass Percentage*
1998-1999	470	135	28.72
1999-2000	452	126	27.88
2000-2001	583	182	31.22
2001-2002	540	181	33.52
2002-2003	649	238	36.67
2003-2004	594	258	43.43
2004-2005	640	329	51.41
2005-2006	773	424	54.85
2006-2007	694	335	48.27
2007-2008	696	352	50.57
Total	**6071**	**2560**	**42.03**

Source: Office Records of Education Wing of Kurnool Municipal Corporation.

In case of Indira Gandhi Memorial Municipal Corporation High School the highest percentage of results was 54 per cent in the years 2004-05 and 2007-08. The least percentage of results was 43 per cent in the year 2002-03. The highest percentage of results was 70 per cent in the year 2004-05 and the least percentage of results was 28 per cent during the years 1999-2000 and 2000-01 in Sri Potti Sreeramulu Memorial Municipal Corporation High School. In case of Dr. B.R. Ambedkar Memorial Municipal Corporation High School the highest percentage of results was 88 per cent during the year 2007-08 and the least percentage was 25.7 per cent during 1999-2000. In case of Sri Tanguturu Prakasam Pantulu Memorial Municipal Corporation High School was 53 per cent during the year 2007-08 and the least percentage was 17 per cent during the year 1999-2000. In the case of Municipal Corporation High School (Urdu) the percentage was 74 during the year 2003-04 and the least percentage was 22 in 1999-2000.

An analysis of Table 5.8 shows that the highest number of candidates appeared in SSC Public Examinations in all the 8 high schools put together was 773 in the year 2005-06 and the highest

Table–5.9

Ranking of Schools Based on SSC Results

Year	*Damodaram Sanjeevaiah Memorial Municipal Corporation High School*	*Nehru Memorial Municipal Corporation High School*	*Cattamanchi Ramalinga Reddy Memorial Municipal Corporation High School*	*Indira Gandhi Memorial Municipal Corporation High School*	*Sri Potti Sreeramulu Memorial Municipal Corporation High School*	*Dr. B.R. Ambedkar Memorial Municipal Corporation High School*	*Sri Tanguturu Prakasam Pantulu Memorial Municipal Corporation High School*	*Municipal Corporation High School (Urdu)*
1998-1999	2	4	3	1	4	4	5	-
1999-2000	2	3	5	1	4	6	8	7
2000-2001	6	2	5	1	6	4	7	3
2001-2002	6	6	7	3	2	4	5	1
2002-2003	4	5	7	2	7	1	6	3
2003-2004	6	3	7	5	4	1	8	2
2004-2005	3	5	6	3	2	1	7	4
2005-2006	3	2	4	5	3	1	7	6
2006-2007	6	6	4	5	2	1	3	7
2007-2008	5	1	7	2	4	1	3	6

Source: Official school records of Kurnool Municipal Corporation High Schools, Kurnool.

Table-5.10
Calculated Ranks According to SSC Results

S.No.	*Name of the School*	*Ranks*							
		I	*II*	*III*	*IV*	*V*	*VI*	*VII*	*VIII*
1.	Damodaram Sanjeevaiah Memorial Municipal Corporation High School	-	2	2	1	1	4	-	-
2.	Nehru Memorial Municipal Corporation High School	1	2	2	1	2	2	-	-
3.	Cattamanchi Ramalinga Reddy Memorial Municipal Corporation High School	-	-	1	2	2	1	4	-
4.	Indira Gandhi Memorial Municipal Corporation High School	3	2	2	3	-	-	-	-
5.	Sri Potti Sreeramulu Memorial Municipal Corporation High School	-	3	1	4	-	1	1	-
6.	Dr. B.R. Ambedkar Memorial Municipal Corporation High School	6	-	-	3	-	1	-	-
7.	Sri Tanguturu Prakasam Pantulu Memorial Municipal Corporation High School	-	-	2	-	2	1	3	2
8.	Municipal Corporation High School (Urdu)	1	1	2	1	-	2	2	-

Source: Official School Records of Kurnool Municipal Corporation High Schools, Kurnool.

number passed was 424 in the same year and the highest percentage of results 54.85 was also in the same year. During the whole study period of a decade 6091 candidates appeared for the examination. Of which only 2560 passed and the coverage percentage of result was only 42.03.

An analysis of Table 5.9 and Table 5.10 give the ranking of schools based on SSC results. During the study period Dr. B.R. Ambedkar Memorial Municipal Corporation High School secured first rank six times, fourth rank thrice and sixth rank once. The Indira Gandhi Memorial Municipal Corporation High School got first rank thrice, twice second and third ranks and thrice fourth rank. The Nehru Memorial Municipal Corporation High School stood once in first rank, twice in second, third, fifth and sixth ranks and once fourth rank. The Municipal Corporation High School (Urdu) secured once the first, second, and fourth ranks and twice the third, sixth and seventh ranks. The Damodaram Sanjeevaiah Memorial Municipal Corporation High School stood twice in second and third ranks, once in fourth and fifth rank and four times the sixth rank. The Cattamanchi Ramalinga Reddy Memorial Municipal Corporation High School stood once in third and sixth ranks, twice in fourth and fifth ranks and four times in seventh rank. The Sri Potti Sreeramulu Memorial Municipal Corporation High School stood thrice in second rank, once in third, sixth and seventh ranks, and four times in fourth rank. Sri Tanguturu Prakasam Pantulu Memorial Municipal Corporation High School stood twice the third, fifth and eighth ranks and once the sixth rank and thrice the seventh rank. Out of eight high schools under Kurnool Municipal Corporation, only four schools could stand in first rank atleast once during the study period. It was only the Tanguturu Prakasam Pantulu High School which tasted the least rank during the study period.

An analysis of Table 5.11, Table 5.12 give the percentage of results in VII class district common examinations held during the study period from 1997-98 upto 2006-07. It is revealed through the study that the performance of the High Schools in respect of VII class examinations was not satisfactory as none of the schools during any academic year of the whole study period could secure cent per cent results. The highest percentage of average results taking the performance of all the schools was 81 per cent during the year 1999-2000 and the least was 70 per cent during 2001-02. Looking into the individual school performance in VII class examinations it was in Sri Tanguturu Prakasam Pantulu High School secured cent per cent results every academic year although the study period. The Nehru Memorial Municipal Corporation High School, Cattamanchi Ramalinga Reddy Memorial Municipal Corporation High School and Sri Potti Sreeramulu Memorial Municipal Corporation High School never achieved cent per cent result during the study period.

Table–5.11

Percentage of VII Class District Common Examination Results in Kurnool Municipal Corporation High Schools From 1997-98 to 2006-07

S. No.	*Name of the School*		*Years* 1997-1998	1998-1999	1999-2000	2000-2001	2001-2002	2002-2003	2003-2004	2004-2005	2005-2006	2006-2007
1.	Damodaram Sanjeevaiah Memorial Municipal Corporation High School	Appeared	94	84	71	54	131	129	132	143	108	120
		Passed	82	51	71	51	114	122	131	119	98	100
		percentage	87	61	100	94	87	95	99	83	93	92
2.	Nehru Memorial Municipal Corporation High School	Appeared	32	35	39	57	54	64	77	46	68	60
		Passed	21	19	27	29	33	36	43	33	39	50
		percentage	66	54	69	51	61	56	56	71	57	85
3.	Cattamanchi Ramalinga Reddy Memorial Municipal Corporation High School	Appeared	164	160	186	179	188	170	179	165	136	129
		Passed	132	127	156	108	170	99	160	124	72	70
		percentage	81	79	84	60	90	58	89	75	53	55
4.	Indira Gandhi Memorial Municipal Corporation High School	Appeared	94	92	123	104	100	101	145	97	87	93
		Passed	88	90	121	104	100	100	141	97	87	93
		percentage	94	99	98	100	100	100	99	100	100	100
5.	Sri Potti Sreeramulu Memorial Municipal Corporation High School	Appeared	53	46	42	39	42	47	42	38	53	54
		Passed	50	30	38	13	24	28	39	31	31	47
		percentage	94	65	93	33	57	62	95	82	58	90

Contd...

S. No.	Name of the School		Years									
			1997-1998	*1998-1999*	*1999-2000*	*2000-2001*	*2001-2002*	*2002-2003*	*2003-2004*	*2004-2005*	*2005-2006*	*2006-2007*
6.	Dr. B.R. Ambedkar Memorial Municipal Corporation High School	Appeared	*	*	*	*	*	75	37	53	53	60
		Passed						54	37	53	53	43
		percentage						74	100	100	100	72
7.	Sri Tanguturu Prakasam Pantulu Memorial Municipal Corporation High School	Appeared	89	86	89	102	85	68	64	37	57	38
		Passed	89	86	89	102	85	68	64	37	57	38
		percentage	100	100	100	100	100	100	100	100	100	100
8.	Municipal Corporation High School (Urdu)	Appeared	30	30	36	30	36	45	49	60	50	34
		Passed	26	24	30	28	25	45	49	60	44	34
		percentage	87	85	83	93	70	100	100	100	87	100
		Appeared	**557**	**553**	**497**	**515**	**579**	**684**	**688**	**625**	**637**	**632**
		Passed	**421**	**398**	**402**	**369**	**407**	**501**	**549**	**493**	**501**	**500**
		percentage	**76**	**72**	**81**	**72**	**70**	**73**	**80**	**79**	**79**	**79**

Source: Official Records of respective schools of Kurnool Municipal Corporation.

Table-5.12
Performance of High Schools in Kurnool Municipal Corporation in VII Class Public Examinations

Year	*No. of Candidates Appeared*	*No. of Candidates Passed*	*Pass Percentage*
1997-1998	557	421	75.58
1998-1999	553	398	72.00
1999-2000	497	402	81.00
2000-2001	515	369	72.00
2001-2002	579	407	70.00
2002-2003	684	501	73.00
2003-2004	688	549	80.00
2004-2005	625	493	79.00
2005-2006	637	501	79.00
2006-2007	632	500	79.00
Total	**5967**	**4541**	**76.10**

Source: Official School Records of Kurnool Municipal Corporation High Schools, Kurnool.

An analysis of Table 5.12 shows that the highest number of candidates appeared for Seventh Class examinations was 688 during the year 2003-04 and the highest number passed was 549 in the same year with 80 per cent of results. The highest number of results was 81 per cent in the year 1999-2000. During the whole study period 5967 candidates appeared for VII class examinations of which 4541 candidates passed the examination and the percentage of pass was 76.10.

An analysis of Table 5.13 and Table 5.14 gives the ranking of High Schools in Kurnool Municipal Corporation based on VII class results. The study revealed that the Sri Tanguturu Prakasam Pantulu Memorial Municipal Corporation High School stood in first rank all through the years. The Indira Gandhi Memorial Municipal Corporation High School stood six times in first rank and four times in second rank. The Municipal Corporation High School (Urdu) stood four times in first rank, four times in third rank and one time in fourth and fifth ranks. Dr. B.R. Ambedkar Memorial Municipal Corporation High School stood thrice in first rank once

Table–5.13
Ranking of Schools Based on VII Class Results

Year	*Damodaram Sanjeevaiah Memorial Municipal Corporation High School*	*Nehru Memorial Municipal Corporation High School*	*Cattamanchi Ramalinga Reddy Memorial Municipal Corporation High School*	*Indira Gandhi Memorial Municipal Corporation High School*	*Sri Potti Sreeramulu Memorial Municipal Corporation High School*	*Dr. B.R. Ambedkar Memorial Municipal Corporation High School*	*Sri Tanguturu Prakasam Pantulu Memorial Municipal Corporation High School*	*Municipal Corporation High School (Urdu)*
1998-1999	3	5	4	2	2	-	1	3
1999-2000	6	7	4	2	5	-	1	3
2000-2001	1	6	4	2	3	-	1	5
2001-2002	2	5	4	1	6	-	1	3
2002-2003	3	5	2	1	6	-	1	4
2003-2004	2	5	4	2	3	1	1	1
2004-2005	2	5	4	1	3	1	1	1
2005-2006	2	5	6	1	4	1	1	1
2006-2007	2	4	6	1	3	5	1	1

Source: Official school records of Kurnool Municipal Corporation High Schools from 1997-98 to 2006-07.

Table-5.14
Calculated Ranks According to S.S.C. Public Examination Results

S.No.	*Name of the School*	*Ranks*						
		I	*II*	*III*	*IV*	*V*	*VI*	*VII*
1.	Damodaram Sanjeevaiah Memorial Municipal Corporation High School	1	6	2	-	-	1	-
2.	Nehru Memorial Municipal Corporation High School	-	-	-	1	6	2	1
3.	Cattamanchi Ramalinga Reddy Memorial Municipal Corporation High School	-	1	-	6	1	2	-
4.	Indira Gandhi Memorial Municipal Corporation High School	6	4	-	-	-	-	-
5.	Sri Potti Sreeramulu Memorial Municipal Corporation High School	-	1	4	2	1	2	-
6.	Dr. B.R. Ambedkar Memorial Municipal Corporation High School	3	-	1	-	1	-	-
7.	Sri Tanguturu Prakasam Pantulu Memorial Municipal Corporation High School	10	-	-	-	-	-	-
8.	Municipal Corporation High School (Urdu)	4	-	4	1	1	-	-

Source: Official School Records of Kurnool Municipal Corporation High Schools, Kurnool.

in third and fifth rank. The Damodaram Sanjeevaiah Memorial Municipal Corporation High School stood once in first and sixth ranks. Six times in second rank and twice in third rank. The Cattamanchi Ramalinga Reddy Memorial Municipal Corporation High School stood once in second and fifth ranks, six times in fourth rank and twice in sixth rank. The Sri Potti Sreeramulu Memorial Municipal Corporation High School stood once in second and fifth ranks, twice in fourth and sixth ranks and four times in third rank. The Nehru Memorial Municipal Corporation High School stood

Table-5.15

School-wise Staff Position in Kurnool Municipal Corporation High Schools as on 31st December 2008

S. No.	Name of the School	H.M.S.	SA (SS)	SA (Maths)	SA (PS)	SA (BS)	SA (Ejng.)	TPs	HPs	SP	PD/ PETs	Drg.	Crafts Music Pvt. Tailoring	SGTS	Total Working Vacant
1.	Damodaram Sanjeevaiah Memorial Municipal Corporation High School	1	3	4	2	2	2	3	2	1	2	1	V	-	21 + 3 = 24
2.	Nehru Memorial Municipal Corporation High School	1	1	2	2	2	1	2	1 (v)	-	1	-	1 (V)	-	12 + 2 = 14
3.	Cattamanchi Ramalinga Reddy Memorial Municipal Corporation High School	1	2	4	4	4	4	4 1 (V)	2	-	1 (PD) 2 (v)	1 (V)	-	-	25 + 4 = 29
4.	Indira Gandhi Memorial Municipal Corporation High School	-	3	2	3	2	2	2 1 (V)	2 1 (v)	-	1	-	1 Music (V) 1 Pvt.	-	15 + 4 = 19
5.	Sri Potti Sreeramulu Memorial Municipal Corporation High School	-	-	3	2	1	1	2 1 (V)	1	-	1 (V)	-	1 Tailoring	-	10 + 2 = 12

Contd...

S. No.	Name of the School	H.M.S.	SA (SS)	SA (Maths)	SA (PS)	SA (BS)	SA (Ejng.)	TPs	HPs	SP	PD/ PETs	Drg.	Crafts Music Pvt. Tailoring	SGTS	Total Working Vacant
6.	Dr. B.R. Ambedkar Memorial Municipal Corporation High School	-	1	1	1	1	1	1	1	-	1 (V)	-	-	1	8 + 1 = 9
7.	Sri Tanguturu Prakasam Pantulu Memorial Municipal Corporation High School	-	1	3	-	-	1	1	1	-	1 (V)	-	1 Pvt. (V)	2	9 + 2 = 11
8.	Municipal Corporation High School (Urdu)	-	1	1 (V)	1	1	1	1 (V) Urdu	-	-	-	-	-	-	4 + 2 = 6
	TOTAL	**3**	**12**	**20**	**15**	**13**	**13**	**16**	**10**	**1**	**10**	**2**	**6**	**3**	**104 + 20 = 124**

Source: Official School Records of Kurnool Municipal Corporation, Kurnool, 2008-09.

once in fourth and seventh ranks, six times in fifth rank and twice the sixth ranks. It is interesting to note that in many occasions the first rank was shared by more than two schools.

Teaching Staff and Teacher-Pupil Ratio

Compared to primary schools, the secondary schools which impart and promote higher standards of education require more number of teachers and these teachers must also be well qualified and appropriately trained. The need for subject specialists is very much felt in High Schools and above all these schools also required qualified technical teachers to give some kind of technical exposition to the students at High School level. Keeping this in view the Kurnool Municipal Corporation had appointed different kinds of teachers to the High Schools under its management.

Table–5.16
Position of Teaching Staff in Kurnool Municipal Corporation High Schools Cadre-wise as on 31st December, 2008

S.No.	*Name of the Post*	*No. of Posts Sanctioned*	*No. of Posts Filed*	*Positions Vacant*
1.	Headmasters	3	2	1
2.	**Subject Teachers**			
	Social Studies	12	12	–
	Mathematics	20	19	1
	Physical Science	15	15	–
	Biological Science	13	13	–
	English	13	13	–
	Telugu	15	11	4
	Urdu	1	-	1
	Hindi	10	7	3
	Sanskrit	1	1	–
	Total	**103**	**93**	**10**
3.	**Non-subject Teachers**			
	PD/PET	10	5	5
	Drawing	2	1	1
	Craft/Music/PVI/Tailoring	6	1	5
	SGTs	3	3	0
	Total	**21**	**11**	**10**
	Grand Total	**124**	**103**	**21**

Source: Official School Records of Kurnool Municipal Corporation, Kurnool.

Table–5.17
Teacher-Pupil Ratio in Kurnool Municipal Corporation High Schools

Year	*No. of Students*	*No. of Subject Teachers*	*Teacher-pupil Ratio*	*No. of Non-subject Teachers*	*Teacher-pupil Ratio*	*Total No. of Teachers*	*Average Teacher-pupil Ratio*
1999-2000	3040	101	30	19	160	120	25
2000-2001	3327	101	33	19	175	120	28
2001-2002	3663	101	36	19	177	120	31
2002-2003	3664	101	36	19	177	121	30
2003-2004	3893	102	38	20	195	122	32
2004-2005	4083	103	40	21	194	124	33
2005-2006	4094	103	40	21	195	124	33
2006-2007	3923	103	38	21	187	124	32
2007-2008	3863	103	38	21	184	124	31
2008-2009	3992	103	39	21	190	124	32

Source: Official records of Kurnool Municipal Corporation High Schools 1999-2000 to 2008-09.

Table–5.18
Teacher-Pupil Ratio During the Year 2008-09 Subject Teacher-wise

S.No.	*Subject Teacher*	*No. of Teachers*	*Student Strength*	*Teacher-pupil Ratio*
1.	B.Ed. Assistants	73	3992	55
2.	Secondary Grade Teachers	03	1727	576
3.	Telugu Pandits	15	3992	266
4.	Sanskrit Pandits**	01	--	--
5.	Hindi Pandits	10	3992	399
6.	Urdu Pandits**	01	179	179

Note: * Secondary Grade Teachers.
**Sanskrit and Urdu subjects are opted by students who knew Sanskrit and Urdu.

Source: Official Records of Kurnool Municipal Corporation High Schools, Kurnool, 2008-09.

An analysis of Table 5.15 reveals that the Kurnool Municipal Corporation have adequate number of teachers required in the light of the pupils strength existing in the high schools including the subjects offered to the students. It is also revealed through the interviews conducted by the researcher as shown in Table 5.16 that some of the posts in these high schools were kept vacant since longtime. There are only three Headmaster posts sanctioned to Eight High Schools in Kurnool Municipal Corporation and out of these three posts one post remained unfilled since long time. Hence in six High Schools the senior most School Assistants are acting as incharge Headmasters.

An analysis of Table 5.17 shows two types of teacher-pupil ratio. One is the ratio between the total students and number of subject teachers like Headmasters who are also B.Ed. qualified teachers in any one of the subjects taught in the high schools, the B.Ed. Assistants, Secondary Grade Teachers, Telugu Pandits, Hindi Pandits, Sanskrit and Urdu Pandits. Under this analysis the teacher pupil ratio during the study period from 1999-2000 to 2008-09, the highest was 1:40 in the years 2004-05 and 2005-06 and the least was 1:30 in 1999-2000. In all the study years the teacher-pupil ratio of 1:40 was maintained by these High Schools. In respect of the other category of teacher-pupil ratio calculated between the total strength of the students and the non-subject teachers, the highest during the study period was 1:195 and the least was 1:160. The teacher-pupil ratio is calculated based on total number of teachers and the total number of student strength.

The procedure of calculating the teacher pupil ratio in respect of High Schools is different from that of calculating for elementary schools. Generally in Andhra Pradesh, at elementary schools level the curriculum would be I to V standards. Depending upon the strength in each standard or class the class will be divided into sections and each section would be handled by one teacher who might be called as 'class teacher' and he or she teaches all the subjects. But in case of Secondary or High Schools the curriculum offered would be VI to X standards or classes and each class would be divided into number of sections depending upon the strength of pupils as in the case of elementary school, but the different subjects offered in the high schools would be handled by different subject experts, besides having a 'class teacher' to each class who would be one of the subject experts to the same students. In addition to these, the other teachers like drawing teachers, sewing teachers, music teachers, PETs, Craft teachers who do not come under the category of subject teachers who teach the subjects on which examinations are conducted. Thus these non-subject teachers would have no interaction with all the pupils in the High School as far as subject matters are concerned. In the same way each subject expert will have interaction with the pupils of that subject. Thus, the teacher-pupil ratio to be calculated is subject-wise-teacher and the pupils and not like the total teaching staff is to total student strength.

Based on the above principle, the teacher-pupil ratio was calculated depending upon individual subject teachers-wise like B.Ed. Assistant, Secondary Grade Teachers, Telugu Pandits, Hindi Pandits and so on which subjects are common to all except Sanskrit and Urdu which were opted by interested students. Thus, Table 5.18 gives the latest teacher-pupil ratio available in the all High Schools under Kurnool Municipal Corporation. An analysis of Table 5.18 shows that the teacher-pupil ratio between the B.Ed. Teachers and the student strength is 1:55. The ratio between Secondary Grade Teacher and the students is 1:576. The ratio between the Telugu Pandits and the Telugu taught students is 1:266 and the Hindi Pandits and the Hindi taught students is 1:399. This clearly shows that the High Schools under Kurnool Municipal Corporation have gravely violated in all respects the teacher-pupil ratio of 1:40. This analysis also reveals the need and urgency for appointment of adequate number of teaching staff to these high schools.

Medical Check-up to Students

Health and Hygiene are the two important things necessary for the students to keep up good strength, vigour, and sound mind. Without good health one cannot have sound mind and without sound mind no student will be alert in his studies. To keep up these things, periodical medical examinations to the students is essential. Especially, all the students in all the schools must be exposed to this kind of check-up by a good medical expert and necessary treatment, medicines and general health tonics and tablets must be supplied. At the time of spread of epidemic diseases like Cholera, Malaria, Chicken pox, Eye sores, Brain fever and various skin diseases, the concerned Headmasters must take necessary steps to invite government doctors or Municipal Health Officers to give preventive treatments to the students.

An analysis of annual reports of the present study period reveals that the camps of medical check-up were not conducted regularly to Secondary School students of Kurnool Municipal Corporation. Further there was no protected water supply to the pupils in most of the schools which kept the pupils nearer to ill-health and disease prone.

Play Grounds

The facility of play ground for conducting physical exercises, games, sports and other extra curricular activities is necessary. In respect of eight secondary schools only four schools namely the Damodaram Sanjeevaiah High School, Nehru Memorial High School, Cattamanchi Ramalinga Reddy, Indira Gandhi Memorial High School have small play grounds and the other four High Schools do not have play grounds. As a result, the Physical Education activities, games, sports and other play activities did not find place. No school under Kurnool Municipal Corporation maintains a gymnasium.

Headmasters and their Dress

Dress plays a very important role for the Heads of the institutions as well as the teachers working in the institutions and it is more important especially to those working in educational institutions. Wearing of proper, decent and dignified dress especially by the Headmasters working in the schools was very well suggested by the State Government. The special committee constituted by the State Government for implementing the recommendations of the Secondary Education Commission suggested that government should prescribe for decent dress for teachers particularly Headmasters in all High Schools. Accordingly, the Director of Public Instruction issued orders to impress upon every Headmaster to wear decent and neat dress like jubba (long sleeves) Dhoti and an upper cloth or a closed coat and a dhoti or pants. Similarly the other members of the staff also to be followed.

An observation of the dressing pattern of the Headmasters and the teachers working in various High Schools in Kurnool Municipal Corporation reveals that none of them are following the instructions given by the government and these male teachers wear half sleaved slacks, and pants, some wear their traditional dresses. Even the management is neither guiding nor instructing these Headmasters as well as the teachers to wear decent dress.

Secular Schools

Secularism is one of the basic principles followed by the Kurnool Municipal Corporation in managing its secondary schools. It is clearly evident at the perusal of the Admission Registers of the schools, all the schools were accessible to children of all classes, castes, communities and religions and hence no separate schools were opened for Scheduled Castes, Scheduled Tribes, Backward Classes or Minorities as could be seen in respect of Panchayat Raj schools which are established in Scheduled Castes and Scheduled Tribe colonies in certain areas in Kurnool district perhaps for the convenience of such communities. Even in respect of medium of instruction, as seen in the analysis of Table 5.2 in some of the Telugu medium schools Urdu language is also offered as second language of instruction. This certainly proved that the Kurnool Municipal Corporation is safeguarding secularism through its educational administration to some extent. Same pattern is also adopted even in case of appointment of teaching and non-teaching staff for its schools.

Finance

The efficiency of administration largely depends upon adequate and timely availability of finances for discharging the varied functions and responsibilities entrusted to it. In order to understand and appreciate the educational administration of the Kurnool Municipal Corporation, it is necessary to know about the financial management practices. Hence, in the financial administration, management of educational institutions also by Kurnool Municipal Corporation occupies an important place. The functioning of schools called for a provision of adequate finances to meet the expenditure on the maintenance of school buildings, payment of rents to school buildings, purchase of furniture, the stationery, the equipment and other necessary overheads.[3]

Education has never been considered as a commercial activity in the traditional sense of the term. Though before independence, voluntary associations and philanthropic organizations were running these educational institutions by collecting donations and contributions from the public, the Government has continuously been involved in one way or the other with the administration of such institutions. Even today there are several private institutions catering to the educational needs of the society. However, as a part of its welfare commitments, the Government has assumed full responsibility for the maintenance of educational institutions in the country. While the Government had directly undertaken the responsibility of the management of schools and colleges in several other instances, it also took up the responsibility for payment of grants on a regular basis. Today, the Government of Andhra Pradesh provides finances for the municipalities to run educational institutions under their management and the salaries of the teaching and non-teaching staff are not from government sanctioned budget.

Grants

In case of secondary schools, the monthly grants to reimburse the expenditure incurred towards contingency and miscellaneous are received by the Kurnool Municipal Corporation.

The expenditure incurred in Kurnool Municipal Corporation for education subject has been increasing gradually. This is due to the increase in the pay scales, whenever pay scales are revised, periodical incremental arrears, Dearness Allowances, House Rent Allowances and so on of both teaching and non-teaching staff over the years.[4] All these expenditure is met by State Government. In addition to this the government is also giving maintenance grant to the Kurnool Municipal Corporation for the proper maintenance of the High Schools. But to what extent this grant is spent is a point of criticism.

The Headmaster of each Municipal Corporation High School prepares monthly pay bills of the teaching and non-teaching staff of their respective schools for the succeeding month and submits the same to the Municipal Commissioner before twentieth of every month. The bills thus received would be scrutinized by the concerned Junior and Senior Assistants in Municipal Corporation Office and the same are passed on to the Municipal Commissioner. The Municipal Commissioner sends these bills to the Banks from where the staff take their monthly salaries.

Contingency Grant

In order to meet the expenditure on contingencies the government also made available to the Municipal Corporation High Schools an amount equivalent to a maximum of two per cent of the total expenditure incurred on the basis of the revised pay scales of the staff.[5] Before the revised pay scales were adopted the contingency expenditure used to be equivalent to a maximum of six per cent of the total expenditure incurred on the salaries of the staff.

Under the contingency grant, the expenditure may be incurred on various items such as the salary of contingent staff like sweepers, purchase of stationery, postage, text books, repairs to school buildings etc.

Table-5.19
Budget Allocations and Amount Spent on Secondary Education in Kurnool Municipal Corporation

S.No.	*Year*	*Amount Sanctioned (Rs. in Lakhs)*	*Amount Spent (Rs. in Lakhs)*	*Difference (Rs. in Lakhs)*
1.	1999-2000	98.50	97.46	1.04
2.	2000-2001	101.00	99.32	1.68
3.	2001-2002	104.90	101.68	3.22
4.	2002-2003	126.53	104.90	21.63
5.	2003-2004	193.00	106.42	86.58
6.	2004-2005	240.35	108.69	131.66
7.	2005-2006	123.37	119.72	3.65
8.	2006-2007	180.00	120.31	59.69
9.	2007-2008	159.57	121.58	37.99
	Total	**1327.22**	**980.08**	**347.14**

Source: Kurnool Municipal Corporation Budget Estimates and Revised Budget Estimates from 1999-2000 to 2007-08.

An analysis of Table 5.19 reveals the clear position of financial status of Kurnool Municipal Corporation in the promotion of secondary education under its jurisdiction. As stated earlier, the salaries of the staff of teaching and non-teaching are met by the State Government. But with regard to giving of maintenance grant, contingency grant etc., the total grant sanctioned by the State Government was not satisfactory.

Table 5.19 gives the financial details of Kurnool Municipal Corporation in respect of secondary education. The total grant received by the Municipal Corporation during the study period from 1999-2000 to 2007-08 was 1327.22 lakhs while the expenditure incurred was 980.08 lakhs resulting an accumulated surplus of Rs. 367.14 lakhs. For all the years of study period the grant released was more than the expenditure. The highest surplus was 131.66 lakhs in the year 2004-05.

Scholarship Grant

The other item of income of secondary schools in Kurnool Municipal Corporation is the scholarship amount given by the Social Welfare Department for the Scheduled Castes, Scheduled Tribes and Backward Classes pupils. The Commissioner and Director of Social Welfare and the Backward Classes Welfare release grants towards payment scholarships as per the proposals sent by the District Social Welfare Officer and as per the applications recommended by the concerned Headmasters of the schools. After the receipt of the amount the Headmasters arrange for disbursement of money to these pupils. Though this is a type of grant sanctioned by the State Government every year but not meant for the institutional maintenance of the schools but only for the welfare of the people. Hence, it does not directly help the schools financially.

Special Fees in Schools

The Headmaster of a Municipal High School is responsible to maintain the accounts of the special fee fund collected from the pupils (VI to X class). The special fee fund is used for purchase of newspapers, library books and sports and games material for the school. Such expenditure can be incurred with the help of the resolutions passed by the special fee fund committee. This Committee consists of the Headmaster, two or three staff members and two or three pupils as members.[6] The Headmaster has to open a savings Bank Account in the post office to operate and maintain the accounts carefully.

Audit and Accounts

All public authorities have to maintain systematic account of the public money spent by them and the Kurnool Municipal Corporation is no exception. It has to maintain the record of all financial transactions showing the income received and the expenditure incurred by it with the support of vouchers. The responsibility for maintaining the accounts relating to secondary education is entrusted to the Commissioner of Kurnool Municipal Corporation himself with the help of one Senior Assistant for Secondary Education.

In order to verify whether the public money is spent honestly and prudently, it is necessary for an independent authority to audit the accounts of the public body. Further, it is imperative to see that the money is spent for the very purpose for which it has been sanctioned. In case of Kurnool Municipal Corporation the task of auditing the accounts is entrusted by the Government to the Audit Officer. Alongwith the accounts of other wings of the Kurnool Municipal Corporation, he also audits the accounts relating to secondary education.

An Overview

The Kurnool Municipal Corporation is playing its role in the promotion of secondary education to the children of Kurnool city by managing as many as eight secondary schools exclusively on secular principles open to all categories of people. However, there are no special schools like school for the Blind, school for the dumb and deaf and school for mentally retarded and so on. The strength of the students in high schools is showing a downward trend. Various reasons have been attributed to this kind of slackness such as starting of good number of English medium as well as Telugu medium convent school in every street and lane in Kurnool city. The performance results as publicized by these private convent schools attracted many parents and put their children in private convents rather than in Municipal Corporation schools. The low percentage of success in the SSC Public Examinations also discouraged the parents to admit their children in these schools and sometimes discontinued their children from Municipal Corporation schools and encouraged them to join in private schools and other reputed institutions. The trend in Kurnool city, today to be the fact is every where. Even the daily wage earners, rickshaw pullers, auto drivers though they have meager income but are tempted to admit their children in English medium convent schools than prefer to admit their children in Municipal Corporation schools. The lack of commitment, sincerity and devotion and dedication to the profession is lacking among the teachers in Municipal

Corporation schools which caused diminishing performance of these schools. The poor physical facilities, weak financial position of these schools also other reasons for their lowered status and reputation in Kurnool city as is revealed by the empirical study conducted by the researcher on selected pupil respondents as discussed in the forthcoming chapter.

REFERENCES

1. Lakshmi, S., *Challenges in Indian Education*, New Delhi: Sterling, 1993, p. 6.
2. Kochhar, S.K., *Secondary School Administration*, New Delhi: Sterling, 1993, p. 7.
3. Inamdar, N.R., *Educational Administration in Zilla Parishads in Maharashtra – A Pilot Study*, Bombay: Popular, 1974, p. 198.
4. Government of Andhra Pradesh, G.O. Ms. No. 65 (Education), dated 28.1.1975.
5. Government of Andhra Pradesh, U.D. No. 471/346/EE-77/11 (Finance and Planning Department), dated 14.3.1977 and Memo No. 452/F1/71, dated 29.4.1977.
6. Government of Andhra Pradesh, G.O. Ms. No. 414, Education, dated 16.4.1977.

6

Pupils' Perceptions

The acid-test for the success or efficiency of any educational institution in general and secondary schools in particular is the achievement of pupils' satisfaction. Pupils' perceptions are the measuring scale through which the pupil's satisfaction in respect of the functioning and performance of the schools and the efficiency and commitment of the teachers and other related staff in these educational institutions is determined. Pupils or the 'learners' are the legitimate stakeholders of the institutions and it is for their purpose that all necessary efforts are mobilized and organized. It is those pupils' who take the focus of the lime light—the pivot and the centre of educational administration. It is for their all-round wholesome development that curricula are designed and planned, the plant is set, qualified teachers and Headmasters are appointed and auxiliary services are arranged. In fact the pupil is the common dominator in the arithmetic of educational administration. Thus, verification of pupils pulse in the light of their academic and social gains which they derive from their study schools is the unique looking glass through which the performance and working of these educational institutions in the light of their objectives and goals *vis-à-vis* the pupils satisfaction is reflected. Pupils satisfaction and their success in their examinations is the bench mark for the efficiency of any educational institution. Particularly, the pupils and the schools are the inseparable ingredients and two halves of a living seed from which the huge tree of education germinates. The pupils are the backbone of any school and it is said that 'no-pupil-no school' and everything a desert.

In particular the secondary schools play a vital role in imparting secondary education to the boys and girls in any country. Realizing this importance alongwith other agencies the local bodies, particularly the Municipalities and the Municipal Corporations jumped into action and have taken up the task of structuring and managing secondary schools which are also called as High Schools in Andhra Pradesh and in all urban areas of the districts. The Municipal Corporations in particular are said to be the custodians of school education also and be active in their task of imparting education to the students in urban or town areas and cities. The children who pass through elementary education will enroll themselves in these schools put up their regular attendance and staying in the school responding to the time-table looking at their teachers. Thus, these schools have emerged as 'places of learning', the teachers as 'Masters' or 'Gurus' and the pupils as 'learners' or 'disciples'. While the teachers in any educational institutions are at the giving end and the pupils are at the receiving end. Thus, these schools are not like other institutions but they are like temples of education to lead the ignorant pupil towards light, illiterate child towards the goal of education. It is here that the pupil gets motivated to plan and lay foundation for his bright career. Hence, these schools are endowed with moral responsibility of moulding the pupil as 'full student' and fill him with highest satisfaction of well taught, well learned and well achieved.

The Kurnool Municipal Corporation in Andhra Pradesh, which is considered to be one of the oldest former municipalities in the State is also striving to achieve its avowed objective of managing and imparting education at secondary level by running eight secondary schools spread over to fifty municipal wards. Of these, six are Telugu medium, one Telugu and English medium and one Urdu medium schools. Of these eight schools one each are exclusive boys and girls schools and the rest of the schools provide co-education.

Today, the performance record of the schools under local bodies in general and under Kurnool Municipal Corporation in particular in providing standard and quality education to the children in Kurnool Municipal Corporation (starting from VI to X Class (S.S.C.)) have been subjected to severe public scrutiny and criticism. An insight into the enrollment of students in these schools, the number of Transfer Certificates (T.C's) given away, the general academic standard of the children, the results achieved in Secondary School Certificate (SSC) Public Examinations revealed that these schools were irresponsible in maintaining and improving the academic standards. The frequent transfers of the pupils from these schools to other private schools and other tutorial institutions reveal that the pupils as well as the parents have lost faith and confidence in Municipal Corporation schools in respect of academic as well as moral standards and individual discipline. It is also branded that these Municipal Corporation schools are the 'poor-child's-school' and there is no other substitute for them except to dwarf in these schools. It is also alleged that the moral, mental and physical abilities of the pupils would be ruined if these children are left study in these schools. There is also a severe criticism focused on the teaching community of Kurnool Municipal Corporation schools that they are more monetary conscious than academically interested.

In view of the above sweeping remarks and impressions, it became necessary for the researcher to test their credibility and establish the truth. The researcher tested this hypotheses from the angle of the perceptions of the pupils in the light of the working of secondary schools under Kurnool Municipal Corporation as discussed in Chapter V (Kurnool Municipal Corporation Schools -- At Work) and ultimately resulting in making suitable suggestions for the promotion of higher functional quality of these schools.

The present study is mainly based on various parameters like curriculum extended by these schools, physical infrastructural facilities, adequacy of teaching and non-teaching staff, strength of the students, examination results and so on.

For the purpose of undertaking the performance evaluation of the secondary schools and their contributions made to boost the satisfaction and achievement of the pupils studying in these schools under the management of Kurnool Municipal Corporation were taken to study.

Besides various other factors like number of teachers and non-teaching staff, number of sections, enrollment of students, results of the pupils, teachers qualifications and so on, the following parameters were also applied to study and analyse the perceptions and measure the satisfaction of the pupils. The following were the parameters used:

1. School building location
2. Strength in each class
3. Classroom discipline
4. Accommodation
5. Lighting in the classroom
6. Toilet facilities and sanitation
7. Furniture
8. Teaching aids
9. Library facilities
10. Laboratory facilities
11. Parent-teachers association
12. Cultural programmes
13. Cancellation of classes
14. Teachers coming late to the classes
15. Non-subject teachers handling the classes
16. Medical facilities
17. Copying in examination and so on.

Sampling

For the purpose of conducting field survey through administration of a well-structured questionnaire to collect pupils perceptions and their reactions, the researcher thought it good to touch every school under the management of Kurnool Municipal Corporation with the questionnaire without applying any theory of sampling in selecting the schools. Infact, it was felt convenient by the researcher to touch each school as all these schools are located in Kurnool city only. Hence, all the eight high schools were visited and surveyed by the researcher. However in selecting the respondents the researcher had followed a purposive sampling method in selecting the respondents starting from VI standard to X standard in High Schools. A total of 400 students were selected from all eight schools. The sampling was arranged in such a way that 50 students from each school representing 10 students from each class were selected on a random sampling method. Each 10 students picked up from each class was representative in character that all the social categories in the city available were represented. That way, two students representing Scheduled Castes, one each student representing Scheduled Tribes and Minorities, three each students representing Backward Classes and others respectively. Table 6.1 gives the details of distribution of sample respondents school-wise.

Table 6.2 gives the distribution of sample students based on social background. Thus out of 400 respondents, 80 students from Scheduled Castes, 40 students from Scheduled Tribes, 120 students from Backward Classes, 40 students from Minorities and 120 students representing other category were selected.

Then the findings of the present study in the light of the above mentioned parameters have been calculated and computed by using a common statistical technique of 'Weighted Average', and the perceptions of 400 pupil-respondents have been weighted and the results were drawn. Based on the results, and the weighted averages, the working of the secondary schools under the management of Kurnool Municipal Corporation have been analysed and assessed based on the said parameters as these parameters have an important bearing on the working of these schools.

Methodology: Weighted Averages

The Weighted Average is used for the three or more point scale of attitudes. These scales are used for measuring the various intensity of the attitudes and perceptions. They are found to be mostly suitable when the opinion is not dichotomous in character as in the case of point scales. Take a three point scale using three kinds of words like Good, Average and Bad.

In a rating scale the central, average or neutral opinion is generally given zero score. On both sides one score is given for each point, plus sign is used for favourable opinion or attitude and minus for unfavourable one. Thus, the weights given for three-point scale are as shown below:

Good = +1

Average = 0

Bad = -1

The following formula is followed to find out weighted average.

Response Category	*Weight (x)*	*Frequency (f)*	*Fixi*
Good	x_1	f_1	f_1x_1
Average	x_2	f_2	f_2x_2
Bad	x_3	f_3	f_3x_3

Weighted Average = (Ef1x1)/n

The weighted average value should be always in the limits of weights (x).

With the help of above statistical scaling technique, the weighted average of all perceptions of 400 pupil-respondents in respect of 17 parameters have been calculated and the same have been tabulated as given in Table 6.3.

Table–6.1

Distribution of Sample Respondents School-Wise

S. No.	*Name of the School*	*Class*	*No. of Students*	*No. of Students in Each Class*					*Total*
				VI	*VII*	*VIII*	*IX*	*X*	
1.	Damodaram Sanjeevaiah Memorial Municipal Corporation High School	VI to X	50	10	10	10	10	10	50
2.	Nehru Memorial Municipal Corporation High School	VI to X	50	10	10	10	10	10	50
3.	Cattamanchi Ramalinga Reddy Memorial Municipal Corporation High School	VI to X	50	10	10	10	10	10	50
4.	Indira Gandhi Memorial Municipal Corporation High School	VI to X	50	10	10	10	10	10	50
5.	Sri Potti Sreeramulu Memorial Municipal Corporation High School	VI to X	50	10	10	10	10	10	50
6.	Dr. B.R. Ambedkar Memorial Municipal Corporation High School	VI to X	50	10	10	10	10	10	50
7.	Sri Tanguturu Prakasam Pantulu Memorial Municipal Corporation High School	VI to X	50	10	10	10	10	10	50
8.	Municipal Corporation High School (Urdu)	VI to X	50	10	10	10	10	10	50
	Total		**400**	**80**	**80**	**80**	**80**	**80**	**400**

Table-6.2
Distribution of Sample Respondents Category Wise

S. No.	Category of Pupil	Number of Respondents VI	VII	VIII	IX	X	Total in each School	Total in each Schools	From each School %
1.	Scheduled Castes	2	2	2	2	2	10	80	20
2.	Scheduled Tribes	1	1	1	1	1	5	40	10
3.	Backward Classes	3	3	3	3	3	15	120	30
4.	Minorities	1	1	1	1	1	5	40	10
5.	Others	3	3	3	3	3	15	120	30
	Total	**10**	**10**	**10**	**10**	**10**	**50**	**400**	**100**

Table-6.3
Weighted Averages of Respondent's Perceptions

S. No.	Perception	Weights (x) Good +1 x1	Average 0 0–x2	Bad - 1 (- x3)	Total (n)	Efixi/n	Weighted Average
1.	Location of school building	46	152	-202	400	-156/400	-0.390
2.	Pupils strength in the classroom	10	134	-256	400	-246/400	-0.615
3.	Classroom discipline	06	128	-266	400	-260/400	-0.650
4.	Accommodation	152	67	-181	400	-29/400	-0.072
5.	Lighting	47	89	-264	400	-217/400	-0.543
6.	Toilet facilities and sanitation	76	182	-142	400	-66/400	-0.265
7.	Furniture	92	97	-211	400	-119/400	-0.298
8.	Teaching aids	45	122	-233	400	-188/400	-0.470
9.	Library facilities	33	102	-265	400	-232/400	-0.580
10.	Laboratory facilities	78	56	-266	400	-188/400	-0.470
11.	Question bank	88	114	-198	400	-110/400	-0.275

Contd...

S. No.	Perception	Weights (x)			Total (n)	Efixi / n	Weighted Average
		Good	Average	Bad			
		+1 x1	0 0–x2	- 1 (- x3)			
12.	Cultural programmes	92	111	-197	400	-105/400	-0.263
13.	Cancellation of classes	17	248	-135	400	-118/400	-0.295
14.	Late coming of teachers to classes	62	137	-201	400	-139/400	-0.348
15.	Non-subject Teachers engaging classes	16	138	-246	400	-230/400	-0.575
16.	Medical facilities	53	212	-135	400	-82/400	-0.205
17.	Copying in examinations	69	168	-163	400	-94/400	-0.235

School Building Location

The school plant or building is a factor of tremendous importance in education. Good learning environment is necessary for speeding up the learning process among the students. It is necessary that the school building location should be congenial to learning process. A school cannot be put up anywhere and everywhere. Its sitting has a great importance and significance. Good location and not the low cost should be the deciding factor. Adequacy and suitability should be the primary consideration. Particular attention should be given to the relationship of site to the existing or the future traffic routes with a view to minimizing the danger to children on their way to school. The school building should be away from traffic noises and road dust smoke etc. The school site should have pleasing surroundings which soothe the eye and please the soul. The site of the school should provide sufficient space for future expansion.

In respect of the location of the schools managed by Kurnool Municipal Corporation located in Kurnool city the respondents were asked to give their experiences and perceptions. Their responses have been tabulated in Table 6.4.

An analysis of Table 6.4 reveals that 202 (50.50%) respondents felt that the location of their schools in Kurnool Municipal Corporation

Table–6.4
Perceptions of the Pupils in Respect of Location of their School Buildings

S.No.	*Perception*	*No. of Respondents*	*% of Respondents*
1.	Healthy Location (Good)	46	11.50
2.	Ordinary Location (Average)	152	38.00
3.	Unpleasant Location (Bad)	202	50.50
	Total	**400**	**100.00**

is unpleasant (Bad) and they face the problem of heavy traffic and traffic noises, road dust and smoke. The surroundings of the school buildings are polluting the academic environment of the schools. 152 (38.00%) respondents revealed that their schools are located in somewhat good locations in which the schools are some how were run without much disturbance. Among the respondents 46 (11.50%) have expressed that they feel the school located in healthy environment and good locality and nearer to their residence. Some of the students also expressed that there is no place for them to built compound walls as their schools are constructed in a very congested business establishments and residential houses.

With the help of weighted average (-0.390) as shown in Table 6.3 Sl.No. (1) it is concluded that the locations of school buildings managed by Kurnool Municipal Corporation in Kurnool City are unpleasant to the respondents.

Pupils' Strength in the Classroom

The number of pupils on rolls and the teacher-pupil ratio plays an important role in making the teachers to pay individual attention on the academic progress and personal development of the pupil. At the same time the student in the class also feels a kind of satisfaction that he is subjected to personal attention of the teacher in the classroom. If the strength is more, the teacher may sometimes be a failure in controlling the classroom. Keeping this in view the government also fixed the teacher-pupil ratio is 1:40. Regarding the strength and size of their classroom, the respondents were asked to react with their personal experiences. The responses have been tabulated in Table 6.5.

Table-6.5
Perceptions of the Pupils on the Strength of the Classroom

S.No.	Perception	No. of Respondents	% of Respondents
1.	Well Manageable (Good)	10	2.50
2.	Manageable (Average)	134	33.50
3.	Un-Manageable (Bad)	256	64.00
	Total	**400**	**100.00**

An analysis of Table 6.5 reveals that 256 (64.00%) pupils felt that the teacher in their classrooms was not able to manage the class effectively as the pupils numerical strength in the class was high and the teacher was unable to concentrate on the progress of the student. In the same way 134 (33.50%) pupils felt that their classroom strength was just manageable and the teacher was just able to manage the classroom through the classroom strength was though large. Only 10 (2.50%) of the students felt that there was no problem in having large number of students in the classroom. They felt that it was good if the classroom was full with large number of students.

Thus, with the help of weighted average of (-0.615) as shown in Table 6.3 Sl.No. (2) it is concluded that the pupils strength in classrooms of high schools managed by Kurnool Municipal Corporation in unmanageable.

Classroom Discipline

Maintenance of discipline in the classroom by the teacher always depends upon his ability to impose discipline on the students, the behaviour of the students, that background and above all the span of control. Generally, the higher the number of pupils accommodated in each section of the class the greater is the difficulty of the teacher to regulate the classroom. The pupils generally observe the teachers ability in the maintenance of the class and if the teacher proved ineffective the indiscipline would increase and spread over to the entire class tempting even the disciplined pupil to associate with the indiscipline classmates and contribute to more indiscipline. The respondents were asked to respond to the question of how their classrooms were maintained with discipline by their teachers and the behaviour of their classmates. The responses are tabulated in Table 6.6.

Table-6.6
Perceptions of the Pupils Regarding Discipline in the Classroom

S.No.	*Perception*	*No. of Respondents*	*% of Respondents*
1.	Good Discipline	6	1.50
2.	Average Discipline	128	32.00
3.	Poor Discipline (Bad)	266	66.50
	Total	**400**	**100.00**

An analysis of Table 6.6 reveals that 266 (66.50%) pupils expressed that discipline in their classrooms is poorly maintained. In the same way 128 (32.00%) students have expressed that maintenance of discipline in their classroom was just nominal. Only 6 (1.50%) respondents expressed that good discipline was maintained in their classroom. They also revealed the goodness of some of their teachers and the hard discipline imposed by some of their teachers. The devotion and dedication of some of their teachers was also revealed by these respondents. Higher number of students felt that in view of unwieldy strength there was disciplinary problem in the classrooms and had created uncongenial environment for academic progress.

Thus, with the help of Weighted Average of (-0.650) as shown in Table 6.3 Sl.No. 3 it is concluded that the discipline in the classrooms of Kurnool Municipal Corporation High Schools is poorly maintained.

Accommodation

Sufficient and comfortable accommodation is highly necessary to the students sliding in the schools to enable them to sit conveniently and listen to the teacher in the classroom. Congested and irksome accommodation will lead to lack of ventilation, air pollution and discomfort to the students. This may also lead to ill-health, spreading of diseases from one student to the other. The school buildings should be housed in beautiful buildings which may not only be stimulating centres of education for children but also vital centres of community life. The accommodation should provide facilities necessary for curricular, co-curricular and extra-curricular activities. The accommodation should also ensure safety of pupils, teachers and all those who use its facilities. Lighting, heating and ventilating should be in accordance with the best practices. The classroom should have not only space for good study but adequate space for using maps, charts, pictures, specimens, models, exhibits, reference books, tools, craft materials, experiment apparatus and the like. Every instructional room should provide a healthful living and working environment for pupils and teachers. The respondents were asked to react about the accommodation available in their schools and their classrooms for effectively pursuing their regular academic activities. Table 6.7 gives the responses of the sample respondents.

Table–6.7
Perceptions of the Respondents in Respect of School Accommodation

S.No.	*Perception*	*No. of Respondents*	*% of Respondents*
1.	Abundant (Good)	152	38.00
2.	Nearly Sufficient (Average)	67	16.75
3.	Insufficient (Bad)	181	45.25
	Total	**400**	**100.00**

An analysis of Table 6.7 reveals that 181 (45.25%) respondents expressed that accommodation in their schools as well as the classrooms is insufficient and difficult to have free movement, free ventilation and good lighting. As many as 67 (16.75%) pupils stated that the accommodation is just sufficient and sometimes they feel shortage of accommodation. But 152 (38.00%) of the pupils came out with their impression that the accommodation is abundant in their school as well as in the classrooms.

Thus, with the help of Weighted Average (-0.072) as shown in Table 6.3 Sl.No. (4) it is concluded that the accommodation in Kurnool Municipal Corporation High Schools is insufficient and very short.

Lighting

The increase of short sightedness among children of school-age imposes an additional responsibility on the management for adequate provision of lighting in the classrooms. The light arrangements should be as much approximate as possible to create conditions in the classroom with reference to brightness in it. The classrooms should be fitted with wide windows and doors and there should be adequate lighting in the classroom so that the students can read the texts and take down their notes when the teacher dictates and also able to see and read what is written on the blackboard by their teacher. The pupil respondents were asked to answer to the question about the quality of lighting available in their classroom at the time of school working hours. The responses of the pupil respondents are given in Table 6.8.

Table-6.8
Perceptions of Respondents in Respect of Lighting Position in their Classroom

S.No.	*Perception*	*No. of Respondents*	*% of Respondents*
1.	Good	47	11.75
2.	Average	89	22.25
3.	Poor (Bad)	264	66.00
	Total	**400**	**100.00**

An analysis of Table 6.8 reveals that as many as 264 (66.00%) respondents reveals that the lighting facility available in their classrooms is poor and they face difficulty in reading the text books and take down the matter written on the blackboard especially when they sit in the last few rows in the classroom. Besides these respondents, as many as 89 (22.25%) respondents stated that the have average lighting in the classrooms and they face light problem during times of rainy seasons and cloudy days. However 47 (11.75%) respondents are at the point of satisfying with the lighting condition of their classrooms.

Thus, with the help of calculated Weighted Average of (-0.543) as shown in Table 6.3 Sl.No. (6) it is concluded that the lighting facilities available in the classrooms of Municipal Corporation managed high schools in Kurnool city are very poor and insufficient to follow the blackboard and other writings in the classroom.

Toilet Facilities and Sanitation

Provision of adequate and convenient toilet facilities for the boys and girls students separately is a necessary arrangement that is to be provided in all schools. There should be one urinal and bowl for 60 students. These should be regularly inspected to assure proper cleanliness and working condition. Toilet rooms should have moisture proof concrete floors which can be easily washed. This will not only improve health and hygiene but also meet the urgent nature calls of the pupils. The pupil respondents were asked to reveal about the toilet facilities and sanitary conditions of their schools and their responses are given in Table 6.9.

Table–6.9
Perceptions of Pupil-Respondents on Toilet Facilities and Sanitary Conditions in their Schools

S.No.	*Perception*	*No. of Respondents*	*% of Respondents*
1.	Good (Adequate)	76	19.00
2.	Average	142	35.50
3.	Bad (Inadequate)	182	45.50
	Total	**400**	**100.00**

An analysis of Table 6.9 reveals that 182 (45.50%) respondents expressed their dissatisfaction about the bad and inadequate toilet facilities and sanitary conditions prevailing in their schools. 142 (35.50%) of respondents revealed that the toilet facilities are normal and the sanitary conditions are minimal. The respondents also stated that few nominal facilities are provided in their school for girls toilet and the boys have no such facilities. They use the open surroundings of their school building as toilet places and as a result they get very bad smell to the classrooms. They also stated that the urinated places and toilets of girls are not properly maintained and sanitated. However, 76 (19.00%) were satisfied with the toilet facilities and sanitary conditions available in their schools.

Thus, with the help of Weighted Average of (-0.265) as calculated and given in Table 6.3 Sl. No. (6) it is concluded that the toilet facilities and sanitation are bad and inadequate in Municipal Corporation High Schools in Kurnool city.

Furniture

If the school plant is to function efficiently suitable furniture and equipment for the pupils to sit and write down in the classroom is highly essential. The municipality must be able to provide adequate furniture for the students as well as teachers in the classrooms. Furniture plays sufficiently an important part in physical, moral and mental welfare of the pupils. It is of course, true that fine teaching can be done with little furniture and very bad instruction can be given with a wealth of appliances. But this is also true that sufficient furniture, good apparatus and useful appliances in the hands of a first class teacher can produce results which cannot be obtained under any other circumstances. The students must have ideal desks with convenient height, comfortable seat and with writing surface. Blackboard is the necessary equipment of a classroom and a hand apparatus at the hands of a teacher. Every classroom should have a cupboard for the accommodation of such stock as is issued daily in the class and for the safe keeping of models, specimens, apparatus etc. The pupil-respondents were asked to respond to the question of availability of furniture in their classrooms with facilities like desks, blackboards and cupboards etc. The responses of the students are tabulated in Table 6.10.

Table-6.10
Perceptions of Pupil-Respondents on Furniture Available in Classrooms

S.No.	*Perception*	*No. of Respondents*	*% of Respondents*
1.	Adequate Furniture (Good)	92	23.00
2.	Moderate Furniture (Average)	97	24.25
3.	No Furniture (Bad)	211	52.75
	Total	**400**	**100.00**

An analysis of Table 6.10 reveals that as many as 211 (52.75%) respondents reveals that they do not have adequate furniture in the classroom. They do not have proper desks, comfortable seating arrangements. 97 (24.25%) of the students expressed that they have moderate furniture in the classroom but many of the wooden planks and desks have been broken. However, 92 (23.00%) of the respondents revealed that they have adequate furniture and comfortable seating arrangement. Though all the schools have blackboards, they have become shiny and became bad in condition to write on them. They also stated that there were many occasions when the teachers failed to use blackboards. They also expressed that the writings on the blackboards were not clear and not visible due to bad quality and poor maintenance of their blackboards.

Thus, it is concluded with the help of Weighted Average (-0.298) as shown in Table 6.3 Sl. No. (7) that there is no adequate furniture in Kurnool Municipal Corporation High Schools.

Teaching Aids

Using of teaching aids by the teachers in the classrooms is a best way of communicating the subject to the pupils concerned. The schools must be provided with separate grant for preparing and purchasing teaching aids and the teachers must be encouraged to use teaching aids whenever necessary in the classrooms. This inturn will help them to follow easily the classroom teachings and understand the lessons. The pupil-respondents were asked to reveal the practices of using teaching aids by their teachers in their classrooms. Accordingly, the responses given by the respondents have been listed in Table 6.11.

Table-6.11
Perceptions of Pupil-Respondents on the use of Teaching Aids by their Teachers

S.No.	*Perception*	*No. of Respondents*	*% of Respondents*
1.	Regularly used (Good)	45	11.25
2.	Occasionally used (Average)	122	30.50
3.	Never used (Bad)	233	58.25
	Total	**400**	**100.00**

An analysis of Table 6.11 reveals that as many as 233 (58.25%) of pupil-respondents expressed that the teachers never used teaching aids in the classrooms. They also said that they did not see what is a teaching aid. But as many as 122 (30.50%) of respondents stated that the teaching aids were used rarely and especially when there was an inspection of their school or classroom by any higher authorities. 45 (11.25%) of the respondents experienced the use of teaching aids regularly by their teachers.

Thus, with the help of Weighted Average (-0.470) calculated and shown in Table 6.3 Sl.No. (8), it is concluded that the teachers are not fairly using teaching aids in the classrooms of Municipal Corporation High Schools in Kurnool city.

Library Facilities

Library is the hub of the academic life of the school. It plays a unique role in any educational institution. With the new techniques of teaching library should be the centre of the school education programme. Especially in high schools the library with useful books for the pupils and the related text books in good number may help the pupils in strengthening their academic standards. It also develops reading habits among the students. The habit of going to the library during outside classroom hours certainly develops the mental horizon of the pupils also. The primary school children must be attracted with good children books, picture books, story books and so on. There must be periodicals, daily newspapers and weeklies which are helpful especially to secondary school pupils. Thus the first essential for a school library to work efficiently is that it must have a separate room, a qualified librarian, furniture, resources and above all calm atmosphere. In relation to these, the pupil-respondents were asked to respond about the availability of library facilities in their schools and their responses are given in Table 6.12.

Table-6.12
Perceptions Relating to Library Facilities Available in Pupil-Respondents Schools

S.No.	*Perception*	*No. of Respondents*	*% of Respondents*
1.	Abundant (Good)	33	8.25
2.	Moderate (Average)	102	25.50
3.	Poor (Bad)	265	66.25
	Total	**400**	**100.00**

An analysis of Table 6.12 reveals that as many as 265 (66.25%) pupil-respondents revealed that the library facilities are very poor in their schools. They expressed that they do not have separate library room, no librarian and no books or newspapers at all. Besides these respondents, as many as 102 (25.50%) of the respondents expressed that they have moderate library facilities with just availability of newspapers. Though they have some books in their library they are under the charge of a teacher who open the library during outside class hours. They also have a small room inside as library with some furniture. But none of the respondent revealed that they have a qualified librarian in their schools. Some respondents also stated that the books and newspapers are not properly maintained in their schools. However, 33 (8.35 %) of the respondents stated that they have good library and possessing plenty of books and periodicals.

Thus, with the help of calculated Weighted Average (-0.580) shown in Table 6.3 Sl. No. (9) it is concluded that the library facilities available in the Municipal Corporation High Schools in Kurnool city are poor and inadequate.

Laboratory Facilities

Laboratory is the nucleus in any High School which is necessary for imparting curriculum in neutral and physical sciences including mathematics subjects. Every High School must possess well planned and well equipped science rooms and laboratories. This will certainly aid the instruction and stimulate the students with greater interest in Science Courses. The existence of a laboratory will enable the pupils to get practical knowledge along with the theoretical base in Science subjects. The pupil-respondents from all High Schools were asked to explain about the laboratory facilities available in their schools and thus their perceptions have been placed in Table 6.13.

Table–6.13
Perceptions on Laboratory Facilities Available in the High Schools

S.No.	*Perception*	*No. of Respondents*	*% of Respondents*
1.	Abundant (Good)	78	19.50
2.	Moderate (Average)	56	14.00
3.	Poor (Bad)	266	66.50
	Total	**400**	**100.00**

An analysis of Table 6.13 reveals that out of 400 respondents as many as 266 (66.50%) of the pupil-respondents have expressed that they have poor laboratory facilities in their schools. 56 (14.00%) of the respondents expressed that the laboratory facilities in their schools are moderate and 78 (19.50%) of the respondents stated that they have abundant laboratory facilities.

With the help of calculated Weighted Average (-0.470) as shown in Table 6.3 Sl.No. (10) it is concluded that the laboratory facilities in Kurnool Municipal Corporation High Schools are poor.

Question Bank

The establishment and maintenance of question bank is a healthy practice and supporting arrangement in any High School which will help and guide the students in their preparation for examinations. What type of questions were given in the past examinations and how to answer them and the mode of questions asked and so on can be made easy by the teachers concerned if there is a question bank maintained and kept opened to the students also. The pupil-respondents were asked to respond about the facility of question bank in their schools and their responses have been given in Table 6.14.

Table-6.14
Perceptions on the Facility of Question Bank

S.No.	*Perception*	*No. of Respondents*	*% of Respondents*
1.	Well maintained (Good)	88	22.00
2.	Moderately maintained (Average)	114	28.50
3.	No such facility (Bad)	198	49.50
	Total	**400**	**100.00**

An analysis of Table 6.14 reveals that as many as 198 (49.50%) of the respondents expressed that the facility of question bank is not available in their schools and never looked at past question papers in their schools. But 114 (28.50%) of the respondents came out with the feeling that though they have such facility but all the question banks are not available and the question bank is ill-maintained. 88 (22.00%) of the respondents stated that their question banks are well maintained. Thus, with the help of calculated Weighed Average of (-0.275) shown in Table 6.3 Sl.No. (11) it is concluded that there is no such facility like question bank in Kurnool Municipal Corporation High Schools.

Cultural Programmes

Periodical cultural programmes outside teaching hours are essential and they should be made as an integral part of curriculum in any school programme. Students must be made to participate actively in cultural and histrionic programmes in the schools and the teachers must organize such type of programmes and motivate the pupils to take active part. This kind of histrionic programmes will broaden the mental horizon of the pupils and inturn will create a kind of relaxation to the study mind. The pupil-respondents were asked to reveal about the cultural programme concluded in their schools and the expressions of these respondents have been given in Table 6.15.

Table–6.15
Perceptions of Pupil-Respondents on Activities of Cultural Programmes in their Schools

S.No.	*Perception*	*No. of Respondents*	*% of Respondents*
1.	Regularly conducted (Good)	92	23.00
2.	Occasionally conducted (Average)	111	23.75
3.	Never conducted (Bad)	197	49.25
	Total	**400**	**100.00**

An analysis of Table 6.15 reveals that 197 (49.25%) of the total respondents expressed that the cultural programmes were never conducted in their schools. Out of the total respondents 111 (27.75%) of the respondents revealed that cultural programmes are occasionally conducted. However 92 (23.00%) of the respondents expressed that cultural programmes are conducted regularly in their schools.

Thus, with the help of Weighted Average (-0.263) as calculated and shown in Table 6.3 Sl.No. (12), it is concluded that the Municipal Corporation High Schools in Kurnool city do not have the practice of conducting cultural programmes for benefit of their students as well as outside community.

Cancellation of Classes

Regular time-table and its faithful adoption is the essential requirement for effective teaching and curriculum. Cancellation of classes frequently in view of various reasons like absence of regular subject teachers, non-filling up of vacant posts in the schools, teachers frequently applying leave and so on affects the steadiness of academic programme in the schools. Sometimes in view of lack of accommodation there will be cancellation of classes during rainy seasons and inclement weather. These practices will hit the academic prospects of the pupils. Keeping these in view the pupil-respondents were asked to reveal about the practice of cancellation of classes in their schools. Their expressions have been placed in Table 6.16.

Table-6.16
Perceptions on Cancellation of Classes

S.No.	*Perception*	*No. of Respondents*	*% of Respondents*
1.	Never (Good)	17	4.25
2.	Occasional (Average)	248	62.00
3.	Frequent (Bad)	135	33.75
	Total	**400**	**100.00**

An analysis of Table 6.16 reveals that 248 (62.00%) of the respondents expressed that their class work was cancelled occasionally. As many as 135 (33.75%) of the respondents stated that their class work was cancelled regularly. But 17 (4.25%) of the respondents stated that their classes were never cancelled unnecessarily.

With the help of calculated Weighted Average (-0.295) as shown in Table 6.3 Sl.No. (13) it is concluded that cancellation of classes in Municipal Corporation High Schools in Kurnool city is a common practice.

Teachers Coming Late to Classes

Punctuality of teachers in attending to the class work according to the scheduled time-table is a healthy feature and ensures discipline among the teachers as well ask students. If the teacher is in time in the classroom that will influence the students and inturn the students will also be in time in the classroom. The students who are kept inside the classroom will be averted in disturbing the other neighbouring classes. Engaging the class for the full allotted time will enable the teacher to bestow full attention on the subject and enables them to complete the syllabus in time and prepare the students well to the examinations. Keeping this aspects in view the pupil-respondents were asked to reveal about the attendance of the teachers intime to the classrooms. Responsively the respondents came out with their impressions on this aspect which are shown in Table 6.17.

Table-6.17
Perceptions on Teachers Coming Late to the Classes

S.No.	*Perception*	*No. of Respondents*	*% of Respondents*
1.	Never (Good)	62	15.50
2.	Now and then (Average)	137	34.25
3.	Frequent (Bad)	201	50.25
	Total	**400**	**100.00**

An analysis of Table 6.17 reveals that as many as 201 (50.25%) of the total respondents expressed that their teachers attend to their classes frequently late. Besides these, as many as 137 (34.25%) of the respondents revealed that their teachers come to class late now and then. However, only 62 (15.50%) of the respondents stated that their teachers come intime to the class always.

With the help of calculated Weighted Average of (-0.348) as shown in Table 6.3 Sl.No. 14, it is concluded that the teacher working in Kurnool Municipal Corporation High Schools come late to their schools.

Non-Subject Teachers Engaging Classes

Each subject is to be taught by the concerned teacher who is trained specifically in the subject. This is a good arrangement and the concerned scheduled teachers only can justify in teaching the subject and make the pupils to understand it. But frequently it has been the practice that in many schools posts are vacant and due to this as a stop gap arrangement other subject teachers are asked by the concerned Headmasters to engage the classes. Especially in respect of subjects like physics, chemistry, mathematics, biological sciences and natural sciences and english this type of arrangements are frequently made. These non-subject teachers either try to teach the same subject with their limited or nil knowledge in the subject or try to teach their own subjects or chit chat in the class leaving the subjects allotted untaught. This will ultimately damage the academic progress of the students and force the students either to leave the schools or take shelter under private tuitions. Keeping these in mind, the pupil-respondents picked up from five high schools were asked to reveal this type of arrangements in their schools. The responses of the respondents have been classified in Table 6.18.

Table-6.18
Perceptions on Non-subject Teachers Engaging Classes

S.No.	*Perception*	*No. of Respondents*	*% of Respondents*
1.	Never (Good)	16	4.00
2.	Now and Then (Average)	138	34.50
3.	Frequent (Bad)	246	61.50
	Total	**400**	**100.00**

An analysis of Table 6.18 shows that 138 (34.50%) respondents revealed that in the absence of regular teachers other non-subject teachers engaged their classes and taught other subjects now and then. 246 (61.50%) respondents revealed that non-subject teachers engaged their classes frequently and taught not only other subjects but also entertained them with stories, songs and jokes. But 16 (4.00%) of the respondents stated that their classes in the absence of their regular teachers were engaged always and everytime.

With the help of calculated Weighted Average of (-0.575) as shown in Table 6.3 Sl.No. 15 it is concluded that it is a common practice that non-subject teachers engage the classes in the absence of regular teachers in Kurnool Municipal Corporation High Schools.

Medical Facilities and Medical Check-up

The home and the family carry the primary responsibility for providing total health of the child, but the school has a unique opportunity and role of play a contributing to the healthy development of each pupil. All the schools must provide free medical facilities to its pupils with a part-time medical officer to check the health conditions of the pupils and to attend to their medical needs. Vision and hearing testings are especially important to improve the pupils ability. Hence visual testing and hearing testing should be conducted regularly every year in all schools. The first aid and emergency service facilities must also be available in the schools. Each school must have one nurse to take medical and health care of the students. Further, all the teachers must be given training in First-aid and other simple medical practices to meet any causalities in the schools. To make meaning of the saying 'sound body will have a sound mind', these medical facilities are necessary to keep the students fit enough for studies. Keeping the importance of these medical facilities in mind the respondents were asked to reveal whether such medical facilities are available in their schools and regular medical check-up is undertaken or not. The responses of the respondents are given in Table 6.19.

Table–6.19
Perceptions of Respondents on Availability of Medical Facilities and School Medical Check-ups

S.No.	*Perception*	*No. of Respondents*	*% of Respondents*
1.	Available always	53	13.25
2.	Occasionally available	212	53.00
3.	Not available	135	33.75
	Total	**400**	**100.00**

An analysis of Table 6.19 shows that 135 (33.75%) of the respondents revealed that the medical facilities in their schools are not available and if there is any causality in the schools they have to rush at any time to the Hospital without any first-aid. But 212 (53.00%) of respondents expressed that medical facilities are available occasionally whenever there is rampant of contagious diseases in the town the school authorities make temporary arrangements to provide these facilities. The point of availability of medical facilities all the time during school hours was expressed by 53 (13.25%) of the respondents.

Thus it is concluded with the help of Weighted Average (-0.205) as shown in Table 6.3 Sl.No. (16) that medical facilities are not available in Kurnool Municipal Corporation High Schools and the medical check-ups were not conducted in their schools for the students.

Copying in Examinations

Copying in examinations halls is an academic-evil penetrated into school system. This habit and practice will damage the career of the student concerned as the habit never motivates him to study but makes him lazy and problematic. Allowing copying in schools will also discourage the intelligent and hardworking students and dishonours honesty and sincerity. Thus copying in the schools is a bad practice and permitting this kind of practice results in indiscipline and damages the reputation of the school. Table 6.20 gives the responses of the respondents on this aspect.

Table-6.20
Perceptions on Copying in Examinations

S.No.	*Perception*	*No. of Respondents*	*% of Respondents*
1.	Never aliowed (Good)	69	17.25
2.	Sometimes allowed (Average)	168	42.00
3.	Regularly allowed (Bad)	163	40.75
	Total	**400**	**100.00**

An analysis of Table 6.20 gives that as many as 168 (42.00%) of respondents revealed that copying is permitted sometimes in their schools during examinations and 163 (40.75%) of the respondents stated that copying is regularly allowed during examinations if they are not public examinations. But 69 (17.25%) of respondents stated that copying was not allowed at anytime in their schools.

Thus, with the help of Weighted Average of (-0.235) as shown in Table 6.3 Sl. No.(17) it is concluded that copying is also practiced by the students in Kurnool Municipal Corporation High Schools and the teachers also don't take any interest in avoiding this practice.

In addition to the above perceptions which were of strong and significant in nature various other flaws in the working of their High Schools were also revealed by the respondents while responding to the questionnaire. The following are the perceptions:

1. Non-adherence of class time-table by the teachers.
2. Poor performance of teachers in the classrooms.
3. Failure of teachers to impose on the students in respect of attendance and regularity.
4. Making use of the services of students by their teachers during school working hours.
5. Reluctance of the teacher towards maintaining discipline in the classroom.
6. No proper check over irregular and mischievous students.

7. Non-conduct of regular tests to assess the academic progress of the students.
8. Absence of co-curricular activities like Quiz programmes, elocutions, essay writing and so on.
9. No proper extra-curricular activities like scouts, guides, games and sports and other social service activities.
10. No preparation of progress reports and not keeping the parents informed about their children academic performance.
11. Absence of good drinking water facility.
12. Smoking of teachers within the school campuses.
13. No Cafeteria in the school premises.
14. Absence of Museum in the schools.
15. No Assembly Hall.
16. Absence of proper playground.
17. No study tours and excursions.
18. No school magazine and school hand book.
19. Absence of school gardens.
20. No Teacher-Parent dialogue regularly.
21. Lack of co-operation and co-ordination among teachers.
22. Poor attention of teacher towards weak and physically handicapped pupils.

An analysis of above complaints clearly shows that these are the few reasons which are responsible and contributing for the poor performance of students of Kurnool Municipal Corporation High Schools in the public examinations. As the Government of Andhra Pradesh had implemented non-detention system in the high schools, the pupils are automatically promoted. If they put up minimum attendance. As the attendance is not so seriously considered by the teachers in the regular classrooms almost all the students are treated in having had put up the minimum attendance and are promoted. In fact there were many occasions when the parents, guardians and general public have made their critical comments on the working and performance of these Municipal Corporation High Schools. When the parents are dissatisfied with the performance of these teachers, there were many instances when the parents took away the Transfer Certificates of their children and got them admitted in some other private schools.

The perceptions of the pupil-respondents clearly show the unsatisfactory performance of the Municipal Corporation High Schools in Kurnool City and thus became reasons for their dissatisfaction. Hence, it is necessary to take immediate steps and make suitable arrangements to improve the performance quality of these schools and bring them to the level of functioning to the fullest satisfaction of the pupils, parents and the public in general. This is the time now that the teachers, and management on one side and the parents and the public on the other side should work together for the improvement of efficiency and growth of popularity of these schools with a degree of reputation. The specific and general problems highlighted and the suggestions offered in the chapter would certainly contribute to the effective organization and successful functioning of secondary schools under Kurnool Municipal Corporation.

7
Problems and Suggestions

Administration has been defined by Ordway Tead as "a comprehensive effort to direct, guide and integrate associating human strivings which are focused towards some specific ends or aims." Educational administration is also a comprehensive effort intended to achieve some specific educational objectives and it deals with the educational practices, whereas educational philosophy sets the goal, educational psychology explains the principles, educational administration tells the do-how of educational objectives and principles. It, in fact, is the dynamic side of education. Educational administration deals with educational institutions right from the schools and colleges to the secretariat. It is concerned with both human and material resources. The human elements include *(i)* children *(ii)* parents *(iii)* teachers, and *(iv)* other employees in general—University or Board of Education at social, state and national levels of government. On the material side there are *(i)* money *(ii)* buildings and grounds *(iii)* equipment and instructional supplies. Beyond these two elements are ideas, laws and regulations, community needs and so on. All of these have a bearing on the educational process. The "integration" of these "parts" into a "whole" is educational administration.

Secondary education is the most important stage in any educational school. Its importance is many times greater in India when we are engaged in national reconstruction. The trained manpower for various developmental projects can be the product of only secondary schools in the country. The future of India is dependent upon the type of education provided in our secondary schools. There has always been a hue and cry for reorienting the secondary education to the political, economic, social and cultural needs of the country. But even after the implementation of Secondary Education Commission Report and the partial implementation of Indian Education Commission Report the secondary education lay at its cross-roads. The scheme of Multipurpose Higher Secondary Schools failed to provide education in accordance with the vocational needs of the students. Sometimes, it seems that we are so bound to the traditional secondary education that nothing but a revolt against it can wean in away from it. Qualitative improvement of secondary education should receive the top priority in all the policy processes and the successive five-year plans. Secondary education needs to be vocationalized and quite a large number of students should take to vocational courses after completing their primary education. In the wake of the 10+2 pattern of education and the critical observation it has gone through, one can hardly deny that educational opportunity at the Secondary level is a major instrument of social change and transformation. So, expansion of Secondary Education should be well-planned and in accordance with the need for personnel in different vocations. Moreover facilities for Secondary and Higher Secondary Education should accordingly be extended expeditiously to areas and classes which have been denied these in the past.

An efficient, adequate and effective educational system in *sine qua non* of social development and cultural maturation. In a democratic developing country like India, education at the secondary school level still stakes more importance in view of its ability and possibility to shape and strengthen individual's future prosperity and progress. Knowledge and literature are like two halves which go together to mould the capability, culture and general awareness of the individuals and thus require a well fabricated sound institutional network.

Educational administration has become one of the most significant and dominant ramifications in the field of Public Administration. The contemporary era has evoked for the concept of institutionalization of agencies of literacy and consequently there has been emergence of various educational institutions which took the shape of a double edged sword to weed out the social evil of illiteracy from the transitional heterogeneous social systems especially a developing country like India. The task of managing these educational institutions is being undertaken by both Central and State Governments, private agencies and more particularly and challengingly by local bodies.

At present – the Secondary Education is in Concurrent List and the Local-Self Governments are treated as a State subject. Even then, the local bodies are trying to copeup with these limitations and trying to utilize the opportunity of undertaking this task of promotion of literacy through establishing primary as well as secondary schools both in rural as well as urban areas. Among the urban local bodies, more specifically the Municipalities and Municipal Corporations have been exhibiting much concern in the field of education by employing various categories of teachers and other personnel for the successful fulfillment of the objectives entrusted to them. The laudable point in respect of the Municipal Corporations in Andhra Pradesh is when there are State Government agencies to impart and spread education to all areas and the local bodies are to a great possible extent meant for providing civic amenities, the Municipal Corporations as an integral part of the latter have also taken a leap further in the task of expansion of education by managing primary and secondary schools. Thus, educational administration has become an indispensable and day to day matter of Municipal Administration in Andhra Pradesh as well as in Kurnool city.

Education, indeed has undergone various social changes both in its approaches and contents. The need of the hour is that these municipal bodies must impart such latest standards of education to the upcoming boys and girls to suit their necessities and the schools managed by the Municipal Corporations must also raise to the level of standards where there should not be any void between the education provided at cosmopolitan cities and at the Municipal Corporation areas and Municipality areas.

Kurnool is one of the four districts of Rayalaseema region of Andhra Pradesh. The Town of Kurnool was brought under the Madras Towns Improvement Act of 1865 and began functioning as Municipality from 1866 A.D. After having travelled a long journey of its performance this municipality crossing its various grades of status finally took the elevation of present status as Municipal Corporation in August 1994.

This Municipal Corporation has got its own claims of credits in respect of educational field. Though primary education is the only task to be taken up by the Municipalities in Andhra Pradesh besides providing civic amenities, the Kurnool Municipal Corporation, while it was at the status of Municipality accepted the responsibility of managing secondary education also. Its contribution to the task of education is considerable and is conspicuous by the fact of its management of as many as 49 primary schools, seven Upper Primary Schools and Eight Secondary Schools in a most secular way. Local languages like Telugu and Urdu, national language Hindi and English as a necessary third language are also followed both as media of instruction and also as study subjects. Equal importance is no doubt given by the Municipal Corporation to both primary education as well as secondary education by managing primary as well as secondary schools. Especially when there are 50 wards in this Municipal Corporation, it has set up 49 primary schools with a view to have atleast one primary school to each ward and more than one in some wards. In respect of secondary education it has given the facility to both boys and girls by managing one boys High School and one girls High School separately and the rest with co-education facility. In order to give adequate importance to all sections in the city of Kurnool whose mothertongue differs one with the other, the Municipality is running one Urdu medium High School and seven Telugu medium High Schools besides adequate number of Urdu Primary Schools. Further in Telugu medium schools Urdu is also offered as one language subject who ever opts. This has no doubt been contributing to enhance communal as well as lingual harmony among the people in the city and strengthening Hindu-Muslim fraternity both in learning and living. The Municipal Corporation personnel are also taking up the task of conducting a survey of the available eligible children who have attained the school going age and dropouts in Primary and Secondary Schools in the city.

But the present study has brought to light many inadequacies and failures in various aspects of educational administration under Kurnool Municipal Corporation which gave a gloomy picture about the working and performance of Secondary Schools in particular and thus provided bases for offering general as well as specific suggestions to make the educational administration more effective, student-oriented and academic spirited.

Statutory Paradoxes–Absence of Preamble

The Andhra Pradesh Municipal Corporations Act, 1994 (Act No. 25 of 1994) was enacted in 1994 followed by the framing of Andhra Pradesh Municipal Corporation Rules, 1994. The *prima facie* anomaly that the said Act suffers with is that is never bears it preamble nor states the objectives relating to Primary and Secondary Education. It simply says that it is an Act to consolidate and amend law relating Municipal Corporations in the State of Andhra Pradesh.

Preamble to an Act provides a window for exhibiting the motive of the Act. It is a prefactory statement explaining or declaring the reasons and motives for an object sought to be accomplished by the enactment of statute. But nowhere it is found that the primary and secondary schools are established under the management of Municipalities or Municipal Corporations to accomplish a particular purpose. If one makes a perusal of the Act, at once one finds Section 74 which makes reference about appointment to the post of Headmaster and Headmistress of a High School without stating anywhere earlier to Section 74 that there are Primary and Secondary Schools managed by Municipalities or Municipal Corporations in the State and the following were the aims and objectives. Further the Act speaks pages about various other subjects like composition of the council, public health, taxation, water supply, public drainage, scavenging, public latrines and so on except education. As a result the Municipalities and Municipal Corporations in Andhra Pradesh are managing primary and secondary schools without any set of objectives and goals. Further, the earlier Act was amended good number of times. Later the Constitutional 74th Amendment Act 1992 passed by the Indian Parliament has elevated the status of municipal bodies from statutory to constitutional. Though the XII Schedule of Indian Constitution mentions 18 subjects on which Municipality and Municipal Corporations would be empowered by the State Legislature by law to exercise its administrative control and the 13th subject happened to deal with provision of educational aspects, still the State Government did not make any attempt to make primary and secondary education as one of the aims and objectives of Municipalities and Municipal Corporations in the State and incorporate the same as an aspect in the Act under a newly drafted preamble.

Hence, it is suggested that the present Andhra Pradesh Municipal Corporations Act must be urgently amended and provide a place for a glorious preamble and definite objectives in respect of primary and secondary education as the purpose of Municipal Corporations can be broadly be stated to be as educational, cultural and social development of children apart from civic amenities. And as the schools play a dominant role in formal education the proposed preamble of the Act must set out not only the mission but also the functions of the Municipal Corporations in respect of these schools. As we stand for democracy, socialism, secularism and rule of law the proposed preamble must reflect such a legislative intent succinctly.

In this context it is suggested to take into consideration the model preamble as given hereunder:

> "Where as it is expedient to organize school education system under Municipalities/Municipal Corporations for the purpose of fostering and promoting the spread of literacy, education and culture, for strengthening the forces of socialism, secularism, democracy and rule of law and for fostering and promoting the establishment and operation of Primary and Secondary Schools for free and compulsory school education in the urban areas of the State and matters connected therewith."

Need to Improve the Business of the Municipal Corporation

An examination into the behaviour of the Municipal Corporation members who constitute policy making body revealed that they failed even to observe the minimum democratic norms. Personal interests dominated the decision making process and there was virtually vertical division for sharing of spoils among the members of ruling groups especially with regard to educational administration. Due to this no decision could be taken on the basis of its merit and extent of its benefit to the students, teachers and also non-teaching component. This is also true in the case of making transfers, promotions and also punishments.

Hence, it is necessary that the business of the Corporation could be improved to some extent to make it a truly democratic and representative body. Firstly, the proceedings of the Corporation must be recorded and kept for the perusal of the public which would not only make the public aware of the happenings in the Corporation in general and with regard to educational administration in particular. This would also enhance public interest towards the developments in educational administration that are going on and make the Corporation members responsible and answerable to these developments which otherwise mar the smooth functioning of educational institutions of the Municipal Corporation. Wide publicity must be given in the local papers, annual inspection reports, performance reports on the actual working of these schools so that the public may be in a position to understand the working of the schools in actual sense.

Need to Co-opt Educationists to the Municipal Corporation

The Andhra Pradesh Municipal Corporations Act provides democratic means for filling up all the positions in the Corporation through election. Under such arrangements there is every possibility of uneducated, and not well educated persons get elected to the Corporation. Same is the position at present as majority of the Corporation members are not well educated. Even the present Chairman is not even a Graduate. As the Kurnool Municipal Corporation is managing Secondary Education, it is sure that the uneducated and little educated Corporation members cannot contribute anything to the effective management of schools and they cannot be effectively participate in deliberations relating to academic administrative matters. Even the Municipal Corporation Commissioner is a graduate but he is not a trained Graduate in Education and above all he is more preoccupied with other works relating to the civic amenities and general administration.

Hence it is suggested that if the trained graduates of education failed to secure positions in the Corporations by means of election, it is thus necessary to co-opt two experienced retired teachers or retired Headmasters who served for a longer period in municipal schools. This arrangement would certainly add strength to the Municipal Corporation and the deliberations on schools management and working would be more constructive and academic-oriented. The Andhra Pradesh Municipal Corporations Act must also be amended to make way for the kind of arrangement.

Role Perception of Individual Members of Municipal Corporation

It is suggested that in the interest of Municipal Corporation as well as its dealing with various subjects, it is necessary to fix up individual responsibility over each member of Municipal Corporation. Each individual member's role, powers and functions must be prescribed. This arrangement would certainly enable the individual members to get themselves identified with the Municipal Corporation as well as with various fields of activity. In respect of secondary schools, let each Corporator of his ward be responsible and accountable for the effective functioning of the school located in his/her ward. Hence, the present Act must also be amended suitably in such manner.

Need to Invite Senior Headmasters of Schools to Sit in Municipal Corporation Meetings

The present study revealed that the Municipal Corporation of Kurnool has lack of good number of educated members to discuss matters relating to schools functioning under its management. Virtually no Corporator is qualified in teacher education and they do not possess any amount of experience in schools management and knowledge about academics. As a result, effective and fruitful decisions are not coming out of the deliberations. Hence it is suggested that whenever subjects relating to schools management, and teachers affairs are to be discussed it is good if three senior Headmasters working in Municipal Elementary Schools, Upper Primary Schools and High Schools one from each are invited to the Corporation meetings and permit them to participate in the deliberations. Their presence certainly help the discussion more effective as they contribute their experiences to the deliberations.

Municipal Corporation Schools as Transmitting Agencies

An insight into the objectives and working of the Kurnool Municipal Corporation schools at present reveals that these schools are just existing for the name sake without any result-oriented output in education. They never took any sort of commitment to act as formal agencies to transmit cultural values to the society. A school is a place of learning and more than, a transmitting agency of cultural values of the society to the people by taking critical view of them. In a democratic country like India responsibility of schools run by Municipalities and Municipal Corporations which are established especially in urban areas must expose themselves to the rural people by spreading advanced culture to them.

Municipal Corporation Schools–As Society Builders

The place of any school is highlighted by glorifying them as agencies to undertake a comparative study of other societies and try to extract the positive characters and place them before the society in which they are existing. This role is not at all played by the Municipal Corporation Schools in general and Kurnool Municipal Corporation schools in particular.

Hence, it is necessary that the Municipal Corporation schools in Kurnool must be made as agencies of social study and society builders. The State Government, the Municipal Corporation authorities and the persons at the helm of affairs of educational administration must see that the curriculum and the activities of these schools are directed in this direction along with imparting of education to the children to achieve social interaction.

Need for Determination of Objectives of School Education

The school education in India especially under Local Bodies suffers from aimlessness today even after the completion of sixty years of Independence. It's sole purpose has become only to allow the student to complete his school studies by somehow or other. In view of this the students who complete their school education earlier fail to get into any further course or job, or join in colleges without any inkling of the ultimate object of their education. Most of the boys and girls attend the schools for the simple reason that they are sent by their parents to schools for studies. But they probably little realize what the aim of their success of this type would be or what position they hold in their life in future. The National Educational Commission, 1986 considered education in general and secondary education in particular as a great challenge. Attention has been focused on vocationalisation of education and a large number of vocational streams were recommended. It stressed the need for a closer relation between education and the life of the people.

Hence, the school education especially under Municipal Schools infact, should be self-sufficient and independent unit in itself and not merely complementary to college or university education. At the completion of secondary education, the student should be able to feel confidently that he has attained a definite age in his academic career and that he is comparatively capable to undertake some independent work. He must feel that he has been prepared for his life as well his university education. The aim of secondary education should be both economic and cultural. The High School should become the backbone of national educational system for it is to the High School that the country must look for the preparatory training of its leaders and experts in all walks of life.

Lack of Perspective Planning

There is lack of perspective planning at the Municipal Corporation level as well as district level in Kurnool as far as running of Municipal Corporation schools are concerned. The Municipal Corporation Commissioner along with the District Educational Officer never sat together to make out perspective planning regarding the running of schools under Kurnool Municipal Corporation. Most of the time the Municipal Commissioner at present is lost in routine matters leaving little time for strategic planning, designing procedures of inspections, supervisions and other related matters of educational administration. Although the Kurnool Municipal Corporation has been managing the Elementary and Secondary schools since a long time, not even a single manual or to that matter any systematized and scientific code of procedures, guidelines and norms were brought out by the Kurnool Municipal Corporation or by the Municipal Administration Department in the State. Consequently, planning activity received a set back.

To overcome the above defects it is suggested that the post of Municipal Educational Officer must be created at Municipal Corporation level and the Municipal Commissioner must be relieved of looking into day to day aspects of educational institutions under his control. The Municipal Educational Officer along with the District Educational Officer sit and chalk out a detailed perspective planning to manage the secondary schools under the Municipal Corporation. Besides this, the Municipal Educational Officer along with the Municipal Commissioner and Inspectors of Schools must convene a meeting of Headmasters of High Schools one time in the first week of June every year before the reopening of schools. After discussing the plan for the year, monthly and quarterly review meetings must be arranged with the Headmasters to review the performance and working of the schools under municipal management. This should be made as a regular practice every academic year.

Educational Administration: Need for Organisational Restructuring

A detailed analysis of the educational administration and organizational structure of Secondary education under Kurnool Municipal Corporation clearly revealed that it is fraught with various lapses. The *prima facie* lapse is that in the entire organizational structure there is no single officer who is a specialist in the field of education to lookafter various problems of the schools, teachers and students. There is no single person in municipal organization who can exercise academic supervision and control over the Municipal Corporation schools in Kurnool. There are only two clerks who are meant for looking after certain clerical functions of Secondary Schools and Primary Schools. The Commissioner of Municipal Corporation is the Chief Executive Officer and he is bogged down with heavy work in looking after the execution of various policies made by the Corporation and to supervise all the subjects. In the case of other subjects like Health, Sanitation, Engineering, Town Planning etc., there are officers exclusively appointed for the purpose. But whereas the subject of Education is left without any competent officer. The Commissioner of Municipal Corporation himself is left with looking after the education administration touching all the primary and secondary schools. As a result he is not in a position to exercise effective control and supervision over these schools. At least a visit once in every month is necessary for an average supervision but it is revealed that while there are 64 schools of various categories under Kurnool Municipal Corporation, the Commissioner is not in a position to visit on an average atleast once in a year.

Hence, there is an urgent need to go for a thorough restructuring of organizational structure of primary and secondary education setup in Kurnool Municipal Corporation. The following are the immediate remedies that are to be adopted.

Firstly, as the Municipal Corporation Commissioner who is not a specialist in educational administration must be kept away from acting as an exclusive controller and supervisor of municipal schools. And secondly, as the Municipal Corporation Commissioner is bogged down with heavy load of work he must be made a general supervisor of educational administration as the case with other subjects.

Provision for Municipal Education Officer

As the study revealed that it is necessary that a separate Municipal Educational Officer like Deputy Educational Officer as in the case of Zilla Parishad must be appointed on a full time basis. He must be kept directly under the control of the Municipal Corporation Commissioner and inturn answerable to him. And the Municipal Educational Officer must exercise supervision and control over primary as well as secondary education of Kurnool Municipal Corporation. He must visit every school at least once in every month, prepare an inspection report and submit it to the Municipal Corporation Commissioner. The Commissioner inturn should place it on the table of the Corporation. If any lapse found at any level, strict disciplinary action must be taken against the defaulter.

The present Senior Assistant and Junior Assistants are overburdened with heavy work load in looking after the secretarial works relating to all the teachers and non-teaching staff working in all 64 schools of Kurnool Municipal Corporation. Hence there is a need to add one more Senior Assistant and Junior Assistant and one Superintendent to assist the proposed Municipal Educational Officer.

There is also a greater need to strengthen the organizational structure of educational system not only by inducting efficient officers but also through systematic perspective planning, timely staffing, effective direction, appropriate co-ordination, perfect reporting and adequate budgeting.

Lack of Span of Control

The present study revealed that there is lack of span of control at the Municipal Commissioner level who is the only officer responsible to look after educational administration in Kurnool Municipal Corporation. Normally, not more than six subordinates can report to the Commissioner but in the case of Kurnool Municipal Corporation there are seven officers of different departments, 49 elementary school Headmasters, seven Upper Primary School Headmasters and eight High School Headmasters accounting to 71 subordinates. To exercise effective supervision over these seventy one subordinates is a tough task which is not a healthy arrangement.

Hence, it is necessary to reduce the span of control at Municipal Commissioner level by creating one cadre of Municipal Educational

Officer as suggested earlier and four to five Inspectors of Schools to have effective supervision and control over the Municipal Corporation schools. These Inspectors of Schools will be under the control of Municipal Educational Officer. For the present eight high schools there must be one Senior Inspector of Schools, for the seven upper primary schools there must by one and for the remaining 49 elementary schools there must be three or four Junior Inspectors who can keep watch on the working of these schools.

Further, this arrangement would also enable to separate the functions of general administration which can be easily performed by the Municipal Commissioner and the functions relating to educational administration as separated from him may be and transferred to the newly created post of Municipal Educational Officer.

Headmaster Posts Kept Vacant for Long Time

It has been now and then the practice of Kurnool Municipal Corporation to keep the posts of Headmasters for a long period vacant due to obvious reasons and keeping these schools under incharge Headmasters and incharge Headmistresses. Regarding this aspect also the Teachers Unions made frequent representations to the Municipal Commissioner for which there was no reaction. This kind of incidents also created a kind of conflict of authority and official ill-feelings between the District Educational Officer and the Municipal Commissioner when the former asked the latter to furnish the reasons for not appointing official Headmasters and placing incharge Headmasters. It is also quite illogical to know that for nearly five Secondary Schools in the Corporation there is no sanction of Headmaster posts.

It is to be understood that the Headmaster is the kingpin of the school and directing force for the progress of the school. Every teacher and student will look at him for any kind of guidance and help. In the absence of a regular Headmaster and placing one teacher as incharge, the effective leadership is lost to the school and the incharge Headmaster had to look after his class work as well as administration. As he is not well experienced in school administration he may fail to command and control the students as well as his subordinates. Hence it is suggested that the Kurnool Municipal Corporation must take necessary steps and appoint Headmasters for High Schools as soon as the posts fell vacant.

Lack of Promotional Opportunities to Teachers

The most discouraging factor prevailing in the educational administration of Kurnool Municipal Corporation is that there is lack of promotional opportunities to the qualified, experienced teachers working in Municipal Corporation schools. This is more in the minds of Headmasters and senior most teachers. While the Government High Schools, and Panchayati Raj High school teachers are enjoying the facility of getting promoted as Deputy Educational Officers, Junior College Lecturers, Mandal Educational Officers, the Municipal High School teachers are deprived off this opportunity.

Hence, in order to encourage the experience and high qualifications the Municipal authorities and the State Government must extend the above promotional facilities to the meritorious, qualified and competent teachers to cadres like Municipal Educational Officer, Municipal Inspectors of schools as suggested earlier and as Junior Lecturers. There is a great need to locate and identify merit and reward them suitably. It is suggested that at least 5 to 10 per cent of higher posts must be reserved to local bodies like Municipalities, Municipal Corporations and Panchayati Raj. Otherwise the Headmasters have to retire as Headmasters, and the eligible senior teachers have to retire as they are.

Further, it is suggested to have a common system of education under one umbrella. This is possible when the educational institutions run by Municipalities, Panchayati Raj and Government be inter-linked so that promotion channels can be multiplied. The distinction as Municipal teacher, Panchayati Raj teacher and a Government teacher must be eliminated in the case of promotions. This is possible only when the services of the teachers working under Municipalities and Municipal Corporations are also provincialised as was done in respect of teachers under Panchayati Raj.

An overall view of the appointments made in the Municipal Corporation schools in Kurnool reveals that the principle of seventy per cent posts to be filled by promotion has not been followed. Even in respect of filling up of posts by promotion also was not regular and perfect. Hence it is suggested that the Kurnool Municipal Corporation must strictly adhere to the principle of 70:30 ratio in respect of promotion posts and direct selection posts.

Need for Strict Observance of Seniority for Promotions as Headmasters

The present study revealed that the Kurnool Municipal Corporation is violating the principle of seniority in making promotions as well as appointments to the positions of Headmasters in its various schools. The teachers associations are also making hue and cry in respect this kind of deviation by the Municipal Corporation. The Director of School Education also issued proceedings to Kurnool Municipal Corporation to follow strict seniority in appointing the teachers as Headmasters in High Schools. It was in the light of the representations made by the individual teachers as well as Teachers Unions. There were occasions when the Director of School Education cancelled the proceedings of the Municipal Commissioner issued in connection with promotions made deviating seniority rules and common seniority list. Hence it is suggested that the Kurnool Municipal Corporation must strictly follow the common seniority list prepared by the Municipal Corporation and accordingly the appointments should be made to the posts of Headmasters in High schools.

Need for Periodical In-service Training Programmes to Teachers

Training is a practical education in any profession and especially it is very much needed to teachers working in the schools who are expected to keep pace with the problems of new methods, skills and techniques to meet the academic needs of the pupils. But it is heart-rendering to note that there is no mention about the word like 'Training' anywhere in Andhra Pradesh Municipal Corporation Act relating to the teachers recruited to serve its schools and no mention about the need to provide training programmes to the teachers. As a result no serious effective training.

Programmes are arranged by the District Educational Officer and the programmes arranged so far are not adequate. The institutional arrangements for providing periodical and schematic training in various methods and techniques are quite unsatisfactory. As a result most of the teachers working in Municipal Corporation High Schools are not exposed to new methods of teaching techniques and models as they received training some years back. Now so many improved techniques have entered into the field of teaching of secondary education and improved standards in syllabi also added to the then existing syllabi.

Hence, it is necessary that all the teachers must undergo refreshers training and orientation courses, and attend summer schools in order to expose themselves to these new techniques and wipe out their obsolete knowledge, improve and put them in practice in their regular classroom teaching. The Central and State level bodies like NCERT and SCERT and the district level institutions like DIET must be utilized in this aspect.

Strength of the Students and Attendance

The strength of the students in some of the secondary schools managed by Kurnool Municipal Corporation has been constantly decreasing every year and there were various fluctuations. The strength of the Girls in High Schools also is not that much satisfactory.

Hence, it is suggested that besides mobilizing boy students to enroll in the High Schools, there is also a greater need to encourage girl students towards completion of secondary education and also for further higher studies. It is to be released that the strength of the students in schools depends upon the reputation of that particular school gained in respect of curriculum, coaching, guidance, discipline, infrastructural facilities, location and environment and above all the parental treatment of the teachers. The present study also reveals that the degree of percentage of attendance in all the High Schools is not cent per cent and also not fully satisfactory. Hence, it is suggested that the attendance is the outcome of the encouragement given to the students from all directions, viz., parents, teachers and the students themselves mutually. Hence it is necessary that everybody must realize this responsibility.

Public Examination Results–Unsatisfactory

It is heart-rending to look at the results of public examinations of the Municipal Corporation schools in Kurnool. As the study reveals that two types of public examinations were conducted at High School level earlier. They were; VII standard common examination conducted at each district level and the other is SSC Public Examination conducted at State level. But the overall percentage of results at SSC level was unsatisfactory. It was horrible that in any school the SSC Public Examination results that never touched ninety per cent. There were also incidents when in some High Schools the result was not even 20 per cent and majority of High Schools secured less than 50 per cent results. This clearly gives us the performance record of the Municipal Corporation High Schools.

Hence, it is suggested that vigorous steps must be taken by the teachers to improve the performance of the students in public examinations. Attention must be paid in the maintenance of optimum teacher-pupil ratio, performance review at the end of each year, conduct of periodical examinations, slip tests, evaluation, extra coaching to weak students, improvement in teaching skills by the teachers through undergoing periodical refresher courses in teaching methods and subjects, timely filling up of vacant posts of teachers and so on would go a long way in giving good output.

Need for Evaluation and Periodical Assessment

The results of the students in Kurnool Municipal Corporation schools especially in SSC Public Examinations are heart-rending. The reasons may be attributed in many ways. However, to improve the situation, adoption of new techniques, periodical evaluation and assessment of the students by the teachers concerned is very essential. To make this evaluation more realistic question banks should be supplied to the teachers. In order to check the evil of stagnation, this type of evaluation should be undertaken to help the deficient children to progress and weak students should be given extra coaching outside school hours and during vacations.

Need for Adequate Teaching Staff for High Schools

It is a naked truth that when compared to primary schools the high schools require more number of teachers who are more qualified and more trained than the elementary school teachers. The present study reveals that the Kurnool Municipal Corporation does not have adequate number of teachers required as per the strength of the students and the subjects at various levels. It is also one of the reasons for poor results in public examinations.

Hence, it is suggested that adequate teaching staff must be put in to the high schools through advance planning, timely recruitment of adequate number of teachers depending upon the requirement of subject wise teachers. This would not only reduce abnormal teacher-pupil ratio but also improve effective teaching hours and bring-out good results.

Lack of Proper Medical Check-up to Pupils

The present study revealed that during the whole study period medical check-up was not conducted in any school under the management of Kurnool Municipal Corporation regularly. Further, there was no provision of protected water supply to the pupils in these schools. The teachers associations and the individual teachers including the pupils have strongly complained about this.

Hence, it is suggested that the health check-up programme for the pupils of all schools under the Municipal Corporation should be undertaken periodically. For this, the Municipal Corporation, the concerned Headmasters must keep in touch with the Medical and Health Departments. It is good if a health chart is also maintained for every child and in case of any contingency, immediate steps should be taken up. Hygienic care of the pupils must also be taken up to them by supplying them soaps, towels etc. The mental abilities of the pupils and their family backgrounds must be studied and their socio-psychological deficiencies should also be identified and attended to.

Provision of Text Books in Time

One of the practical problems generally faced by the schools in general and the schools in Kurnool Municipal Corporation in particular was non-availability of prescribed text books in time. Sometimes these text books were supplied to the students only after completion of the first quarter of the academic year. This was directly putting the students and teachers in a great hardship and the students were taught without text books. The case was more severe if new revised books were prescribed to the students. Hence it is necessary that either the Municipal Corporation authorities or the State Government must make proper arrangements to see that the text books are available to the students in time.

Lack of Adequate Teaching Aids

The educational curriculum will be more effective and interesting only when good teaching aids are used by the teachers in their teaching process. The pupils will exhibit keen interest and understand the lesson more quickly and easily through these teaching aids. The present study reveals that even the most essentially required teaching aids such as maps, globes, audio-visual equipment like televisions, video cassette recorders, radios, slide projectors, 16 mm projectors, charts and other tools were not adequately provided in the schools. If even few such aids were available in the schools the teachers were reluctant to make use of them.

Hence, it is necessary that the Municipal authorities must take necessary steps to supply the required teaching aids to all its schools. For this purpose, the maintenance grant given by the State Government and some other fees collected from students can be utilized. Each school must also be equipped with good audio-visual equipment. Further, latest 'programmed teaching methods' in a book form must be supplied to all teachers to be followed by them as it is existing in Western countries.

Lack of Library Facilities

It has been noticed by the researcher through his personal visits and also as revealed by the pupils that most of the schools run by Kurnool Municipal Corporation do not have libraries at all. Even the daily newspapers and small magazines and journals of educative value are also not subscribed by them. When they are asked, they complained that funds are not available to the schools.

In the light of this it is suggested that each school must have a mini library with required reading facilities and equipped with good number of class text books, related books of academic value and daily newspapers and few magazines. Each school must have a Librarian to look after the library. To have this sort of library facility for each school the Municipal Corporation must divert a portion of its income to the schools. The Municipal Corporation must keep in contact with the State Library Authorities and request them to divert some amount for the libraries in the schools and send related books and journals every month at suitable time to all school libraries.

Lack of Furniture and other Facilities

It is found during the study period and as expressed by the pupils as well as teachers that most of the schools under Kurnool Municipal Corporation are facing the problem of lack of minimum furniture to the students as well as teachers. Sometimes, the teachers are also forced to adjust with the available inadequate furniture along with their students. As a result both teachers and students are facing lot of practical problems during their school time.

Hence it is necessary that facilities like furniture, chairs and tables to the teachers, desks to the students should be provided adequately.

Inadequate Laboratory Facilities

All the secondary schools run by the Municipal Corporation in Kurnool are facing an immediate problem of lack of laboratories. As it is revealed by the Science Assistants it has become very difficult to conduct experiments without laboratory facilities and as a result most of the science students are handicapped when compared to other schools. Further, the State Government has introduced new syllabi in mathematical, physical and natural sciences and the same syllabi is followed by the Municipal Corporation High Schools. But correspondingly the laboratory facilities are not provided. Hence, the Municipal Corporation must see that these high schools are provided with good laboratory facilities accordingly.

Lack of Toilet Facilities

The present study on the schools of Kurnool Municipal Corporation reveals that there are no adequate toilet as well as sanitary facilities available in all the schools. There are no urinals and sceptic laboratories for staff and students in the schools. Especially, the women staff members and girl students are facing this problem a lot.

Hence, it is necessary that toilet and sanitary facilities must be provided giving top priority which would lead to good health and hygienic conditions of the children. Further, waiting rooms both for teachers and girls students must also be provided adequately.

Need for Work Experience

One of the most important suggestions made by the Eswari Bhai Patel Committee appointed by the Ministry of Education, Government of India in 1978 was the introduction of socially useful productive work not only at secondary school curriculum but also at primary education level. The students will be given a practical class based on the theory of 'learn while learning'. This work experience will be useful to the students in their future lives. Hence, they should be encouraged to learn self-employment schemes to inculcate the spirit of self-confidence and self-reliance among them. The students must be taught by specialized teachers to enable them to do practical work efficiently. This system must be introduced in all secondary schools run by Kurnool Municipal Corporation also.

Need for Improving Competency of Teachers

As stated earlier, teacher is the key person in any educational system. The competency of the teacher is a major determinant of the quality of education and competency is not a one time acquisition. It has been erroneously assumed that initial education of a teacher is sufficient for life. This assumption is based on the view that the task of the teacher is constant. This is a fallacy. It is essential to have continuing education of all teachers at intervals throughout their career. For this the municipal teachers must be exposed to outside training institutions and provide in-service training to update their knowledge and improve and sharpen their teaching techniques for effective results.

Regularity and Sincerity – Primary Importance

The present study also brought into light some of the irregularities except in to the functioning of schools of Kurnool Municipal Corporation. Frequent cancellation of class work, teachers coming late to the classes, regular absenteeism among the teachers and so on. This is also due to non-filling up of the post of Headmasters in the schools for a long time or keeping the post unfilled by not promoting the qualified teachers. This always affected the regular tempo of academic atmosphere. Hence, it is necessary to observe the code of conduct in respect of the rule position and follow the same without any hesitation by the officials concerned. In this respect the Headmaster concerned must be a model to other teachers and unless he is sincere and honest he cannot administer the code of discipline. In addition to this, the inspecting staff must make frequent and surprise visits to the schools to check these irregularities. Above all the teachers concerned must have self-imposed discipline, honesty, sincerity, dedication and devotion to duty which require no super-imposed discipline.

Lack of Adequate Inspections

It has been revealed that there are no proper and adequate inspections on Municipal Corporation schools by the officers concerned. It has been expressed by the teachers as well as union leaders that some of the schools were not visited even once in a year. As a result the teachers are least bothered about their performance in the schools even in the case of teaching and attendance. The main reason is that there is no adequate number of inspecting staff to supervise 64 schools. As there is no appropriate, Education Officer in the Municipal Corporation who is entrusted with the task of conducting periodical inspections, the schools are left free without any accountability. The Municipal Commissioner is busy with his other duties and spared no time to visit these schools. Same is the case with DEO and his staff.

Hence, it is essential as suggested earlier that the post of Municipal Educational Officer must be created and under him there must be at least four or five Municipal Inspectors of schools to inspect primary and secondary schools respectively. In addition to this, the academic inspection can also be strengthened by the District Educational Officer and his staff whenever possible.

Need for Question Bank

The present study revealed that the high schools under Kurnool Municipal Corporation do not have 'Question Bank'. The question bank may be defined as a kind of reservoir of number of year-wise sets of question papers on each subject in which an examination was held. The question bank also helps the teachers to guide the students and get them prepared for the forthcoming examinations. Hence it is suggested that each school must have a question bank with a collection of past years question papers. Further, the Headmasters of the high schools must insist upon the concerned subject teachers to maintain question banks in their respective subjects as these have various advantages.

The Problem of Discipline

The present study also revealed that discipline was lacking among the students of Municipal Corporation high schools in Kurnool. The problem of discipline is regarded not as that of secondary education exclusively and the secondary schools under Kurnool Municipal Corporation but it is a country wide problem. Though the problem of discipline is not directly related to educational organization, yet Indian system of education, educational organization, method of teaching and the mode of examinations exercise a profound influence upon the aspect of discipline as a whole among the students. In addition to this, the student receives manifold social influences indirectly and unconsciously. Majority of the students, teachers, parents and guardians, forgetting higher aims and values of life have grown irresponsible and indisciplined. The political revolutions that instigated the students to participate prematurely in political movements or to observe strikes, the defective mode of examinations which make the students not to hesitate to adopt the foullest means to get through the examinations, the negligence of the parents and guidance, lack of extra-curricular activities and so on are the reasons for indiscipline among the students.

Hence, it is necessary to check this problem and proper remedies are to be invented. The secondary education is the foundation upon which the mansion of future career of students is built. It is the duty of all concerned to engender in them higher and noble virtues of humility, politeness and discipline.

Absence of Cultural Activities

The present study also brought out the fact that the schools under Kurnool Municipal Corporation are not exhibiting any amount of interest either in organizing cultural programmes by the students or encouraging them in histrionic talents. Keeping in view the mental development of the students and to improve moral and intellectual abilities of the students it is necessary to encourage cultural activities in the schools. They should be trained to perform school prayers daily and celebrate important local, regional and national festivals. The teachers should make their students to learn songs, stories, rhymes, dances and mono actions and so on. These cultural activities will improve the power of expression and communication skills and inculcate national outlook among school children. Hence, cultural activities and programmes should form part of the curriculum. At least one hour must be allotted on every day for generating cultural interest among the children of Kurnool Municipal Corporation schools.

Need for Well Estimated Financial Budget Allocations

Though the systems of non-formal schooling are available, universal education and mass literacy cannot be achieved without the establishment of universal formal schooling. Universal schooling also requires that school education must be made compulsory. Compulsory school education in turn requires mobilization of financial resources. Further, the quality of available schooling facilities is also deplorable. For instance, the NCERT Report says that twenty eight per cent primary schools in the country wide are single teacher schools and many schools remain without any teacher for varying periods of time. The same report also says that forty per cent of primary schools do not have pucca school buildings and nine per cent schools have no buildings at all. Public expenditure on education was growing at a positive rate over the last forty-five years and the expenditure also remained grossly inadequate and is also very low when compared to other developing countries.

As the costs of getting every child into school in the state in the next five years are large and hence, a well estimated financial budget allocations must be made for primary as well as secondary education to make the policy of universal primary schooling meaningful. However, resources alone cannot transform conditions without appropriate socio-political changes and commitments from the governments, teachers and the parents.

Inadequate Contingent Grant

The financial assistance provided by the State Government to the Municipal Corporation to run the schools is inadequate and untimely to meet its minimum requirements. All the Headmasters of secondary schools have expressed their strong feeling and protested against this meager amount. As the contingent grant is more inadequate it is revealed that the secondary school Headmasters are spending their own money for the purchase of stationary like white papers, chalk pieces, dusters and registers etc. The expenditure incurred in Kurnool Municipal Corporation for school education has been increasing gradually. But total grant sanctioned by the Government in respect of contingency and maintenance is highly inadequate, and the grant is not proportionate to the expenditure. There is lot of margin and this is met from Municipal internal funds sometimes. It seems that the State Government is not encouraging the municipal bodies in a right way to manage school education by sanctioning adequate contingent and maintenance grant in time.

Hence, it is suggested that if the municipal bodies are to be properly encouraged in the promotion of secondary education the State Government should increase the contingent grant and maintenance grant to a moderate extent and release the same well in advance.

Need for Parent-Teacher Associations

Formation of parent-teacher associations will have healthy effect on the administration of educational administration in Kurnool Municipal Corporation. These associations will act as balancing factors and make the educational institutions more effective and efficient. But the present study reveals that the formation of these Associations is only on paper but not effective in their functioning.

Hence it is necessary as suggested by the Programme Evaluation Organisation of Planning Commission in 1965 to organize parent-teacher associations with a view to establish direct rapport with the concerned teacher. Each school must organize parents day, school day and cultural day and invite and involve all the parents in these functions. The parents day along with the students and their parents must be a time when the problems of the children observed by the parents and the teachers can be exchanged, discussed and solved.

In addition to the above suggestions the Kurnool Municipal Corporation and the teachers and the related officers must also take into consideration the following suggestions to make the educational administration under Kurnool Municipal Corporation more effective.

1. The provision of deputing the competent teachers to foreign countries under educational and cultural exchange programmes must be extended to municipal teachers also every year in order to expose them to improved teaching methods applied in foreign countries and adopt the same in their schools after their return. Every year atleast one from each school must be selected under this programme to visit countries like Britain, Canada, USA, USSR, Japan etc.
2. There is a greater need to have good relations between the Headmasters concerned and the teachers of the school and among the teachers. They must have espirit de corpse and group responsibility in making the school administration more effective and performance oriented.
3. Mass copying during public examinations is also noticed many times and it seems many students were debarred from the examinations. In this respect the teachers must give orientation to their concerned students about this

malpractice and motivate them to regular study habits and honesty in writing examinations.

4. Educational and study tours play a vital role in exposing the students to other environments and this will help in a way to the learning process. State-to-state tours must be arranged every year for every school and give the students coaching from outside classroom. This would also improve interest and motivation among students.
5. Most of the teachers working in Kurnool Municipal Corporation Secondary schools expressed their unhappiness that they do not have an opportunity to meet all teachers at one place at least once in every month. Hence, it is suggested that the Kurnool Municipal Corporation Secondary school teachers must have this facility to meet atleast on every Second Saturday, so that there would be some get-together and acquaintancy with each other and discuss their common problems and evolve suitable solutions. This is possible if all the teachers form into a local association and elect one President, Vice-President, Secretary and Treasurer etc., as office bearers.
6. It is also expressed by majority teachers to keep all the teachers of Municipal Corporation in touch with Panchayati Raj teachers and Government teachers and coordination must be maintained. This would enable exchange of ideas, solutions to certain problems etc.
7. It is essential to keep the school premises clean and tidy. Hence, the teachers must make arrangements to make the students involve themselves in campus cleaning, slum cleaning, plantation activities in addition to regular drill, scout, games and sports.
8. It is also noticed that these schools are not equipped with first aid and the fighting facilities. Hence it is necessary to provide these facilities to treat and protect the children from various unforeseen accidents.
9. Strict adherence to time tables in the schools by the teachers.
10. Exhibiting effective academic performance in the classroom by the teachers.
11. Strict observance of attendance of pupils.
12. Avoidance of making use of students services for domestic works by the teachers.

13. Preparation of progress reports of students periodically and sending them to the parents.
14. Repairs to school buildings, black painting to wiring boards have to be taken up.
15. Plantation programme should be taken up in the school premises.
16. Today Art and Craft are neglected in all Municipal Corporation schools in Kurnool. Moral Instruction classes are replaced by socially useful productive works. But no utensils and implements are supplied to schools. Hence, these aspects are also to be set right.
17. The municipal management must organize extra coaching classes to students of all classes.
18. Family card for each student furnishing all his family background and accordingly the student must be taken care of.

Conclusion

Democratic and goal oriented-country like India which is passing through the phase of transition to modernity is well in need of social, cultural, political as well as economic progress. Education, more specifically at secondary levels need effective planning, organization and administration in view of the fact that this is the most valuable stage where the country can be more successful in strengthening its educational base on which future mansions of nation's progress is built. The local bodies, especially the Municipal Corporations in urban areas are emerging as agencies of urban development in general and Primary and Secondary Education in particular and have marked their contribution by establishing various schools for primary and upper primary and secondary education. The municipal bodies have taken up the task of promoting primary and secondary education with an avowed objective of effective educational administration and bringing every urban boy and girl into the fold of school education.

The Municipalities and Municipal Corporations have been identified as agencies of primary as well as secondary education in Andhra Pradesh and provision has been created to them to establish secondary schools, provide infrastructural facilities, enroll good number of boys and girls and motivate their parents through social education who inturn encourage their children to prefer Municipal Corporation schools and avoid dropouts, create viable conditions for further studies, establish feasible environment and study atmosphere for the students, adopt code of conduct and maintain discipline in the schools and finally mould each student to grow to a level of emerging as an asset to the nation.

It is very difficult to evaluate the working and performance of any organization such as local bodies in general which always suffer from certain institutional limitations and drawbacks. More in particular, to add fuel to the fire the Municipalities and Municipal Corporations are always subjected to the search light of public scrutiny and criticism where even a minor and insignificant lapse is regarded sometimes as a big failure. It is evident especially when we talk of the mode and media through which the Municipal Corporations are undertaking the educational administration and managing secondary schools. Obviously it is true even in case of Kurnool Municipal Corporation where it is involved in its task of undertaking educational administration. The present case study conducted on the educational administration carried out by Kurnool Municipal Corporation of its secondary schools and the role played by it in this task offered mixed reactions. It is quantitatively not bad but qualitatively it requires lot of improvement. Achievements of Kurnool Municipal Corporation in certain aspects of educational administration undoubtedly marked its laudable performance. But the other side face of its working also is very important where one could see its negative performance which provided some bases for criticism. This is the most important and necessary part of any study conducted as it provides scope for making constructive suggestions as it is done in this thesis. The Kurnool Municipal Corporation is not successful in evolving a productive organizational as well as administrative structure to effectively manage educational institutions under its control. Starting from the question of its developmental activities to the point of just provision of protected drinking water supply to the students in the schools, all have got a kind of pitfalls and lapses. The results of the students in the public examinations is an acid-test to evaluate the performance of the Secondary Schools which inturn have a direct impact on further admissions, and enrollment in the schools. This is true in respect of Municipal Corporation High Schools in Kurnool when it yielded unsatisfactory results in S.S.C. Public Examinations for years together.

In the initial stages when the Kurnool Municipal Corporation entered into the field of educational administration only primary education was taken care of. Later, realizing the need of secondary education to its citizens the government had brought the secondary schools in Kurnool town under municipal management also and thus shifted its responsibility to the municipality to a large extent and later to Municipal Corporation. But today if we see the treatment given to these schools by the government it is really heart-rending. The government tries to continue its hold over the administration part but left the management part to the destiny of Municipal Corporation. As a result the entire education system under Kurnool Municipal Corporation is lopsided.

The District Educational Officer at the district level controls all schools in the district. In respect of Municipal Corporation schools he is the academic controller but rarely reacts to give administrative guidance. He is also expected to supervise and inspect the Municipal Corporation schools as frequently as possible along with his departmental staff. But here also the District Educational Officer serves step-motherly treatment. During the course of personal interviews with some of the Headmasters, it was revealed that the District Educational Officer never visited their schools so far. Sometimes the inspection is only on paper but not physical. The Headmasters carry the visit books and account books to the District Educational Office and get his signature as a token of his visit to that school. Same is also the case with the Commissioner of Municipal Corporation in fulfilling his administrative responsibility of supervision.

Even in respect of financial sanctions to Municipal Corporation schools there is a ocean gap in respect of government's touch and treatment between the Municipal Corporation schools and the social welfare residential schools managed directly by the Government. In view of the absence of physical facilities in Municipal Corporation schools most of the parents tend to look down the Municipal Corporation schools and get their children admitted in other private institutions. Further, the failure of these Municipal Corporation schools in their performance is also one of the reasons for abnormal rise and growth of tuition shops and tutorial markets in the town. Being tempted by monetary attractions, some of the teachers who are good in the subjects working in Municipal Corporation schools deviate from their moral line and tempt the students to join in private tuition shops where they are handling classes. As a result, just for attendance purpose the students are joining in Municipal Corporation schools and their entire academic treatment and guidance is received from outside agencies. Today the pupils, the parents, the teachers, and the government put together are responsible for this kind of sorry state of affairs of the Municipal Corporation schools. In turn today none of them have confidence on these schools. Is the local politician, the Municipal Corporation Chairperson, the Corporator, the District Educational Officer or even the teacher working in Municipal Corporation schools ready to admit their children in Municipal Corporation schools? The answer to a greater extent is negative.

It has also been arrived at the discussions with the retired Headmasters and few Headmasters who are in service working in Kurnool Municipal Corporation schools that there is a need for creation of 'District Education Board' on line with 'State Board of Secondary Education' which can extend academic guidance to all the educational institutions of primary and secondary education including those schools functioning under Kurnool Municipal Corporation. The District Educational Officer and the other officers who are specialized in the subjects concerned should constitute the Board and stand to meet all the academic requirements.

Mutual cooperation, understanding and respect have been eroded among the teachers and Headmasters working in Municipal Corporation schools. The experiment of 'joint inspection' by the Headmasters concerned and the Inspector of Schools to inspect the ongoing teaching classrooms in every school became a failure due to the reason that the teachers in the school could not tolerate the visit of their own Headmaster to their classroom along with the Inspecting Officer and overseeing his performance. Further the teachers felt that this kind of experiment would boost up the image of their Headmaster which they do not like. Today we find not teachers in the schools but 'inspecting teachers' and 'inspecting Headmasters' directing inspections on each other without attending to their fundamental responsibilities.

While making some suggestions by retired Headmasters, they felt that the Municipal Corporation is a misfit to manage secondary education. Only primary education can be managed under municipal management and the secondary education can be handed over to Board of Intermediate Education where the Junior Colleges can have High Schools also by which the children after elementary education join in High school cum Junior Colleges and complete their S.S.C. and plus two course from one institution.

Opening of 'suggestion boxes' in each school is a needed arrangement today. Every teacher as well as students can put their suggestions in that box. Every morning the Headmaster must collect these suggestions, put them before the teachers at the end of every evening session and evolve suitable plans and programmes and execute them. The student's suggestions and remarks are more important and valid which are to be attended to first. This would surely act as an 'Inward Camera' of the school which gives the real picture about the performance of teachers and problems of students. Every teacher must feel that the 'backwardness of the student is the backwardness of the teachers'. Self academic inspection of the school is better than any formal administrative external inspection.

One of the major complaints made by the students is that the syllabus is not completed in all subjects every year by the teachers. In certain schools certain subjects were left untaught. This is due to the dearth of teaching staff. No interest, and attention is paid to maintain laboratories in the schools as there are no practical examinations for the science and mathematical subjects. Hence, laboratories are totally neglected. The Government is much interested on the first 10 ranks secured in S.S.C. Public Examinations but forgetting about thousands of students who are failing in the examinations. In the light of these, it is necessary that the Government should come out with its definite educational policy and act accordingly.

The Teachers' Unions also have a role to play. They can promote the welfare of the teachers on a larger scale if they follow the code of discipline by way of having one union for all the municipal teachers in Kurnool district and by ironing out internal differences and avoiding unhealthy competition, by streamlining the settlement procedures and increasing the membership and finally by improving their financial position and unitedly exerting pressure on the management and so on.

Now it is right time to look into the problems of school education and its success with an appropriate right perspective. The State Government, the district administration as well as the Kurnool Municipal Corporation must have a co-ordinated approach in strengthening the educational administration in respect of secondary education. The policy makers at local bodies level, the administrative machinery for education at district level including the Department of Municipal Administration and Director of School Education all must act in a co-ordinated and devoted way with a commitment to strengthen school education under local bodies. The Government must come forward liberally with its Grants to provide all necessary requirements and infrastructural facilities to educational institutions functioning under the management of Municipal bodies in general and Kurnool Municipal Corporation in particular.

The teachers, students and their parents are like a triangle network who can contribute for the success of secondary education. There must be honesty, sincerity, devotedness above all commitment among the teachers to serve for the cause of the students. The parents must have enough understanding, motivation and interest in sending their children for studies. Above all the students who once get into the mainstream of school education must be sincere, hard working and disciplined and realize the aims of their studies and act in such a way to grow further and further, if any lapse on any side of these three supporting pillars may finally damage the future prospects of the students in general and the nation at large in particular.

Fundamentally, the purpose of educational administration is to bring the pupils and teachers together under such conditions which promote the end of education successfully. Hence, the issues discussed in the last chapter with regard to educational administration need ready treatment as it requires qualitative improvement. The suggestions made in this thesis and their prompt and effective implementation by the concerned would certainly go a long way in systematizing the educational administration under Kurnool Municipal Corporation and further enable its secondary schools to work with a noble commitment and performance-orientation filled with academic spirit.

Bibliography

A. BOOKS

Agarwal, J.C,. *Theory and Principles of Education*, New Delhi, Vikas, 1995.

Aleem and Shammeem, *State Administration in Andhra Pradesh*, Hyderabad; Allied, 1984.

Alfred Holbrook, *School Management*, New Delhi: Cosmo, 2005.

American Association of School Administration, *Staff Relations in School Administration*, Washington A.A.S.A., 1955.

Argal, P., *Municipal Government in India*, Allahabad: Agarwal Press, 1960.

Avasti, A., (Ed.) *Municipal Administration in India*, Agra: Lakshminarain Agarwal, 1973.

Basrao, Sharda, *Municipal Government in Rajasthan*, New Delhi: Chand, 1975.

Bharadwaj, R.K., *The Municipal Administration in India*—A Sociological Analysis of Rural and Urban India, Jullandar: Sterling, 1970.

Bhatia, B.D., *Theory and Principles of Education*, New Delhi: Doaba House, 1970.

Bhatia, H.R., *Elements of Educational Psychology*, New Delhi: Orient Longman, 1975.

Bhatia, K.K.; *Modern Indian Education and its Problems*, Ludhiana: Prakash Brothers, 1990.

Bhatnagar, R.P. & Varma, I.V., *Educational Administration*, Meerut: Local Book Depot, 1978.

Bhattacharya, M., *State Municipal Relations – A Functional Analysis*, New Delhi: NIPA, 1972.

Bhaskara Rao, B., *Decentralised Management of Education: Management of Education in Panchayati Raj and Municipal Bodies*, New Delhi: Discovery, 2001.

Bhaskar Rao, D., *Educational Administration*, New Delhi: Discovery, 2004.

Bhaskar Rao, D., *Principles of Secondary Schools*, New Delhi: Sonai, 2007.

Braham Dev, *Educational Administration*, New Delhi: Vohra Publication, 2007.

Bela Rani Sharma, *A Handbook of School Administration*, New Delhi: Sarup, 2007.

Barik, G.D. and Mishra, B.C.H. *Organisational Climate of Secondary Schools*, New Delhi: Sonali, 2008.

Bryce, James, *Modern Democracies*, New York: Macmillan, 1921.

Cambell Ronald, F., Corbally, John, A., *Introduction to Educational Administration*, Boston: Allyn and Bacon, 1962.

Chabe, S.P., *Secondary Education in India*, New Delhi: Atma Ram, 1956.

Corbally, Jensen, Staub, *Educational Administration – The Secondary School*, Boston: Allyn and Bacon, 1961.

Cox Phillip, *et.al.*, *Education in Democracy*, New York: McGraw Hill, 1961.

Dash, M., and Neena Dash, *School Management*, New Delhi: Atlantic Publications, 2008.

Elsbree, McNally, *Elementary School Administration and Supervision*, New York: American Book Company, 1959.

Everest Reimer, *The School is Dead*, England: Penguin, 1971.

Gaind, R.P. Sarma, '*Educational and Secondary School Administration*, Agra: Ram Prasad, 1971.

Govardhan Lal Bhakshi, *Towards Better Education*, New Delhi: Chand & Co., 1978.

Gyanchand, *Local Finances in India*, Allahabad: Kitab, 1947.

Goutam N.C., *Educational Administration*, New Delhi: Shree Publication, 2005.

Harris, P.B., *Changing Conceptions of School Discipline*, New York: Macmillan, 1928.

Hennessy, J., *Indian Democracy and Education*, New Delhi: Orient Longman, 1977.

Herald, F. Alderfer, *Local Government in Developing Countries*, New York: McGraw Hill, 1964.

Hussain, M.A., *Urban Politics in India*, New Delhi: Criterion, 1987.

Ivan Illich, *Die Schooling Society*, England: Penguin Books, 1971.

Jagannatha Mohanthy, *Indian Education in the Emerging Society*, Bangalore: Sterling, 1982.

Jaswanth Sing, *Successful Head Master*, Jullundhar: University Publications, 1964.

Johnson, Faunce, *Student Activities in Secondary Schools*, New York: Ronald Press, 1972.

James, C. Laurence, *Changing Role of Teachers in Education*, New Delhi: Rajat, 2007.

John Jacob, *Educational System in the Computer Age*—New Delhi: Commonwealth, 2005.

Jandhyala, B.G. Tilak, *Financing of Secondary Education in India*, Delhi: Shipra, 2008.

Jalaja Kumari, C., *Job Satisfaction of Teachers*, New Delhi: Discovery, 2007.

Janardhan Prasad, *Panorama of Indian Education*, New Delhi: Kanishka, 2008.

Kale, S.V., (ed.), *Child Psychology and Child Guidance*, Bombay: Himalaya, 1980.

Kande, I.L., *Studies in Comparative Education*, London: George G. Harrap, 1933.

Kochhar, S.K., *Secondary School Administration*, Jullundhar: University Publication, 1997.

_________, *Pivotal Issues in Indian Education*, New Delhi: Sterling, 1996.

_________, *Successful Supervision and Inspection*, Delhi: Kalyan's Publishers, 1974.

Kamlesh Gupta, *School Management*, New Delhi: Penguin, 2006.

Laxminarasaiah, M., *Education and Globalisation*, New Delhi: Discovery, 2008.

Leena Datla Bharati, *History of Higher Secondary Education*, New Delhi: Anmol, 2006.

Lakshmi, S., *Challenges in Indian Education*, New Delhi: Sterling, 1993.

Leyland Bric., *Libraries in Schools*, Chicago: American Library Associations, 1961.

Lulla, B.P., *Study on Educational Administration in the United States and in India*, Baroda: Acharya Book Depot, 1956.

________, *Current Trends in Modern Education*, Ludhiana, Prakash Publishers, 1978.

Lulla, B.P., and Murthy, S.K., *Essentials of Educational Administration*, Chandigarh: Mohindra, 1975.

Marlow Edigar and Bhaskar Rao, D., *Administration of Schools*, New Delhi: Discovery, 2007.

Mishra, R.C., *Classroom Management*, New Delhi: A.P.H. Publication, 2007.

Mishra R.C., *Encyclopaedia of Educational Administration*, New Delhi: A.P.W. Publication, 2007.

Manju Mishra, *Modern Methods of Educational Administration*, New Delhi: Alfa Pub. 2007.

Manzoor Ahmed, *et.al*, *The State of Secondary Education*, Bangladesh: Popular, 2006.

Marlow Edigar and Bhaskar Rao, D., *Successful School Administration*, New Delhi, Discovery, 2006.

Maheswari, S.R., *Local Government in India*, Agra: Lakshmi Narain, 1987.

Mochaiman Arthur, B., *School Administration*, Boston: Houghton, 1951.

Mohanty, B., *School Administration and Supervision*, New Delhi: Deep and Deep, 2005.

Mohanty, J., *Current Issues in Education*, New Delhi: Cosmo Publishers, 1993.

Mohanty, J. S.N., (Ed.), *Administration of Education India – Symposium*, New Delhi: Acharya, 1962.

Mukherji, S.N., *Education in India, Today and Tomorrow*, Baroda: Acharya, 1964.

__________, *History of Education in India, Modern Period*, Baroda: Acharya, 1955.

__________, *Secondary School Administration – Its Principles and Functions in India*, Baroda: Acharya, 1969.

Naik, J.P., *Educational Planning*, New Delhi: Allied Publishers, 1961.

________, *Elementary Education in India – A Promise to Keep*, New Delhi: Allied, 1974.

Narayana Rao, K.V., *Emergence of Andhra Pradesh*, Tirupati: Bhargava, 1974.

Netar Singh, *Municipal Administration in India*, Delhi: H.K. Publishers, 1990.

Nigam, S.R., *Local Government*, New Delhi: S. Chand, 1983.

Nurullah Syed & Naik, J.P., *A History of Education in India*, Bombay: Macmillan, 1951.

Nwankwo, J.I., *Educational Administration – Theory and Practice*, New Delhi: Vikas, 1958.

Oltway, A.K.C., *Education and Society*, London: Routledge, 1962.

Patel Rambhai, *Educational Evaluation: Theory and Practice*, Bombay: Himalaya, 1980.

Pickering, George, *The Challenge of Education*, London: Penguin Books, 1967.

Pillai, K.K., *History of Local Self-Government in the Madras Presidency (1856-1919)*, Bombay: Local Self-Government Institute, 1953.

Prasad, S.N., *Education and World Hunger*, Delhi: Mittal, 1985.

Pramila Chandra Sekharan, *Educational Planning and Management*, New Delhi: Sterling, 1997.

Premanath, *The Bases of Education*, New Delhi: S. Chand, 1979.

Premchand Patanjali, *Development of Secondary Education in India*, New Delhi: Shree Publication, 2005.

Ramanujachari, R., *An Introduction to the Philosophy of Education*, Tirupati: Department of Education, S.V. University, 1973.

Rao, V.K.R.V., *Education and Human Resource Development*, Bombay: Allied, 1966.

Rao, V.V., *Hundred Years of Local Self-Government and Administration in Andhra Pradesh and Madras State 1850-1950*, Bombay: AILSG, 1960.

Rai, B.P., *Sociological Foundation of Education*, Lucknow: Prakashan Kendra, 1995.

Ralph, R.G., *Library in Education*, London: Turnstile, 1949.

Ramachandra Pillai, *General and Technical Education in Andhra Pradesh*, Hyderabad: Telugu Academy, 1961.

Reddy, R.S., *Administration of Secondary Education*, New Delhi: Rajat, 2006.

Ranjan Sharma, *Effective Teacher-Parent Communication*, Jaipur: Book Enclave, 2008.

Ramanna, R.K., *Elements of Secondary School Administration*, New Delhi: Rajat, 2006.

Reddy, R.S., *History and Development of Secondary Education*, New Delhi: Rajat, 2006.

Ramanna, R.K., *Issues in Educational Administration*, New Delhi: Rajat, 2006.

Saiyidian, K.G., *Problems of Educational Reconstruction*, Bombay: Asia, 1957.

Sampath, K., *et. al.*, *Introduction to Educational Technology*, New Delhi: Sterling, 1987.

Sharma, Sitaram, *Educational Development in India*, New Delhi: Anmol, 1990.

Sinha, R., *Educational Administration in India*, Ambala: Kantt, 1965.

Sinha, S.P.P., *Teachers and their Training*, Patna: Gian Pith, 1972.

Smeaton, J., *School Libraries*, New Delhi: Ministry of Education, Government of India, 1968.

Smith, D., *Measurement and Evaluation in Secondary Schools*, New Delhi: Commonwealth, 2005.

Sukla, P.D., *The New Education Policy in India*, New Delhi: Sterling, 1990.

Sukumar Mitra, E.E., *A History of Education in India*, Calcutta: Oxford, 1978.

Shankar Mukherjee, *Contemporary Issues in Modern Indian Education*, Delhi: Authors Press, 2007.

Shouriamma, B., *Education Administration*, New Delhi: A.P.H., 2008.

Sitaram Sharma, *Educational Administration*, New Delhi: Sri Sai, 2005.

Susmitha Sony, *Educational Management and Administration*, New Delhi: Adhyan Publication, 2007.

Shipra Vidya, *Educational Reforms*, New Delhi: Deep and Deep Publications, 2005.

Sunil Chavan, *Educational Supervision on Pupils Development*, New Delhi: Rajat, 2006.

Sinha, G.S. and Rao, V.K., *Encyclopaedia of Educational Administration*, New Delhi: Commonwealth, 2002.

Sharma, R.S., *Issues in Educational Administration*, Jaipur: ABD, 2005.

Satyanarayana, P.V.V., *et.al*, *School Administration and Management*, New Delhi: Sonali, 2004.

Tead Ordway, *The Act of Administration*, New York, McGraw Hill, 1955.

UNESCO, *School Buildings*, Paris: 1957.

Vakil, K.S., and Natarajan, S., *Education in India*, Bombay: Allied, 1966.

Venkata Rao and Niru Hazarika, *Local Self-Government in India*, New Delhi: S. Chand, 1959.

Venkata Rao, V., *Local Self-Government in India*, New Delhi: S. Chand, 1983.

Vishnoo Bhagavan, *Municipal Government and Politics in Hyderabad*, New Delhi: S. Chand, 1974.

Wadia Khorished A., and Rohila Pritam, K., *Guidance Services in Schools*, New Delhi: Albian Press, 1964.

Yadav, C.P., *Education for All by 2015 A.D*, New Delhi: Anmol, 2007.

B. ARTICLES

Ajit Singh, Priorities of Research in Teacher Education, New Frontiers in Education, Vol. XXXIV, No. 3, July-September 2004.

Amartya Sen, Children and Human Rights, *Indian Journal of Human Development*, Institute for Human Development, Vol. 1, No. 2, July-December 2007.

Amita Pandey Bhardwaj, Interactive classroom behaviour patterns of Secondary School Science Teachers, Vol. 1, No. 2, December 2004, *Indian Journal of Teacher Education.*

Amruth Rao, A., Personal Administration in the Municipal Corporation of Hyderabad, *Nagarlok*, P(1), 1977.

Anna Saiti, The Development and Reform of School Administration, *Educational Management Administration and Leadership*, Vol. 37, May 2009.

Appa Rao, T. and Bapuji, N., The Municipal Chairman in Andhra Pradesh, *Quarterly Journal of Local Self-Government Institute*, 44 (1), 1973.

Balachandran, M.K., Legal Framework of Municipal Management, *Nagarlok*, Vol. V, New Delhi: IIPA, 1974.

Bhaskar Rao, D., Participation of Secondary School Students in Sports and Games, *Journal of Educational Research and Extension*, Vol. 40 (3), July-September 2003.

Chandrasekharan, S., Essential Values in the Text Books of Secondary Education, *International Educator*, Vol. 19, No. 1, June 2007.

Charasia, G., Innovations of Teachers Education, *Miracle of Teaching*, Vol. 3, No. 3, September-December 2003.

Chopra, R.N., Municipal Personnel Administration, *Indian Journal of Public Administration*, New Delhi: IIPA, 1968.

Deva Raj, The Political Context of Municipal Management, *Nagarlok*, Vol.VI, New Delhi: IIPA, 1974.

Hemalata Talesara, Innovational in Teachers Education, *Miracle of Teaching*, Vol. 3, September-December, 2003.

Kumaraswamy, R.P., & Salivahana Sarma, P., Job Involvement of Secondary School Teachers, *International Education*, Vol. 17, No. 2, December 2005.

Malhotra, D.D., Municipal Personal Management, *Nagarlok*, Vol. VI, IIPA, New Delhi, 1973.

Manjuvani, E., Ramakrishnaiah, D., School Environment and Mental Health Students of High School Students, *Experiments in India*, Vol. 32, No. 2, February 2004.

Marlow Ediga, Role of the School Administration, *EDU TRACKS*, Vol. 7, No. 5, January 2008.

Masooda Jamal, Examination and Evaluation at Secondary School Level, *Indian Journal of Psychometry and Education*, Vol. 38 (2), July 2007.

Mercy Bhavan, N.K. Arjunan, Environmental Interest of Secondary School Students in Relation to their Environmental Attitude, *Perspectives in Education*, Vol. 21, No. 2, April 2005.

Mohit Bhattacharya, Motivating Municipal Employees, *Nagarlok*, Vol. VI, IIPA, New Delhi, 1974.

Mudaliar, A.L., 'The Changing Pattern in Secondary Education in India-Priorities' *Education Quarterly*, November, 1956.

Muttalib, M.A., The Municipal Commissioner, London: *The Journal of the Royal Institute of Public Administration*, Vol. 45, 1967.

Pradeep Kumar, T., The Impact of Mass Media on the Academic Achievement of Secondary School Students: A Theoretical Analysis, *MERI Journal of Education*, Vol. 3, No. 1, April 2008.

Rama Rao, S., Municipal Revenue in Andhra Pradesh, *Nagarlok*, 6(2), 1974.

Richard, C. Hunter, Public School Administration, *Education and Urban Society*, Vol. I, April 2009.

Sachdeva Pany, Parent Child Interaction in relation to creative thinking ability of Secondary School Learners, *MERI Journal of Education*, Vol. 3, No. 1, April 2008.

Saramma Chandy, Fostering Research Ability through Science Teaching among Secondary Schools, *Miracle of Teaching*, Vol. 9, No. 1, January to April 2009.

Shahapur Nagappa Panchaliingappa, Self-Confidence, Anxiety, Study Habits and Mathematics Achievements of Under Achievers at Secondary School Level, *Question in India*, Vol. 30, No. 3, July 2006.

Shamshuddin, 'Teaching as a Career' *Educational India*, April, 1968.

Sharma, M.D., 'Providing of Facilities in Secondary Stage—Whose Concern', *Secondary Education*, October-December, 1961.

Sindkhedkar, S.D., In Service Teachers Education for Primary and Secondary School Teachers—*The Primary Teachers*, Vol. 31, No. 1-2, January to April 2006.

Srinivasan, K.V., and Haragopal, G., 'Changing Trends of Municipal Administration in Andhra Pradesh', *Journal of the Lal Bahadur Sastri National Academy of Administration*, 20(4), 1975.

Swamy Suvirananda, Value Education in Secondary Schools: Methodology, *Journal of Value Education*, Vol. 5, No. 1&2, January & July 2005.

Uniyal, B.P., Computer Assisted Teaching-Learning—A Study of Awareness among the Teachers and Students of Secondary Schools, *Quest in India*, Vol. 30, No. 3, July 2005.

Upall, J.S., 'New Secondary Education and Multipurpose Schools in India', *Education Quarterly*, November, 1956.

Venkateswara Rao, D., Municipal Personnel System in Andhra Pradesh, *Nagarlok*, 6(4), 1994.

Verma, V.K., 'Teacher and Professional Status', *Educational India*, August, 1962.

C. GOVERNMENT REPORTS AND PUBLICATIONS

1. Lord Rippon's Resolution, Gazette of India, (Supplement), April to June, 1882.
2. Report on Local Government Administration in Hyderabad State Government Central Press, Hyderabad, 1947.
3. Report of the Secondary Education Commission, (1952-53), Ministry of Education, Government of India, New Delhi.
4. Report of the State Re-organisation Commission, Government of India, 1955.
5. Andhra Pradesh Educational Inspection Code, issued by Director of Public Instruction, 1956.
6. Report of the Committee on the Training of Municipal Employees, New Delhi, 1963.
7. Report of the Committee of Ministers on Augmentation of Financial Resources of Urban Local Bodies, Government of India, New Delhi, November, 1963, (Zakaria Committee).

8. Report on Teacher Training—Committee on Plan Projects, New Delhi, Planning Commission, 1964.
9. NCERT—Elementary Education—India Year Book of Education, New Delhi, 1964.
10. Report of the Education Commission (1964-66), Ministry of Education, Government of India, New Delhi.
11. Andhra Pradesh Municipalities Act, 1965 and 1994.
12. Report of the Committee on Urban Policy, Ministry of Health, Government of India, New Delhi, 1965.
13. The Andhra Pradesh Municipalities Rules, 1965.
14. The Andhra Pradesh Municipalities Manual (Panchayat Publications, Hyderabad), 1965.
15. Government of India, The Constitution of India, The Manager of Publications, New Delhi, 1965.
16. Report of the Secondary Educational Survey in Andhra Pradesh, 1965-66.
17. Kothari Committee Report, Ministry of Education, Government of India, New Delhi, 1978.
18. Eswari Bhai Patel Committee Report, Ministry of Education, Government of India, New Delhi, 1978.
19. Andhra Pradesh District Gazetteer, Kurnool 1982.
20. Government of India, National Policy on Education, Ministry of HRD, New Delhi, 1986.
21. The 74th Constitution Amendment Act, 1992.
22. Annual Administration Reports of Kurnool Municipality from 1995-96 to 2007-08.
23. India 1997 to 2008.
24. Government of India, Five Year Plans I to X.
25. Hand Book of Statistics, Government of Andhra Pradesh, 2006.
26. Hand Book of Statistics, 2006-07, Kurnool District.
27. Andhra Pradesh Human Development Report, 2007.
28. Andhra Pradesh Statistical Abstract, 2008.

D. JOURNALS AND PERIODICALS

Adhyapaka Darshini
Andhra Pradesh Purapalaka Darsini (Data News Features)
Anweshika Indian Journal of Teachers Education (NCERT)
British Journal of Educational Psychology
Civic Affairs
Data News Features—A.P. Year Books
Economic and Political Weekly
Education and Urban Society
Education Quarterly
Education Quarterly—Ministry of Education

Educational Evolution and Policy Analysis
Educational India (Monthly)
Educational Management Administration and Leadership
Educational Planning and Administration
Educational Policy
Educational Research Quarterly
Educational Researcher
Experiments in Education
Ikyaupadhya
Improving Schools
Indian Educational Review
Indian Journal of Adult Education
Indian Journal of Human Development
Indian Journal of Psychometry and Education
Indian Journal of Public Administration
Indian Journal of Training and Development
Indian Journal Political Science
International Education
International Journal of Adult and Lifelong Education
International Social Science Journal
Journal of Educational Administration
Journal of Educational Research and Extension
Journal of Indian Education
Journal of Local Administration Overseas
Journal of Local Self-Government in India
Journal of Value Education (NCERT)
Management in Education
Manorama—Year Books
Miracle of Teaching
Municipal Review
Nagar Lok
National Municipal Review
New Frontiers in Education (Islamabad Journal of Education)
Perspectives in Education
Political Quarterly
Public Administration Review
Quest in India (Quarterly)
Secondary Education (Quarterly)
Social Science
Teachers Journal
The Education Digest (Monthly)
The Educational Review
The Indian Teacher
The Primary Teacher (Quarterly)
The Progress of Education

Upadhyaya
Upadhyaya Vani
Vidhyodaya
Vidyarthi

E. ENCYCLOPAEDIAS

Encyclopaedia of Americana
Encyclopaedia of Britanica
Encyclopaedia of Social Sciences
Encyclopaedia of Education by R.S. Sharma, Anuradha Sarma
Encyclopaedia of Educational Terms
Encyclopaedia of Great Thinkers on Education
Encyclopaedia of Educational Measurement and Evaluation
Encyclopaedia of Educational and Vocational Guidance
Encyclopaedia of Dictionary of Education
Encyclopaedia of Education in 21st Century
Encyclopaedia of World Psychologists
Encyclopaedia of Modern Techniques of Teaching
Encyclopaedia of Educational Technology
Encyclopaedia of Modern Techniques of Educational Testing
Encyclopaedia of Teacher Training
Encyclopaedia of Teaching Techniques
Encyclopaedia of Guidance and Counselling

F. NEWS PAPERS

Andhra Jyothi (Telugu Daily)
Andhra Prabha (Telugu Daily)
Deccan Chronicle
Eenadu (Telugu Daily)
Hindustan Times
Indian Express
Sakshi (Telugu Daily)
Surya (Telugu Daily)
The Hindu
Vaartha (Telugu Daily)
Visalandhra

G. INTERVIEWS CONDUCTED

1. Sri. S. Raghurami Reddy, Mayor, Kurnool Municipal Corporation, Kurnool on 25.11.2008.
2. Sri. N. Sreeramulu, Corporator, I Ward, Kurnool on 10.10.2008.
3. Sri. B. Adenna, Corporator, IV Ward, Kurnool on 11.10.2008.
4. Sri. P. Dhanunjaya, Commissioner, Kurnool Municipal Corporation on 14.11.2008.

5. Sri. Veeraiah, Schools Supervision, Kurnool Municipal Corporation on 5.9.2008.
6. Sri. Subramanyam, Manager, Kurnool Municipal Corporation on 4.6.2008.
7. Sri. Krishna Rao, District Educational Officer, Kurnool on 9.10.2008.
8. Smt. Gousia Begum, Retd. Deputy Educational Officer, Kurnool on 16.2.2008.
9. Sri. H. Ananda Rao, Head Master, DSMMCHS, Kurnool on 4.1.2009.
10. Sri. S. Narasimha Rao, Head Master, CRRMMCHS, Kurnool on 10.2.2009.
11. Sri. T.K. Viswanatham, Head Master, NMMCHS, Kurnool on 28.01.2009.
12. Sri. Akthavur Rahiman, Head Master, IGMMCHS, Kurnool on 4.2.2009.
13. Sri. K.C. Venkata Swamy, Head Master, SPSMMCHS, Kurnool on 24.01.2009.
14. Smt. S. Vasantha Kumari, Head Mistress, Dr. BRAMMCHS, Kurnool on 29.12.2008.
15. Smt. N. Vahida Khanam, Head Mistress, STPPMMCHS, Kurnool on 22.12.2008.
16. Smt. Khaisar Jahan, Head Mistress, MCHS (Urdu), Kurnool on 31.1.2009.
17. Sri. D. Venkata Reddy, Sr. Asst, Dr. BRAMMCHS, Kurnool on 27.11.2008.
18. Smt. M.D. Sakunthala, Sr. Asst., DSMMCHS, Kurnool on 9.7.2008.
19. Smt. Shobha Rani, Sr. Asst, IGMMCHS, Kurnool on 14.12.2008.
20. Sri. Pratap Reddy, Retd. Head Master, DSMMCHS, Kurnool on 2.6.2008.
21. Sri. Ramana, Junior Asst, Dr. BRAMMCHS, Kurnool on 6.7.2008.
22. Sri. S. Kantha Rao, Union bearer, DTF on 11.9.2008.
23. Sri. Narasimhulu, President, UTF, Kurnool on 13.10.2008.
24. Chi. Suresh, Student of VII Class, NMMCHS on 3.1.2009.
25. Chi. Hussain Peera, Student of VIII Class, STPPMMCHS on 1.2.2009.
26. Chi. S. Ranganayakulu, Student of X Class, DSMMCHS on 5.1.2009.
27. Kum. D. Deepika, Student of IX Class, SPSMMCHS on 9.12.2008.
28. Sri. P. Sunkanna, Father of Pavan Kumar, Student of VII Class, Dr. BRAMMCHS on 19.1.2009.
29. Smt. A. Narayanamma, Mother of Laxmi Devi Student of X Class, SPSMMCHS on 18.12.2008.

Index